LASTING IMPACT

ONE TEAM, ONE SEASON.
WHAT HAPPENS WHEN OUR SONS
PLAY FOOTBALL

KOSTYA KENNEDY

NEW YORK TIMES BESTSELLING AUTHOR

Also by
Kostya Kennedy

Pete Rose
An American Dilemma

56
Joe DiMaggio
and the
Last Magic Number
in Sports

LASTING IMPACT

ONE TEAM, ONE SEASON.
WHAT HAPPENS WHEN OUR SONS
PLAY FOOTBALL

KOSTYA KENNEDY

NEW YORK TIMES BESTSELLING AUTHOR

Book design by Stephen Skalocky

Published by Liberty Street, an imprint of Time Inc. Books
225 Liberty Street
New York, NY 10281

Liberty Street and Sports Illustrated are trademarks of Time Inc.

ISBN 10: 1-61893-157-1
ISBN 13: 978-1-61893-157-3
Library of Congress Control Number: 2016931936

First edition, 2016

1 QGF 16

10 9 8 7 6 5 4 3 2 1

We welcome your comments and suggestions about Time Inc. Books.
Please write to us at:
Time Inc. Books
Attention: Book Editors
P.O. Box 62310, Tampa, FL 33662-2310

timeincbooks.com

For Amy

Contents

INTRODUCTION

The Question

OULD YOU let your son play high school football? Sure you would. Meaning your son, my son, the collective son. You'd let him play high school football, right?

He would learn about discipline and camaraderie, respect and humility. He'd learn lasting lessons, like the importance of being on time and of giving honest effort and of being part of a team. He might learn how to lead, and he would learn how to follow wisely. He'd learn to aid a struggling teammate, and to be lifted by a determined one. At the right school, with the right coach, he could find real guidance. It would be good for the son to have a community like that, good for him to have responsibility.

"You know, of all the people I meet in sales, and I meet a lot, the guys who played football are the best," says Lynda Radosevich a marketing guru for start-ups in New York City. "They understand being part of a team, how to follow through. I don't think it's a coincidence."

It's *not* a coincidence, not at all. Many studies show it—that employers like to hire former student-athletes, believing they will be more confident, over the whole, than non–student athletes. And it seems those employees may be right, in the short run and in the long. "Men who participated in varsity-level high school sports an average of 60 years earlier appear to demonstrate higher levels of leadership and enjoyed higher-status careers," posits an academic study done through the Dyson School of Applied Economics and Management at Cornell University. They also gave more to charity and engaged in more public service. "And," says Kevin M. Kniffin, that study's lead author, "when you begin to look at sports independently, there appears to be an even greater correlation among collaborative, demanding sports such as football and success in the professional workplace."

Or maybe, aside from any values, maybe you'd let your son play football just to have fun—how he loves this game! You'd be happy to see *him* happy, playing the most popular sport in the land, the sport that makes cultural heroes of boys and men, a game that even at this early level, in high school, is bound inextricably to the rich and glittering NFL shield.

He would have something to do every day after school, something he *wanted* to do. No hanging around in the parking lot, getting into things you wish he wasn't getting into. No coming home to fall into the couch and stare at the screen in the palm of his hand, the hours of his youth ticking away, formlessly, in texts and video bytes. Football would get him out into the autumn air, give him something to point to each week—Friday night or Saturday afternoon, those three hours of game day. He'd lose some weight, get into shape, burnish his self-esteem. He'd *belong* someplace, to a world where sacrifices are made and rewards are reaped. Playing this game in this time, in this country, in these high schools, can be a first step, can't it? A first step on a bridge to adulthood and to a better life.

Maybe playing high school football would lead this son to play the sport in college. Maybe he'd even be one of the few to get a scholarship. Maybe he is one of the hundreds of thousands of young men who believes he could play for a powerful Division I program, get that long arrow shot at the NFL. Maybe he is one of the minute few who actually has a chance to make it there.

Or maybe, and for most of the boys this is it, he plays his four years of high school ball, two at jayvee, say, two at varsity, and pretty much never puts on the shoulder pads or the helmet again, takes those high school football years and keeps them with him forever, the time of his life. Walking the halls in his uniform on a Friday afternoon, catching the right girl's eye, knowing he has a direction, a purpose, and a whole team behind him and with him, every day of those earth-shifting, uneasy teenage years. Who could deny him that?

He is your son and my son, and he is you and he is me and he is all of us, a kid looking for a place to fit in, a mission to accomplish, a way to walk, someone to guide him and, yes, some real fun in life. Football can be all of that and more. So sure, you'd pack an extra sandwich in his lunch bag all season long, and you'd leave work to pick him up from the practice field in the evening darkness, and sure you'd be right there on hand, there among the buzzing crowd, every Saturday afternoon cheering for him, cheering for the team.

———————————

BUT NO. Wait. No. You're not letting your son play *football*, no way. Knowing the things that we now know? Absolutely not. Not when you've heard the stories, seen them right in your neighborhood (or experienced them yourself), of the kid who comes home from that week's game, or that day's practice, with his head dull and ringing. And then for weeks he can't run or read or look at a computer screen without feeling like he's about to throw up. Not when head injuries are even more frequent in high school football than they are in the college game. Not when the President of the United States says he would not let his son—his figurative son, the collective son—play in the NFL. Not when one former NFL star after another says exactly the same thing. Not when there's a White House Summit on concussions in youth sports and millions of dollars devoted to researching that very same subject, as if this were now an epidemic of some kind, as if we were in a moment pushed to a crisis.

True, it's not only football. Boys and girls get knocked loopy playing soccer too. Hockey. Lacrosse. Hoops. But football, well, football . . . that's the game of real collisions, play after play after play. That's the game where you're *supposed* to smash someone to the ground. No way your kid plays football four years and doesn't get his brain bounced around in his skull a few times. Inevitable. Now, is that worth it for the time of his life? You wouldn't let your son be a boxer would you?

"We are a no-football family," says Greg L., a 42-year-old financial analyst at Standard and Poor's who has a son and a daughter. "Basketball, hockey, sure, and there are injury risks there too. But football is just too much for us, too risky. If our son really got hurt out there we'd never forgive ourselves."

Certainly football has evolved far from its most treacherous roots, from back more than a century ago when college kids died on the field each month and the great bare-knuckled boxer John L. Sullivan (he of all people!) said he would never have the stomach to get out on the football field. "There's murder in that game," Sullivan said. Yet all through football's changes and right through to today, the awful-horrible stories keep coming in. Rutgers linebacker Eric LeGrand who went to make an ordinary tackle on an ordinary kickoff return in an ordinary game, October of 2010, and has never walked again. Or the running back from Navy, Will McKarney, a freshman kid coming back from a head injury, who collapsed and died in spring practice 2014. Or the whole of it, that in the last year alone, 11 American boys died directly or indirectly through playing high school football. That risk of catastrophe has always been there, that risk that you'll suffer the kind of impact injury that happens as a matter of natural course on the football field, but nowhere else in everyday American life.

We have heard the unhappy voices of old football stars, so many of them—the Hall of Fame Dallas Cowboy Rayfield Wright, the all-world running back Tony Dorsett, the late, great Detroit Lion Alex Karras and hundreds, even thousands, more. NFL players whose lives were given over to confusion, who slipped into darkness and dementia, their later years of life taken from them by the game that made their names. No wonder a judge looked at the $765-million concussion settlement the NFL reached with its retired players and threw it out, worried, she said, that the money would not be enough, not nearly, to cover the human damage done. There have been other concussion lawsuits too (same concern: the diminution of lives) and a recent suit arguing that playing in the league forces players, by the sheer fact of the pounding and punishment they receive, to become addicted to painkillers. Even among the best preserved of the retired players, those unclouded in their minds, so many are early-arthritic, carrying about on their old torn knees, their shredded ankles.

The touchdowns may be glorious, the spirit at times divine, but is this the sport you want your son to be playing?

High school football is not the same game that's played in grand stadiums on Sunday afternoons. It's not *that* kind of violent—not by a long shot given the NFL players' ferocity and heft and speed. But the mission and the parameters of each play are the same, from Pop Warner to high school to college to Super Bowl Sunday: Hit and be hit. Public school districts are facing concussion lawsuits too, levied by young men whose lives were reordered, thrown off course and slowed down by head injuries sustained while playing the game. Even if you got your son into the best-built helmet around (and isn't it vexing that the national federation of high schools hasn't updated helmet safety standards since the early 1970s?), and even taking into account the new rules penalizing headfirst hits in the high school game, could there ever really be protection against the collisions and the crashes? Against the violence both intended and incidental, that occurs, play after play, on the football field? Studies show that even for players who don't suffer a formal concussion, the repetitive, subconcussive blows absorbed over a high school season's worth of practices and games is enough to wound the brain.

You know about those helmet standards and you know about the research because you've been looking into it all, weighing the odds as it were, trying to decide what to do.

Yet maybe, you figure, football isn't really as dangerous as all that. That there's just so much hype about it all, that so many kids play the sport joyously and (essentially) unharmed, that they seem to come through just fine, stronger even. Surely football isn't as dangerous now as it was two, three, five decades ago, when a player would absorb a head-bashing and his coach would send him right back into the game for another. Maybe, given all the education we have gotten in recent years, all that research, and all the little precautions and safeguards now in place, maybe football really is safer today? The coaches know more about it all now and they've got good common sense (and so does your son!), and maybe the high school's concussion protocol could even protect this son from harm.

You think about all of that, and other things too. You imagine the son with his helmet in hand, staring at the front door, like the dog with the wagging tail and the leash in his mouth. And so, then, finally, *Yes!* you decide. You would let him play football. You'd swallow your fears about the head injuries (and about broken collarbones and ripped knees and splintered ankles). You'd acknowledge how football could nourish and educate and elevate the son, have an impact on his life for years to come, forever. That's it, decision made.

Except then you let yourself think the unthinkable one more time, the darkest possible thoughts right there with you as you stare up at your ceiling at night, and more of those nightmare numbers come pressing back into your head: The fact that about 30 boys a year suffer a serious or catastrophic head or spine injury playing football in high school; the fact that in the average year a dozen high school football players die. Okay, you tell yourself, but that's 12 out of more than a million players, and a few of those deaths come about during taxing workouts in high summer heat that you might be able to guard against, and one or two more might stem from a preexisting heart ailment that you are pretty sure this son does not have. Yes, football is dangerous as sports go, you acknowledge to yourself, but the truth is the kid has worse odds every time he gets into a car and goes for a ride with a peer. Much worse.

So, what is it, one death out of every 100,000 kids who plays high school football in America? You can frame those odds a little better, you think, if you massage the numbers, take some cautionary steps. One in 150,000? Who can really pinpoint the odds anyway, given the variances in human conditions, the variances in environment. We aren't actually rolling dice or flipping coins here. These are people! In any case, it's long odds to be sure. Really long. *One in 150,000.* But then, what if that one is yours?

A Note About This Book

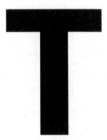T HERE'S AN old, good story, perhaps apocryphal, involving the British novelist and playwright W. Somerset Maugham. A writer friend told Maugham that he was having difficulty choosing a title for his just completed book.

"Are there drums in it?" Maugham asked.

"No," the friend replied.

"Are there trumpets?"

"No, not those either."

"Then call it 'No Drums, No Trumpets.'"

In describing *this* book, it seems also relevant, given the history and suggestion of the general subject matter, to first describe some of the things that this book is not. It is not about football at a high school in rural Texas, where the Friday night outcome can determine an entire town's mental well-being. It is not about a high school football factory that recruits players of superior talent and thwacks them into shape and mints them for use by Division I colleges and the NFL. Nor, in this book, did a tornado or earthquake or flood or other natural disaster devastate a team and town before folks and athletes rallied together in a stirring revival. This book is about a high school football team in a fairly ordinary suburban town, a big suburb where football is valued but not revered, a suburb with a gulf between the haves and have-nots, a suburb of great diversity, of many races and many abilities and many circumstances. This is a school, and a football team, populated by lives that can represent notions that every one of us might relate to, that we all understand, and a team that in its own particular and ordinary ways can say something large.

Another thing to note: This book takes place in the summer and autumn of 2014, a time unlike any other in the game and institution of football—the most critical and portentous months (riddled as they were with news and revelation) that the sport had yet known. Football had never, it seemed, had more far-reaching appeal, had never enticed more fans; and yet at the same time football had never been under greater attack, never more subject to judgment, even revulsion.

These were months when the extraordinary prevalence and troubling consequences of head trauma in the game were part of many, many conversations; when prominent football players, one after another after another, were arrested for domestic violence; when the dip in youth participation in the game, begun a few years before, began to raise true alarm. And these were months when—even as college and pro football drew more viewers than ever before, and millions of fans signed up to play in NFL fantasy leagues—a series of deaths in the high school game caused the full foundation of football to tremble.

Once, and not so long ago, the idea of suggesting that football be abolished was seen as radical, way out on the edge of reason. But at times during those baleful months of 2014, and then beyond, if you were in certain (wine-sipping) circles and you were reading certain (high-culture) magazines, the really radical thing to do was to stand in *support* of football, to defend the game and to say, "Let them play."

In whatever ways football evolves and devolves over the decades ahead, whether it survives and thrives or whether it feints and founders, it may well be that when we look back across the many years to see when things started to change, when football was able to strengthen its empire or began irrevocably to erode, we will say with a historian's wisdom that the tipping point of everything came then, in the summer and autumn of 2014.

CHAPTER 1

Hey, Coach D

HEY ARE as young as 14, and as old as 19. They play in public schools and at private academies. They play alongside unpaved country roads and beside busy city corners. They play on balding, unseeded fields, and they play on newly sewn synthetic turf. Many fields have single-bulb scoreboards; a few have spectacular Jumbotrons, others have no scoreboard at all. They play at football powers like De La Salle and St. Thomas Aquinas and they play for small schools, with incidental programs, that have never sent a player anywhere close to the NFL.

By the reckoning of the National Federation of State High School Associations, a total of 1,085,182 teenagers (all but a tiny fraction of them boys) played 11-man high school football in this country in 2014, more than any other high school sport by far. No other sport attracted even 600,000 boys. Those million-plus football players make up 14,154 teams. They play high school football from sea to sea in America, from Anchorage, Alaska, to Zephyrhills, Florida.

About 165,000 of those high schoolers play in football-mad Texas beneath the hot Friday night lights of autumn, where a community's culture and even its sense of self might be wound up and reflected in the team. There are towns like that in Oklahoma and Florida, and other places too. Another 104,000 of those teenagers play high school football in California, and 43,000 more play in Ohio, and 31,000 in Alabama. Football, everywhere. The state of New York, for its part, counts nearly 36,000 high school football players, engaged in 572 high school programs. Among those 36,000 kids are those who play in the southeastern swing of the state, in the suburban county of Westchester, including, for many decades now, the four dozen or so teenage boys who each fall pull on their bright purple and white uniforms to play an eight- or nine-game schedule for the Huguenots of New Rochelle High.

It's a big school, 3,389 students, and markedly diverse: a melting pot of African-American students, Caucasians, Latinos, Asians and children from India and the Middle East. The flag of every country in the world hangs in the school's entrance lobby. By definition a city district—New Rochelle has a population of 78,000—the school system is populated largely by suburbanites.

Many families here have ample means, although many others have little means at all. New Rochelle graduates go to Columbia and Stanford and Yale. They go to state schools and junior colleges, and many don't go to college at all. There is trouble to be found if you want it. "The joke is that we send as many kids to Sing Sing as we do to Harvard," a school administrator said. "But we do send them to both." In a given year, the football team's roster might include the child of a woman who works as a housekeeper for a teammate's parents.

Along with the football Huguenots (two-time New York State Class AA champions, three-time runners-up), New Rochelle High has a national champion cheerleading squad, a successful, avidly watched basketball team and 21 other varsity sports. There's a sprawling array of academic electives to complement the core courses. Students can strive for any or all of nine honor societies, and there is a rigorous, locally renowned performing arts program that gives kids a chance to perform at venues such as Carnegie Hall, and that each year yields graduates to places like Oberlin as a first violin or NYU's Tisch School as a promising actor. Yet for the many high achievers there are others of lesser success—some 38% of the student body is classified as disadvantaged, and New Rochelle High operates a series of sought-after special-needs programs that lure parents from neighboring towns whose children are compromised, physically or otherwise, in how they learn.

So there are all-state oboists, and grant-winning science projects, and budding stage performers, and the lure of gangs, and trips to the opera and the museum, and killer weed in the second-floor bathroom for $45 an eighth, and dozens of honor-roll kids bound for the Ivy League, and scores of learning-disabled kids with aides to lean on as they work their way through the grades, and two dozen interscholastic sports, and a kick-ass Model Congress. The school's got a big lunchroom and a smaller one, two gyms and a swimming pool, and the light blue paint on the hallway lockers is beginning to wear. Kids congregate by the parking lot during free periods to do skateboard tricks and to share music and to flirt. Some do homework on their laps, and others might disappear into the stand of trees across the way to smoke stuff. In May and June, the ice cream truck parks over by the school's side entrance, away from the long line of yellow buses, right around the time of last bell.

And in all of that, the chances are very good that someone in this high school would remind you a lot of yourself, or of your child—that you might look at certain students and their experiences and say to yourself, *This is like where I went, these are things that we did.* This could be your public high school and this could be my public high school. A school in which a cross-section of America's children are raised. And for each of those 3,389 kids at New Rochelle High, some kind of future, any kind of dream.

THE HIGH school building itself, a kind of marvel from the outside, opened in 1926 and sits on a broad-lawned campus adjacent to a town park. Wide, three-storied and made of brick, the building looms with an ornate French Renaissance architecture: towers, gargoyles, finials, arched doorways—everything it seems but crocodiles in a moat. It was

3

constructed in that style as a nod to the town's founders, a group of Huguenots, French Protestants who had fled persecution centuries earlier. Some of those Huguenots, including a core from the coastal town of La Rochelle in France, sailed into the region in 1688 and made land at Bonnefoy's Point in nearby Echo Bay. The land was hospitable and a community began to form and to thrive and in the early 1700s, many more Huguenots came over from La Rochelle as well.

In the 1930s New Rochelle, N.Y., was the third-wealthiest city per capita in the United States and it adopted the moniker "Queen City of the [Long Island] Sound." Lou Gehrig lived in New Rochelle as did Norman Rockwell and Elia Kazan, and later, in the '60s, the town served as the fictional setting of the classic and ultrapopular TV series *The Dick Van Dyke Show.* The '60s was also the decade in which New Rochelle's Lincoln Elementary School made history when it was court-ordered to desegregate, the first such order to any school in the North. E.L. Doctorow's novel *Ragtime*, published in 1975 and still very much in print, begins: "In 1902 Father built a house at the crest of the Broadview Avenue hill in New Rochelle, New York."

New Rochelle is no longer ranked the third wealthiest area in the country; despite some sizeable pockets of high-net-worth families, it now comes in as only the 198th wealthiest locale in *New York State.*

The freshwater pond carved into the High School's sprawling front lawn is the remnant of a family ice-making business that closed in the early 1900s. The pond's shoreline runs the length of the school, making it easily visible from the built-in metal bleachers that overlook the newish turf football field, with the school name painted in signature purple in the end zones, and ringed by a synthetic running track. The field is named William H. McKenna Field, and it was first dedicated in 1946 to coach Bill McKenna who, as the commemorative plaque by the flagpole declares: "produced some of the finest football and baseball teams New Rochelle has ever fielded by building the character of every athlete who played for him. From 1932 to 1935, his football teams had a 21-game winning streak and an overall record of 31-1-1. During that streak New Rochelle High School defeated the Illinois State Champion, Chicago's

Lane Tech, 36–0. The Huguenots were crowned National Champions in 1932." When the turf surface and the new scoreboard were installed in 2007, the field was rededicated to coach McKenna once again.

There's a grass practice area next to the game-day football field, and beside that a soccer space and then the baseball diamonds beyond. To get out to that sports area, you might walk through the school hallway that houses the athletic department—the coaches' offices, the rubber-matted exercise area, the player locker rooms. It's in this hallway, at just about any time of the school day, that you might hear the voice of a teenager call out. It might well be a football player, but perhaps not. It might be someone looking to make up a gym class, or to use the weightlifting equipment, or just a kid with a problem, hoping for a little practical advice on this matter or that. What you'll hear that voice call out is: "Hey, Coach D. You got a minute?"

———————

LOU DIRIENZO is 54 years old and has been the head football coach at New Rochelle for nearly 25 seasons. In that time he has become, in the way that teachers and coaches can become, a confidante of sorts, a father figure to many. He wears T-shirts, usually gray, and sweatpants and sneakers, and a yellow stopwatch on a cord around his neck. His skull, covered now and then by a ball cap, is predominately bald, and though he could not be described as muscular, he is quite broad across the chest. DiRienzo seems larger and taller than he actually is (big voice) and he is not at all afraid to hug one of his football players when the situation calls for it.

Each year DiRienzo stresses to the newest members of his team that "once you are in this program you are part of a family. There is nothing we don't do for each other." He means it at once as a promise and a caution, a reminder of responsibility. DiRienzo has accompanied players to court after an arrest. He has picked them up from parties when they were in no shape to drive. (And then benched them for the next game.) He has walked players to their classrooms on test days and he goes into their homes during college recruiting season. Each player's parent has DiRienzo's cellphone

5

number; many use it, at all hours. Coach D might be the first adult a player comes to when he learns that his girlfriend is pregnant. And Coach might be the first to get the news that a player scored 95 on a Regents exam.

DiRienzo spends most of his time at school (when he's not bellowing through a gym class) in a large, open and somewhat disarrayed space. It's a football community room, a short hallway removed from his office. The cinderblock walls are painted white and there are a couple of desks and computers that he and his assistant coaches use. No windows, and all the light comes from long cylindrical bulbs in the gridded fixtures in the ceiling. On the coaches' desks sit packets of papers delineating approaches to football: formations, bits of strategy and other pieces of wisdom that DiRienzo has lately gleaned or taken an interest in. He is an avid student of football and has incorporated aspects of the game from numerous programs at every level—Don Bosco Prep, Columbia University, the New England Patriots and so on. When in 2012 DiRienzo was intrigued by a particular aspect of Auburn University's offense that he'd noticed while watching the team play on television, he cold-called an Auburn assistant and probed for details. That led to a new suite of offensive plays that remains in the New Rochelle arsenal.

The community room also houses a large screen, around which coaches and players gather for daily film sessions, and there's also a wall-length whiteboard loaded with X's-and-O's diagrams, and with code names for play-calling, as well as with DiRienzo maxims. Things like: "The play doesn't care who makes it" and "Humble enough to prepare. Confident enough to perform." On the door of DiRienzo's office proper hangs a sign that reads, in block print: DISCIPLINE: DO WHAT HAS TO BE DONE/ WHEN IT HAS TO BE DONE/AS WELL AS IT CAN BE DONE/DO IT THAT WAY ALL THE TIME. Throughout the day, DiRienzo dips tobacco (Skoal, Original Wintergreen), continually refreshing the pinch beneath his lower lip and spitting quietly into a paper cup.

DiRienzo has two sons, Lou Jr. and Andrew, both of whom played small-college football and both of whom played for their father at New Rochelle. "The highs on the field were higher with them and the lows were lower," coach DiRienzo says, "but in most ways they were just like any other members of the team." Both boys embraced the game, took on prominent roles as Huguenots, and both have sustained concussions—while playing at New Rochelle and afterward. Over the years DiRienzo has developed a level of expertise in recognizing when a head injury has been concussive. Once, in the fall of 2013, he was talking by phone to his younger son Andrew, who was playing at Springfield College. Andrew had taken a hit in practice a couple of days before, he said, and during the conversation, he would become suddenly irrational and angry, not like his usual self. That led DiRienzo, who has seen such things in his players, to take him for the testing that confirmed the head injury. When Andrew got his next concussion, and the symptoms lingered, that was it; his playing days, everyone agreed, were done.

In the early 1980s DiRienzo had his own small-college football career cut short not by concussion but when his legs swelled up dramatically after making a routine block. He was a lineman at West Chester State in Pennsylvania, having made the team as a walk-on. "I was so far in back on the depth chart I couldn't see the line of scrimmage," he says. DiRienzo, though, became a three-year starter as an offensive lineman—not easy at barely 5' 9"—and it was four weeks into his senior year that he took his last hit. Blood clots, a resurfacing of an old problem, had made the leg balloon. "I woke up the day after that hit and I'm telling you my calf was the size of my thigh," DiRienzo says. "Football can be dangerous. Cutting granite with a sledgehammer can be dangerous too."

DiRienzo grew up in Tuckahoe, N.Y., the grandson to Italian immigrants and a youngest child with two older sisters. DiRienzo's mother did clerical work, and his father, Carmine, and uncles ran a stone quarry in Yonkers, N.Y. As a boy in the 1970s, working through the height of summer, DiRienzo learned to drill into the granite and to carefully pack in dynamite so as to blast large slabs off the mountainside. He learned to wrap the massive chunks of rock in thick chains so they could be hoisted and carried by a crane. He learned how to drop a sledgehammer just so, and to curb the granite into their 12-inch chunks for sale. "Quarry work is unforgiving, man," DiRienzo says. "The hardest work I have ever done. My dad did that pretty much until the day he died. He never played a down of football, but he left me the tools and values of my football life." The experience at the quarry, says DiRienzo, yielded the bedrock of his coaching philosophy: "Loyalty, humility and a belief in an honest day's work for an honest day's pay."

The bond in his nuclear family is thick. "We are like this," said his sister, Carmen, raising a clenched fist as she watched a New Rochelle game from the bleachers during the 2014 season. "And when you have that in your life you can pretty much do anything. You can get through anything. It's the most powerful strength there is."

Carmen is a lawyer who spent part of her career as the vice president of corporate affairs for WNET in New York, and Lou's other sister, Joan, is a nun and the principal of St. Bernadette Catholic parish elementary school in Brooklyn. "They were the ones who got the real education, who got the idea," Lou likes to say. "I think my parents should have quit after two. They gambled one time too many."

Coach DiRienzo's sisters and mother, Lucretia, often come to New Rochelle games (Carmen in particular) and in the state playoffs Joan has created a happy stir by sitting in the stands in her nun's habit, cheering loudly for the Huguenots and holding up a DE-FENSE sign. (She also follows the team avidly on Twitter.) Joan's first year as a playoff figure was in 2000, an emotional season in which DiRienzo led a team that had gone 4–6 the previous year to an 11–0 record and an unexpected berth in the state final game at Syracuse. The stunning run unfolded after Lou's father, Carmine, had died of congestive heart failure in late September, coloring it all. "My father was still with us that season," says Carmen. "We all felt it and you could see my father's values in Lou and how they kept him grounded. That's really what it is with Lou: He is amazingly well-grounded, straightforward, no-nonsense, comfortable in who he is. And he is very kind. Really he is very much like my dad. These are the things that make kids relate to him and believe in him, and why they keep him in their lives."

Even after they have left New Rochelle High, sometimes long after, many of DiRienzo's former players come back to him, continuing a dialogue they have come to depend on. Some may have been backups. Some were ordinary players. Some were the stars and leaders of the team. Some of the former players have gone on to notable football careers or to high-paying corporate jobs. Others have been less fortunate in the game and less fortunate in life. Some might come looking for jobs—the district's coaching ranks are peppered with former DiRienzo players—but most come just to talk, reminisce, seek advice, feel a sense of affirmation. Around coach D, as Khalil Edney, who graduated in 2013, says, "We're all kind of the same. We all want to listen to him and follow him. When you are with coach D some of the confidence that he gave you when you were with the team comes back."

The New Rochelle football program, and the mentoring that goes into it—the study halls and the college prep, the off-season workouts, the early morning meetings, the hallway bantering, the holding up of oneself in a certain light with a certain humility and a certain confidence—begins and ends with Lou DiRienzo. The tenets and teachings of the program are sustained by his commitment and avidity, and strongly supported by a loyal and long-tenured staff of assistants.

"Football is my father's life," says Lou DiRienzo Jr. "It's who he is, it's how he understands the world. Football is a way for him to communicate the things that he believes in. And it's a way for him to help the rest of us understand the world as well."

CHAPTER 2

Camp Brookwood

ACH YEAR at the end of August, after holding the preseason's first, long days of official practice at the high school, coach DiRienzo takes his New Rochelle varsity football team away for a four-day retreat. It's just the team—in 2014 that meant 46 kids and six coaches—and during the getaway the group aims to lay the groundwork for the season ahead. They put in the new offense, add some defensive alignments, work on a few stunts, hone the language of their play-calling and grow to understand one another better. The coaches will learn some things about the players. The players will learn some things about each other. Some starting positions will be won and lost. A level of mettle will be tested. "It's scary the first time you go up there," says senior Jonathan Forrest, the team's star running back who made varsity as a freshman and thus has been to the preseason camp four times. "You don't know what to expect, not from the coaches, not from the other guys, not from anything. You just kind of know that you're all up there together, four days nothing but football—and each other. It works out."

DiRienzo's teams attended other late-summer camps over the years before he settled, in the mid-2000s, on Camp Brookwood, a collection of bunkhouses on a 160-acre spread deep within the wooded and hilly countryside of Sullivan County, New York. For most of the summer Brookwood is a conventional, sports-oriented sleepaway camp. The kind of place, as DiRienzo puts it, "where the rich kids, the doctors' and lawyers' kids, go." But in the last weeks of August, after the final sleepaway session has ended and the campers and counselors have gone home or back to school, Camp Brookwood, like many other, similar camps, rents its sleeping and eating facilities to high school sports teams. At the same time that New Rochelle was at Brookwood, so were football teams from Canarsie, Fort Hamilton (both in Brooklyn) and Monsignor Farrell (Staten Island). There was also in residence a soccer team from Fieldston, an upscale private school in the Bronx.

The camps that New Rochelle teams went to in earlier years under DiRienzo were more plush—with bright, permanent field lights for night practice; stocked arcade game rooms; heated swimming pools; better options at the canteens—but DiRienzo likes the no-frills, no-nonsense feeling at Brookwood (for one thing, swimming in the lake or pool during this week is forbidden by the camp directors), and he likes the sleeping situation. Rather than in open dorms, the kids stay in small bedrooms, three or four players in each. The players' rooms occupy one wing of a single-floor bunkhouse, while the coaches sleep in an adjacent wing, just on the other side of a common room that has a television on which the team watches practice film and the players are sometimes afforded time to play video games after the day's work is done. The kids get to their rooms by 10:30 or 11 each night; the wrestling, the pranking, the loud laughter and general horseplay commences—and it is lights out by 11:30. An assistant coach tries to stay in the hall outside the players' rooms each night until the shenanigans have quieted for good and the kids (so far as he can tell) are truly asleep.

The closer quarters can lead to important relationships for the season ahead, and also means more accountability to the coaches. "Now if I walk into someone's room and it looks like a hurricane hit, if there's crap all over or the window screen is broken or whatever, I know it's got to be one of four guys," says DiRienzo. "I don't have to whack the whole team." For the most part friends on the team can choose to bunk together but the coaches also employ some strategy to the arrangements, rooming some of the less confident, more vulnerable kids with the team's established and trusted figures, the players DiRienzo has explicitly asked for leadership. The leaders tend to protect the weaker kids, and this, the coaches hope, fends off some of the bullying, keeps the hazing pretty much innocuous, clean and safe.

The coaches (and players) also like Brookwood for the fact that despite the weathered and eminently penetrable cabins, despite the debris from foodstuff that inevitably lands outside the rooms or windows, and despite the woodlands all around, there are noticeably fewer "vermin" here than in other camp locations—that is, not too many rats or squirrels or hedgehogs or raccoons nosing around. "Well," says DiRienzo, "I *used* to like the fact that there weren't many small animals, but then someone told me that the reason there are no small animals is because the big animals ate them. So now at night when we're coming off the practice field I've got my head on a swivel, keeping my eyes out for brown bears or coyotes. You hear them sometimes, I'm telling you. I don't like 'em." Camp Brookwood is a little more than a two-hour drive from the crowded, concrete center of New Rochelle.

TWO LONG, white coach buses left the New Rochelle High School parking lot at 8:30 on Sunday morning Aug. 24, 2014, and headed northwest by highway. Already the players had had a week of intensive practice at the school, arriving at 7:30 each morning and staying, through the hot August afternoons, until 7 or 7:30 at night. On the first two days, per school district rule, the team practiced without putting on any gear at all. Then the helmets and shoulder pads came on and, in DiRienzo's words, "In helmets and shoulder pads you can pretty much do whatever you would do in full gear." There's running, of course, agility exercises and numerous tackling drills. Defensive formations are put in place and tested time and again. The offensive and defensive lines crash into each other for a while each day, the quarterbacks take snap after snap, and lessons that were learned a few months earlier in spring football get reinforced. There's some weightlifting mixed in during these days as well—a continuation of the off-season free-weight program most of the kids have been doing since the start of January.

During that week of August practice (it is known, predictably, as "hell week") the kids eat breakfast, lunch and usually dinner at the high school. They take naps on the rubberized floor of the weight room or on the long, sticky benches in the boys' locker room. Each evening, as Justice Cowan, a senior linebacker, describes it, they go home "tired enough to fall asleep until it is time to wake up and go back in and do it again." The understanding among all of them is that this is a first taste of the season, a warmup for the full-gear and full-on camp experience ahead.

With hell week behind them, the players were chatty and jokey as the bus ride to Brookwood began, though soon, as the highway exits began to roll by, a quieter mood set in. Players dozed in their seats or listened to music or played on their smartphones. A few read books or magazines; others ate food packed for them at home. A movie played on the television screens above the aisle: *Cabin Fever*, a 2002 horror film in which a group of college kids rent a cabin in the woods for vacation. Rather than just relax out there in the wild, the young vacationers in *Cabin Fever*—as young vacationers to cabins in the woods tend to do— encounter a strange hermit and kill him. They go on to meet a child with a vicious biting habit, a deeply corrupt police officer and other memorable characters. And, as might also be reasonably expected on such an excursion, they all begin to fall prey to a deadly flesh-devouring virus. After a while, one of the college kids gets eaten alive by a dog. "Just a little something to set the mood, I guess," said New Rochelle assistant coach Keith Fagan, laughing. The setting of *Cabin Fever*, with the woodlands and the nearby lake, is not an environment many of the New Rochelle players are familiar with in real life. And it's also quite a bit like the surroundings at Brookwood.

The bus turned off the highway, then traveled along industrial boulevards before emerging north of the old railroad town of Port Jervis, N.Y. (where the local high school has been playing football since 1897), onto winding rural roads, the last stretch of the journey. The remoteness of Brookwood, the far-from-homeness, is another part of its appeal to the coaches. About five miles out from camp, just before entering a thickly forested and stream-strewn town called Lumberland, the road to Brookwood climbs and wends alongside a steep drop to the Delaware River. It's a narrow, two-lane road, a bit disconcerting when riding in a bus, but the view is spectacular and locally renowned. There are occasional cutaways where drivers can pull over and get out of their cars to look at, or take postcard-worthy pictures of, the glinting river scene below: a few kayaks, a small fishing boat, a couple sitting together on a large rock by the water's edge, the river moving swiftly and swollen by summer rain.

By this time of year, the trees along both banks—here New York, there Pennsylvania—loom large and lush: rich canopies of deep green. The feeling among the Huguenot players, stirring now as the destination neared, was, along the lines of, *Whoa, we're not in New Rochelle anymore.* And while the bus did not stop and pull over to allow for taking in the view, some of the kids, those confident enough to slough off the façade of teenage indifference, rose in their seats to look out the window. Senior noseguard Jasper Baskerville, who at maybe 5' 10" and 236 pounds is built thick as a young bear and is the team's hands-down weight-room hero, shook his head slightly as he stared out at it all—the deep ragged gully, the splendid, broad river split here by a small green island, an osprey turning overhead. "Damn," Jasper said softly, and he and the others stayed half-risen from their seats looking out the windows until the bus rolled past, into Lumberland, and then on to Brookwood, leaving that scene behind.

"THAT WILL be your field over there," camp director Scott Fiedler was saying, gesturing in the direction. The players had just spilled out of the two buses and were standing together in a loose semicircle on the gravel-and-sand parking area, receiving some Brookwood ground rules. "And that's where you'll eat—the dining room closest to your bunk. Each team has its own dining room and own eating times, your coaches will tell you when."

Brookwood's customer base—those wealthy, white-collar suburbanites that DiRienzo described—was hit hard by the economic recession of 2008. The camp's annual sleepaway enrollment dropped by roughly a third, and even six years later had not yet fully recovered, a circumstance which had led Brookwood's operators to further develop and lean more heavily upon the specific sports programs they have long had in place. Ken and Donna Fiedler, both already experienced camp directors at the time, had bought Brookwood in 1986 and have run it, along with Scott, their son, ever since. When Ken underwent his second open-heart surgery in 2012, forcing him to limit his workload, Scott's younger brother, Jay, increased his involvement with Brookwood, becoming a full-time camp director in 2013. Jay and Scott were now delivering this orientation speech to the Huguenots together.

"It's a beautiful lake," Jay told the kids. "But don't go near it. And when you're back in your bunks for the night, stay in your bunks. You want your sleep. This is the time of year to get some important football work in and that starts with being rested."

"Listen up. This is an NFL player talking," New Rochelle assistant coach Greg Foster reminded the players as Jay finished up his orientation. "This is a guy who has been there."

Indeed, Fiedler, who played high school football in Oceanside, Long Island (a town with precisely the demographics that Camp Brookwood has depended upon), starred at quarterback at Dartmouth College and spent 10 seasons in the NFL, playing for five teams. Twice he went to the playoffs with the Miami Dolphins, leading them to an overtime win against the Colts in a December 2000 wild-card game. In 2005, as a backup with the Jets, Fiedler suffered shoulder injuries that would end his professional career. Over 76 career NFL game appearances, he completed more than 1,000 passes and threw for 69 touchdowns. He is among the most accomplished NFL quarterbacks to emerge from the

Ivy League in the past 65 years,[1] certainly the best out of Dartmouth, and he has been inducted into the National Jewish Sports Hall of Fame.

Jay is a young man, 42 years old in the summer of 2014, and he remains powerful across the chest and shoulders. A solid jaw and an athlete's neck. He admits, though, that his back hurts almost all the time ("Mornings suck," he says), and surgeries on both hips have given him a stiff, labored gait. Jay usually travels around the Brookwood grounds—surveying the teams at practice, checking on the bunks, helping stock the kitchen—in a golf cart. He was sitting in that golf cart, casually reflecting, as the New Rochelle team dispersed. "My body hurts, but I think my head is O.K., my brain," he said. "For now anyway. You don't know what will happen. You see things all the time about the head injuries and the mental and psychological stuff that guys are going through, guys you played football with. Of course it's scary. It has to be. You don't play that long without getting your bell rung a bunch of times.

"Things are different now though. Not just in the NFL. When I was in high school and college they didn't track concussions like they do these days. Even now you can't do anything to prevent them. This is football. Head injuries are going to happen. They're going to happen more than you want them to. But at least people are trying to track them, and to treat them the right way. That's a start."

Fiedler adjusted his baseball cap and stretched out his right leg and rested a forearm on the steering wheel of the cart. Ahead to his right, New Rochelle players were a couple of hundred yards out, making their way down to their bunkhouse, bags slung over their shoulders. Ahead to Fiedler's left, and further off, was Brookwood's network of football fields, laid out on cascading levels, some parallel to the ones above, others perpendicular. Grassy berms section off the fields, yielding a

---

[1] That is, since the great and pioneering Columbia product Sid Luckman retired from the Bears in 1950. More recently, Harvard alum Ryan Fitzpatrick, who has played for six teams and who, through the end of his 2015 season with the Jets, had thrown for more than 23,000 career yards, has established himself as the NFL's reigning Ivy quarterback king.

kind of Opus 40 effect; there's at once a sense of continuum among the playing areas—one enormous man-made lawn cut and fashioned from the earth—and at the same time a degree of privacy on each of them. At that moment the Canarsie team was practicing on the farthest field, sunken out of view. You could hear the distant clack of bodily contact and the sharp, urgent voices of players and coaches calling out.

Fiedler loves football and he loves teaching it to young people, which he does at clinics and camps throughout each year. Since his days at Oceanside in the 1980s, and through his Brookwood involvement, and over the course of leading hundreds of multi-day football and quarterback camps in many locations over many years during and after his career, Fiedler has seen a lot of high school football teams and known a lot of high school football coaches. "I can tell you something," he said, nodding toward the bunk-house where the last of New Rochelle players were carrying their things inside. "No one does a better job at this level than Louie DiRienzo does."

AFTER FINDING their assigned bedrooms (names were posted on the doors, as in Room 2: Haitam Coughlin, Manny Walker, Greg Powell, Eric Stenroos) and dropping off their bags, the players were quickly due at the field to begin warmups and then a series of agility drills. The coaches had set up the familiar SPARQ equipment, neon-and-black plastic contraptions of varying shapes and purposes that the players, doing this drill or that, began to hop over, dodge around and high-step through. Even here in the mountains it was hot—high 80s, low 90s— and now, at a little past noon, the sun was bright and high and beating down on the field. Off one of the sidelines, beside a small section of bleachers, a rack of spigots had been set up, each spigot attached to a garden hose that went to a shed farther off. The players, dressed in T-shirts and shorts (no helmets or other gear), were given regular breaks to drink and to douse their faces and heads. During one such break coach DiRienzo went over to his assistants, who were gathered on the field, and said, "O.K., time to run."

The running in this case meant ladder sprints, or the cheerfully named "suicides," a staple conditioning drill across sports, and common, with variations, on preseason football fields. The players lined up in the end zone and at the coaches' "Go!" sprinted to the 10-yard line and back, then to the 20-yard line and back, then to the 30 and so on. They did this up to the length of the field, 100 yards. Then they worked back down, sprinting at descending lengths, to 10 yards. As the sprints wore on, the rests between them grew successively longer—10 seconds, 30 seconds, a minute—as the boys wearied. The coaches stood on the field, just outside the running area, rallying the players with claps and encouragement. "Let's go! Keep working it, keep working," Keith Fagan shouted, "Finish! Finish the sprint! Which one of you is going to be first? Who is going to lead?"

The players, busy breathing, did not say much at all. Some, upon reaching the end of a sprint, would bend to rest in a half crouch, hands on his knees. A couple of kids went down to all fours or rolled onto their backs. They didn't seem troubled or even unhappy. Just tired. "Do not go down, stay up!" shouted Brian Violante, a heavy-set and well-liked assistant. Violante, 32, is also New Rochelle's varsity lacrosse coach and his father, Frank, won 227 games as a high school football coach in Dobbs Ferry, N.Y. "You're making it harder for yourself when you go down like that— because you've gotta get back up!" Violante added sharply. "Don't even bend over. Stand up straight. If you're tired, put your hands on top of your head." As dozens of hands went to the top of dozens of heads, one player turned to Fagan and said quietly, "Coach, I think I have to vomit."

This was about halfway through the ladder sprints and the kid feeling queasy was Alex Gaudio, at 6' 2" and 278 pounds the largest player on the team, a senior lineman low on the depth chart. He wore glasses with metallic rims and despite the heat had dressed in black three-quarter length shorts and a black Nirvana concert shirt. His bangs were matted to his forehead.

A player needing to vomit during early season ladder sprints is not a new or unusual phenomenon at New Rochelle or anywhere else. If anything, football coaches like to know the kids are truly pushing themselves. "O.K. then, do it, get it out. Go on over there to the side, away from the field though," said Fagan. "Up and out. Get it out. You'll feel better."

The summer running, as a general rule, tends to be hardest on the heaviest players and along with Gaudio that included 6-foot, 270-pound Shameek Miller, also a senior offensive lineman. Not so long before, Shameek occupied much more space, weighing in at more than 300 pounds. Through football, and during his time on New Rochelle's wrestling team the previous winter, Miller had steadily brought his weight down and, his schoolmates say, his confidence up. "It's like you could see his self-esteem rising as he was losing weight and having some success in sports," says DiRienzo.

Shameek (nicknamed Mickey) suffers from asthma and the fact that he was doing these sprints, even at his new weight, was an achievement in itself. At times when the players restarted their sprints Shameek wasn't ready, still winded, lagging. He would stand alone in the end zone, bent slightly, trying to gain control of his breathing, looking out at his teammates 50 yards away. And then, suddenly, he would take off toward them, his arms flailing, his running form ruined by fatigue. A cheer always went up from the boys and clapping—"That's it, Mickey! That's it, Mickey!" DiRienzo called out—and when Shameek chugged his way across the 50, he was greeted with high fives and back slaps.

"They're picking me up," Shameek would say afterward, walking toward the dining hall for lunch. "These guys are always picking me up. You know? It makes me feel good."

IT WAS a full day of practices: special teams drills, inside drills, heavy work on defense. DiRienzo explained to the players that he'd had them run those midday suicides right off the bus because "I wanted you to know that we are here to work, not to play. I know it's different up here, and you're all together. You'll have some time to blow off steam, you'll get your free time together, but this isn't four days of summer camp. This is four days of football camp."

Lunch was spaghetti with red sauce, deep-fried chicken cutlet, salad. The boys went back for seconds, some for thirds, and many took extra bowls of a sweet pale-beige substance identified by a camp cook as "some kind of pudding." They drank water or else the red juice that passed for punch. The team was back on the field from 2:30 until past 5 o'clock and then again for a couple of hours after dinner, and during the breaks in between they unrolled their sleeping bags on their dorm beds and squirreled away the candy they'd brought and hollered at each other and went up and down the hallway seeing just who was in which room. The team started a *Madden NFL 25* tournament on a small TV that someone had brought up, then later moved the tournament out to the game-film screen in the lobby. Five bucks each in the pot, winner-take-all. About 30 of the guys got in, and the eventual victory—after three days of games—went to junior Manny Walker, before a hooting and hollering crowd of teammates gathered around him. Winning not only put some good money in Manny's pocket, it also earned him increased acceptance, a clear measure of respect, even, among the team elders.

Other times, when they were in their rooms and allowed on their phones, kids called their parents or girlfriends (cell reception was spotty depending on where you stood) or took naps. Late in the day, before dinner and after the sun had dropped a bit in the sky, a few of the more determinedly energetic of the kids played a loosely run game of basketball on the cement court just outside the bunkhouse. "There's Aleve and Tylenol and Nyquil in my room," coach DiRienzo had told the team before the afternoon practice, as he helped them wrap ankles and knees and wrists. The Aleves and Tylenols sat in oversized, industrial-looking plastic jars, like vats almost, and after alerting DiRienzo, players were free to go in and take what they thought they needed when they needed it.

Overall, you sensed a heady buzz, even a degree of giddiness among the players—*damn, boys, can you believe we're up here?*—mixed as it was with a feeling of apprehension about what needed to be done on the football field and the concern, on the part of each boy, whatever his level or stature, about whether he would perform well enough or not; whether, as the junior split end and defensive back Haitam Coughlin said, "the coaches will like what they see in you, whether your teammates will like what they see in you."

The scene on the practice field that afternoon, as well as the scene at other practices at Brookwood and then at New Rochelle throughout the season, was similar to scenes on so many football fields at so many levels. The players were divided into position groups, squadrons of a kind, with each group developing and honing particular required skills, the. players work-shopping their talents in the hopes of impressing the coaches and doing so with the drummed-in mind-set that their varied assets would ultimately operate together as a larger and efficient whole.

Those on the offensive and defensive lines, who toil for the most part in close spaces, bullied their way or maneuvered their way through and past opposing bodies. Linebackers and defensive backs, who work in more open areas, were being taught how to cover ground more efficiently—as well as just what ground to cover, and when. And those who throw and catch and carry the ball were running through some basic plays, undefended against. (The kickers, and the players who aid them, were, at times, yet another small group.) Each group had its own, if not entirely unrelated, requirements for footwork and positioning, approach, philosophy and execution, the players embracing (or succumbing to) the fact that along with strength and speed, a true understanding of the game and each player's role within it was essential.[2]

Each collection of players had a coach directing them, hands-on. Guiding the interior lineman through their blocking drills was the burliest and biggest-voiced of the assistants, Greg Foster, who played (well, and at times heroically) for DiRienzo during the coach's first year at New Rochelle in 1990, then went to the University of Albany. Brian Violante,

---

[2] The concept of dividing a sports team into specialty groups for practice is hardly unique to football. Infielders snagging ground balls here, outfielders chasing fly balls there; hockey defensemen doing lateral skating drills on one half of the ice, forwards honing breakaways on the other; and so on. But football is unique for both the size of the team, and for the sheer number and nuances of the specialties required. Small matters of hand placement and "hip wiggle" may seem picayune to a defensive back (or for that matter to most of the civilized and noncivilized world) but it can be the difference between an offensive guard's success or failure on a given play. Such examples, across all the moving parts on a football field, abound.

the varsity lacrosse coach, ran a drill in which linebackers wrapped up running backs as they burst mid-stride across the line of scrimmage. Rich Tassello, the team's fitness and conditioning expert, who was a water boy at Roosevelt High in Roosevelt, N.Y., when DiRienzo was an assistant there in the late 1980s, led the secondary with help from first-year assistant Vic Chiappa. ("I kid Richie about his water boy days now," says DiRienzo. "I say 'I'm going to send you for coffee if you don't watch out.' ") And Keith Fagan had the two quarterbacks and a few receivers over on one side of the field getting down some intermediate routes.

DiRienzo went from drill to drill, offering advice here, admonishment there, exhorting the groups, keeping the tempo high. He would lean in and watch, talking with a coach, or come over and take a player aside and break down something he'd just observed. Coach D would holler when he wanted everyone to stop and drink water or to take off their heavy shoulder pad gear ("packs" as they're called) to cool down. It was hot enough that you sweated just standing still and when the players drank water—from the spigots or from the plastic bottles they shared among themselves—they invariably doused their heads and necks and faces between slugs.

DiRienzo moved with a pronounced limp, one he had not had a few months before at spring practice. After a while, to continue making his rounds, he clambered into a golf cart. "I hate riding in this thing on the field. Hate it," he said. "It gives off the vibe of a lazy person, and I am *not* a lazy person. In other parts of life maybe sometimes, but on the football field no one could ever say I was lazy."

He needed the cart, though, because he was having real trouble with his left leg. In July he had needed surgery to repair a bleeding ulcer and now, he said, there were complications with the internal wound, and blood kept pooling down in his left foot. He felt pain, a strange almost toothachy sensation in his leg, and he had been instructed to keep off his feet much more than he was actually doing. On the field at Brookwood, after he drove over and parked alongside a drill to watch, DiRienzo lifted his left leg and rested it over the nose of the golf cart.

DiRienzo has had circulatory issues ever since a childhood hernia surgery led to blood clotting and thrombosis and forced him to miss his junior and senior years of football at Tuckahoe High. It was the same issue that later ended his self-made Division II career as an undersized lineman. "But that was then and I thought that was it. This thing now, it's killing me," said DiRienzo. "I had three weeks going out of my mind lying on the couch trying to find football movies on ESPN. Did I get a bleeding ulcer because we only went 6–3 last year and the team drove me crazy?" he asked laughing. "I don't know about that. I guess maybe. It is true that I didn't have an ulcer the year before, when we won the state championship."

RETREATS OF the Brookwood kind are commonplace among teams in numerous sports, not only at high schools but also among college and pro teams. Nonsports companies go on retreats too, as a way to foster employee bonding. At such company off-sites and at some sports retreats, the schedule of events is often littered with various team-building, trust-building exercises. (Blindfold yourself, let yourself fall, a teammate catches you, that kind of thing.) Participants climb rope courses and scale rock walls—a numbers guy from cube 412 belaying for the creative director with the office down the hall— or sit in a circle and toss a ball of yarn among themselves and tell personal stories. Some football teams do things like this, but it is far less common, because as a means of team-building and trust-building football teams have, well, football.

"All team sports can create a bonding relationship, but in football you really need each other in the most basic sense," said Jay Fiedler that first night at Brookwood. "You have to protect one another. If you're playing baseball and the leftfielder misses the ball, yes it hurts the team—but the ball isn't going to hit the rightfielder in the face. Miss your assignment in football, do the wrong thing, and there's a good chance one of your guys will get walloped. Do things the right way and you might be taking punishment that someone else did not have to take. That's a big part of everything in football."

It was late in the evening now, 8:30 or so, and the sky was clear and dark gray and already peppered gently with stars. Fiedler was in his golf cart at the side of the field, watching New Rochelle work drills under the yellow cast of two generator-run floodlights. All of the other teams in residence had gone in for the night. There were a few trees on one sideline of the field and, a bit farther off, thick woods circling the property, the treetops in silhouette. The land the team was playing on had been cleared and leveled and developed many decades before, yet those tree tops and the dark mountain ridges against the moonlit sky, and the absence of artificial light when you looked away from the camp, made it easy to imagine centuries back when the terrain was worked and lived on by clans of the Lenni-Lenape tribe that controlled the region. You could hear distant clucks and hoots and other indiscriminate noises come sporadically out of the woods, and the steady croak of crickets and the mechanical hum of the generators running the floodlights, as well as the sound of the coaches and the boys playing football. Foster and Violante were again running offensive and defensive line drills, urging the players to break hard off the snap and really larrup one another, so that into the still night came also the sound of colliding bodies and grunts, and of the clackety-clack of helmets knocking into helmets, play after play after play. The Lenni-Lenape clans played a version of football too, those centuries ago, both men and women together on the field, using a ball sewn of deerskin and stuffed with animal hair.

DiRienzo, out of his cart, was directly overseeing a drill, implementing a short curl pass play—virtually a screen—into the offense. The quarterback, junior Greg Powell, was out to the right. The receiver, set far left, would break out a couple of strides, curl down and away, come back toward Powell just ahead of the line of scrimmage, catch the football and turn upfield. There were no true offensive linemen out there, just some defenders in linebacker positions with big foam blocking shields who would cover the nonreceiving receivers as they ran their decoy routes. Then, after the reception, they would close in and blunt the ballcarrier's progress.

The play, like most in football, depends upon at least some level of deception, and Powell had been instructed to drop back and quickly move his feet exactly this way, then that, before throwing. His footwork, the coaches knew, needed improvement. DiRienzo took his white ball cap off his head and set it on the ground three strides behind the line of scrimmage, telling Powell that this was the spot he should always get back to and stop at.

They ran the curl over and over, Powell calling hike, then flicking off this short cross-field pass 10 times, 20 times, 30. . . . Too often Powell threw the ball a little low and slightly behind the play so that it came to the receiver by his right hip, forcing him to slow slightly and reach backward to make the catch. Ideally in this play the ball should arrive higher and out front, at the height of the receiver's left, downfield shoulder. It is a difference of maybe 21 inches from where Powell kept delivering the ball, and the proper throw leads the receiver in the direction he wants to be going. He can snare the football, tuck it and take off.

Coach D reminded Powell of this, quietly, patiently—it was a new play they were working on after all—but the misthrows began to irk one of the receivers in rotation, senior CJ Anthony. CJ is a well-raised football junkie (his father coached in the New Rochelle youth league for close to 30 years) and he is in fine physical shape. He likes to wear his jersey hiked up to reveal the impressive definition in his stomach muscles. CJ often corrals his bushy, dyed-blonde hair with a headband, and he can be a determined jokester, a smart aleck. On the practice field, during breaks, Anthony likes to strut around, imitating and exaggerating coach D's long-strided, arms-swinging gait, patrolling the area and pretending to be doing the caricature only when Coach doesn't see him, though everyone knows that Coach *does* see him but won't blanch. CJ's father worked for a while as one of DiRienzo's assistants.

"You're throwing the ball down here at my waist," Anthony, peeved, snapped at Powell after dropping a pass. "You've got to put it up here so I can catch it."

"Just stop whining and catch the ball," Powell snapped back. Anthony stood and glared at Powell and Powell glared back.

DiRienzo didn't say anything about this exchange, just kept running the play, another 20, 25 times as he stood there, shifting his weight to take pressure off his aching left leg. Practice was going on elsewhere on the field as well, in another linemen exercise, and a few of the team's younger players, not needed for the moment, were standing off to the side, watching.

DiRienzo made a small adjustment on the receivers' route, honed in again on Powell's feet—"Right to here, Greg, right to here, and then you turn." Occasionally DiRienzo pulled a kid from the linemen's drill or from the sideline to switch in and play linebacker on the curl play for a while. Finally, he called out "One more rep!" and after it the players took off their helmets and drank water and bantered a bit and then gathered along with the assistant coaches near the center of the half-lit field, down on one knee, looking up at coach D. It was well past 9 o'clock by then and the stars were more plentiful in the black sky. The loudest sound now was coach D clearing his throat. The players were at Camp Brookwood, first night, and there was no place any of them could have gone if they wanted to. Though by the looks on their glistening faces there was no place else they would have rather been.

"There are things here that we need to address," said DiRienzo. "It was a good practice but not great and I am seeing things, for those of you in the curl drill especially, that we need to address." The players and the assistant coaches were at this point expecting a technical assessment, a critique of the execution. "I have a receiver complaining to the quarterback that the ball is coming in too low. And I have a quarterback complaining that the receiver should just catch the ball," DiRienzo continued. He was loud now and suddenly his voice had a charge in it that's not always there. "Well guess what. You don't do that here. You don't point. If we make a play on the New Rochelle football team it's because 'WE' make a play. 'I' don't make any plays here. The time will come when a quarterback throws you a ball and it's going to hit you right in your hands where it should be and you are going to drop it. The time is going to come when a quarterback is going to throw the ball way too high and somebody is going to make a circus catch. And 'WE' are going to make a great play. When we make a play, we all do it. We are all in.

"If we miss a play, if someone misses a block, 'WE' missed it. If we sack the other team's quarterback when we are only rushing four men, it's because we had good coverage in the back. 'I' don't make a play at

New Rochelle. *'I'* have never made a play at New Rochelle. *'WE'* make a play at New Rochelle."

His voice resounded in the quiet night and the boys, tired from the long day, were nonetheless fixed upon him. Though some of them knew the identities of the quarreling boys he was talking about, DiRienzo never mentioned Anthony or Powell by name. He went silent for moment, and then said, "You are going to find out, and find out in a real hurry, that this"—DiRienzo pounded his left pectoral, his heart—"means a whole lot more than this," he swung his right leg in a hard kick. "That *THIS*"—he said it again and pounded his left pec again—"means a whole lot more than this.

"O.K. Get back to the bunk, get out of your uniforms, get something to drink. In 15 minutes meet in the front room. We've got some film to go over, then you've got an hour to yourselves."

Jay Fiedler had been watching all this and as the team began to walk off toward the bunkhouse, he climbed off his golf cart and hobbled toward the middle of the field where he picked up a football. "Hey, Louie," Fiedler called out. "Someone I can have a catch with? I want to throw."

"Powell!" shouted Keith Fagan. "Powell, turn around and catch the ball." Fiedler was on the 40-yard line, and Powell was near the closer end zone, walking off toward the bunk. He stopped and turned and tossed away his helmet, ready to catch. Fiedler released the ball with an easy, even graceful, motion (accompanied though it was by the grimace of a man with a body well-worn), and sent out a splendid, high spiral that descended 40 yards later, right into Powell's hands. Powell, quiet and expressionless, caught the ball and threw it back. He has the arm for this distance, and though the light from the floodlights was poor, the back-and-forth toss went on for a while, no words between them. Some of Powell's teammates stopped and watched, pulling on their water bottles and jibing good naturedly when Powell mishandled the ball in any way. And so it was that Greg Powell, a 17-year-old preparing for the first start of his high school career, played a game of catch with Jay Fiedler, a man who appeared in 76 games in the National Football League, and it all seemed entirely natural, two quarterbacks linked through the long and lasting continuum of football.

CHAPTER 3

Mess Up Your Baseline, Bro

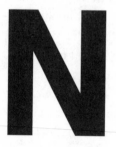**OT EVERY** member of the New Rochelle team took part in the on-field drills at Brookwood. A small group of injured players (the group grew larger as camp went on) was relegated to the sidelines, to sitting on the small metal bleachers or hovering on the outskirts of the field. They brought water bottles to their teammates, helped set up cones, fetched ice—biddable, when needed, to the coaching staff. At other times the boys on the sideline tossed a football back and forth or stretched or simply sat, wrapped in the ennui of the hot, hot day, talking intermittently with one another and watching what was happening on the field as time passed. "This sucks," said Alex Xhokaxhiu, a senior lineman, leaning back on the bleachers on the second day of camp. Alex, a marginal player and one of the larger kids on the team at 6' 1", 218 pounds, goes not surprisingly by Alex X (or simply X) and he, along with Justin Cossifos, a 15-year-old junior and the Huguenots' second-youngest player, were being held aside for suspected concussions.

X, an easygoing and immensely likable kid who crosses easily through the team cliques, had first been concussed while doing fundamentals during spring football in early June. He's not sure how it happened—a solid hit or two during tackling circuits perhaps—but after practice he began to feel nauseous and dizzy, "like I had just drunk a whole bottle of wine, but a bad, sour wine. It was not a good feeling." He was driving away from school, he said, when things started "moving and swaying," forcing him to pull to the side of the road and then, after contacting his parents, to go to a hospital emergency room where the concussion was confirmed. He had symptoms for five days. Spring football was over for him.

During the first August week of preseason practice, X had complained off-handedly of a headache and asked for an Advil, and this had been enough for the team's trainer and the team's doctor to remove him from the field and require him to take an ImPACT test to determine whether he showed any evidence, cognitively, of a concussion. X was forbidden to practice until the results of the test were evaluated and he was still waiting on the outcome of that evaluation on the Sunday morning that the team had to leave for Brookwood. Alex's head-injury issues followed on the heels of his missing most of his junior season due to a fractured vertebra in his back, also suffered on the practice field.

Alex, whose mother is from Italy and whose father is Albanian (the surname, Xhokaxhiu, thus explained), only began playing football in sixth grade, late by most towns' standards, and certainly by those in New Rochelle, where many first-graders have already been schooled on how to react to the play-action fake. X was a running back then, but now he played exclusively on the offensive and defensive lines. Both of his parents are dancers and choreographers and they run the Ajkun Ballet Theatre in the Bronx. "I'm not a big fan of football, it's pretty hard stuff," says Alex's mother, Chiara, "but I'm glad he loves it and has a passion for it. Passion is always good." Each year in December, the Ajkun Ballet puts on a performance of *The Nutcracker* in the auditorium at New Rochelle High School.

"Some of the guys say I'm faking with the concussion, that I don't want to play," X said. "I'm confident enough in myself to try to ignore that but it does bother me. I just want to get the clearance in time to play in our scrimmage tomorrow. Those are intense. Last year we went up against some pretty mean-looking guys from this other high school. There was one *really* big kid on their offensive line and I pushed him down and got to the quarterback. That was like the greatest play of my life."

Cossifos, who is burly at 5' 8", 212 pounds and full of chatter—"Of the kids I know on the team, he's the one I would say is most obviously excited about being on varsity and who is always talking about it," an editor at the school newspaper told me—had himself suffered an earlier concussion, as well as a neck injury, when his head was snapped back during a drill at Champions Camp, a weeklong football camp held in July at New Rochelle. Now, because Cossifos had felt recurring neck pain and stiffness (although no explicit concussion symptoms) during the last days of preseason practice at the school—hell week—he too had been required to take the ImPACT concussion test before being allowed to continue playing. And while Cossifos was the sprightliest of the group of injured Huguenots at Brookwood, at times even being allowed on the field as a decoy or nontackling bystander during a drill, he too was anxious to get into his gear and join the team, and he too was waiting on the results of his test.

THE TEST, ImPACT, which stands for Immediate Post-Concussion Assessment and Cognitive Testing, is the most popular football concussion test of its kind. (Companies such as Axon Sports offer comparable ones.) Not dissimilar from tests used to help assess head injuries in the military, ImPACT was developed and branded in the 1990s by neurologists and concussion experts who later worked at the University of Pittsburgh Medical Center. The test is a staple in the treatment and assessment of players in the NFL—for which it was initially developed—and the NHL. In the recent years of heightened attention to concussions, ImPACT has also become increasingly popular, almost de rigueur, for colleges and high schools. This has been an especially worthy development for that younger set: high school athletes, according to the independent Institute of Medicine are nearly twice as likely to suffer (and report) concussions as athletes in college.[1]

Each state has its own concussion policies for public-school athletes and New York, building off the Concussion Management and Awareness Act that first passed in 2011, requires coaches, athletic trainers, nurses and gym teachers to take an online course in concussion education and management. The state also mandates that a student who is believed to have sustained a concussion be held out of "athletic activities" and be symptom-free for at least 24 hours. Everything else in terms of concussion management—what procedures to follow, what precautions to take and, specifically, whether or not to use cognitive testing as an assessment tool—is left up to individual school districts. In New Rochelle every athlete in every collision sport beginning in middle school has to take an ImPACT baseline test once every two years in order to be allowed to play.

"The baseline tests cost us one dollar an athlete," says Stephen B. Young, the school district's Chairperson for Physical Education, Health and Director of Athletics. "And when a kid needs a postconcussion test it costs about three to four dollars. We have a lot of tough budget decisions to make every year, across 70 teams in three schools. But the ImPACT testing, from my point of view, is nonnegotiable."

At New Rochelle the student-athletes take the baseline test sitting at a computer, often in a classroom with 25 others, though sometimes in smaller groups or on their own. A nurse, a physical education teacher or Young himself oversees the test. ImPACT essentially measures short-term memory and response time, as well as, to a lesser degree, the abilities to comprehend and interpret. While a test-taker can do well or poorly on the exam, that performance is relevant only in establishing a personal baseline. Unlike just about

---

[1] *Sports-Related Concussions in Youth: Improving the Science, Changing the Culture Committee on Sports-Related Concussions in Youth.* Oct. 2013. Robert Graham; Frederick P. Rivara; Morgan A. Ford and Carol Mason Spicer, Editors; Institute of Medicine and National Research Council of the National Academies. The National Academies Press, Washington, D.C.

every other standardized test a student takes, his or her performance on this one doesn't get stacked up against others. The test-taker will only be graded, as it were, against him or herself. This means that, in theory, ImPACT can be equally valuable in assessing students who have a wide range of intellectual ability and acumen.

The idea is to record how an individual performs on the test in a normal (that is nonconcussed) mental state (the "baseline") and to then compare that against his (or her) performance when the test is administered a day or two after he is believed to have suffered a head injury. If the test-taker is markedly less accurate or slower in response on the postinjury test than he was on the baseline that may mean he has concussion symptoms. By New Rochelle protocol he will be kept off the field for two or three more days and then he'll take the test again. This will continue until he improves his score to at or very near his baseline level.

The players are well aware of these parameters, of course, which explains why some of the guys on the football team say—jokingly, though it is a joke soaked in reality—that they intentionally do worse than their best on the baseline test, screw it up on purpose, so that if they get a concussion the symptoms won't be as apparent on the retest and they can return to the field sooner. "You didn't mess up your baseline?" one New Rochelle player scolded X and Cossifos on that Brookwood sideline. "You *gotta* mess up your baseline, bro. Then if you get a concussion and you do really bad when you take the test again, they will think you're fine, you're like normal, so you can get right back in there. I always mess up my baseline at the start of the year." Then he added, laughing: "What I should've done is taken my baseline in Hungarian." ImPACT offers its exam in 17 languages: Spanish, Mandarin and Japanese, not surprisingly, but also 14 others including Finnish, Afrikaans, Czech and, yes, Hungarian.

The test, for which you need about 20 minutes to complete, goes like this: After answering a series of self-identifying questions—what sport you play and what position; whether you have learning disabilities, hyperactivity, dyslexia or autism; whether you've had previous concussions; whether you've been treated for migraines, meningitis or anxiety; how much sleep you got the night before; whether you're experiencing any of a long list of symptoms from vomiting to numbness to light-headedness; and several other interrogations of that ilk—the test proper begins. First you're shown a series of 12 words one by one. "Liquid" and "dog" and "music." Then a longer series of words appears, also one by one, and you're asked to identify whether or not a word in this second batch was also in the first batch. Next comes a similar assignment with, instead of words, a collection of abstract designs made out of squiggly lines. Then there's a section in which you're asked to memorize the location of numbers, and of X's and O's, and finally a speed test that involves arranging numbers and letters in a 5-by-5 box. There are not exactly any *Call of Duty* or *Minecraft* analogs here, but for the video game generation, this test is not without appeal. "It's pretty fun, actually," said Alex X.

For all the value of a test like ImPACT, and it certainly appears that it can help determine how well someone is recovering from a head injury, it also has significant limitations and flaws. The test has hardly proved to be a perfect predictor. Some studies suggest false positive and false negative rates of more than 30%, perhaps because test-takers can manipulate results and also because factors aside from the presence of concussion symptoms can influence performance: A noisy or distracting classroom; nervousness about taking the test; the teenager's mind wandering after a hard breakup with a girlfriend or boyfriend a few days before.

Also, the valuable information that an ImPACT test yields relates almost entirely to cognitive function. Head injuries, though, can also significantly disrupt vision, balance, coordination and emotional stability, none of which are measured by ImPACT. Cognitive testing is meant as only a part of an assessment and treatment plan for head injuries, as the founders and directors of ImPACT agree. The test is but a handheld flashlight pointing into the vast, dark and as yet largely unknowable world of concussions, their implications and the treatment they require.

Dr. Robert Cantu, a true guru in the modern wave of concussion research,[2] suggests also incorporating additional testing such as the King-Devick Test which can be administered quickly, on the sideline, and which is designed to catch impairments of vision and speech. But, as Cantu said during one of our discussions, "These tests can be useful and important, but they are not perfect. They aren't close to perfect, even if you rely on more than one of them."

The New Rochelle coaches, football lifers, are naturally no strangers to concussions. "You can see it in a kid," DiRienzo says. "When he gets a concussion he can't stand looking at the light. He'll become very emotional. Noise bothers him. I usually know when a kid has had a concussion without any doctor telling me."

As far as the current attitudes and treatment of concussions (the cognitive testing being just one significant piece of it), the coaches at New Rochelle have not applied themselves to learning the smaller details. Discussing the ImPACT test, for example, one coach, having not understood or been made aware of the individualized baseline aspect that is central to the test, said he was under the impression that a kid needed "to get at least a 75 on it to be able to play after a concussion. And that's not fair, because we have a lot of kids with learning issues, so how are they going to get a 75?"

Or as another assistant, Greg Foster, said, "I don't get involved in what to do with a kid as far as the head injuries go. Knee injuries, ankle injuries, wrists, shoulders. Those are the things I help the kids deal with. Decisions about concussions are for the team doctor, the trainer, the athletic director. That's above me."

Foster was saying this from the bunkhouse at Brookwood. He had just put down his cellphone after arranging for the team's affiliated doctor, Sergai DeLaMora at NY Orthopedics, to take an appointment with senior running back Jonathan Forrest when the team returned

---

[2] Among numerous other responsibilities, Cantu is a professor of neurosurgery at Boston University School of Medicine and at the school's CTE center, which has pioneered much of the modern research on NFL player brain injuries. He is passionate and deeply learned on concussions and sports brain injuries, and his dozens of books include 2012's *Concussions and Our Kids* (cowritten with Mark Hyman) in which he addresses a wide range of important issues including ImPACT testing.

from camp. Forrest, whose left foot was badly sprained after having been kicked and then wrenched in practice, is New Rochelle's marquee player, a returning captain who, as a sophomore in 2012, was an important part of the Huguenots' New York state championship team, scoring the first touchdown in the title game. Forrest has been featured in area newspapers and magazines, and is renowned in football circles even outside the school, all a part of what leads his teammates to refer to him with a degree of reverence. The respect, though, derives even more from his high level of production and from the general feeling that, as Jasper Baskerville says, "We've got some pretty tough dudes on this team,"—and Baskerville, incidentally, is one of them—"but on the field, no one is any tougher than Jonny."

Forrest's injury at Brookwood was acute. His ankle was immensely swollen, his limp extravagantly pronounced, and he iced the foot almost perpetually. It was clear he would not play at all throughout the camp and before calling Dr. DeLaMora, Foster had suggested to Forrest that it might make sense for him to leave, get a ride back to New Rochelle and have the foot examined even sooner. "There is no way I am going to do that," said Forrest quietly (he says most things quietly). Later he added, "I am not leaving the team. It's something to be part of this. Brookwood is a big deal to me, and it's a big deal to the team. It may be the most important time of the whole season for us, for the things we learn and how we bond. And also, you know, it's *fun*. Like a four-day sleepover with the football team, with your friends."

No other player on the team had been to four of these camps as Forrest had, and over the days he was often pestered to tell stories of heroics and shenanigans past. He recalled his nervousness before his first Brookwood experience, in August of 2011, and how that camp had been roiled by Hurricane Irene, the players and coaches gathering together in the dimlit bunkhouse through the biblical rains and the high blasting winds. The storm's damages, along with the unshakable sense of unease many of the players' parents felt at having their children so far away in the immediate aftermath and recovery, led DiRienzo to bring the team home two days early.

This year, as he nursed his battered foot, Forrest made it a point to pay close attention to the action on the field, often going to the edge of the sideline and leaning down on one knee to watch. When coach D gave one of his short soliloquies at the end of each practice session,[3] Forrest limped over to listen, then afterward occasionally took aside a teammate to talk. A linebacker as well as a running back, Forrest thoroughly understands the New Rochelle defense and offense, and is adept at absorbing and executing the new and various wrinkles that the staff puts in. ("We can kind of use him as a coach out there by now," DiRienzo confided.) At Brookwood, Forrest said he wanted to "coach up" some of his teammates who were having trouble learning or who weren't yet feeling connected to all the coaches. "I wish I could do something with Gaudio," he said one afternoon of the team's largest player, the bespectacled kid in the Nirvana tee shirt who was driven to the point of retching during the first-day suicides. "He's big and he's strong, and he wants to do good," said Forrest. "I'm just not sure he has in him what I'm trying to get out of him."

Forrest began playing tackle football at age 6—as a kindergartner. His father, Randy, coached him in New Rochelle's competitive Youth Tackle League. Janice, Jonathan's mother, says she was "worried at first. You watch these kids get hit, and any parent would get scared"; but there was never much doubt that Jonathan would play the game and stick with it. He showed natural talent from the start, and he was following

---

[3] During Brookwood, especially as the days wore on, DiRienzo kept looking for ways to extract some extra effort out of what seemed to be a bedraggled bunch, beaten by the heat and rigor. An example: "Boys, there is no one, from Pop Warner to the NFL who isn't sore and tweaked in camp. That's the nature of it. That's what you signed up for. When we come back out here later today I need a little more grind from you. I need a little more juice out of the orange, another sip." When the team made its way off the field CJ Anthony sidled up by DiRienzo and asked, "Hey, Coach, bro. Do you rap? Are you a rapper?" DiRienzo gave him a mildly suspicious look that said Huh? "I'm talkin' about those metaphors that you make up right on the spot!" CJ said. "Do you rehearse?" After a palpable silence, DiRienzo shook his head, gave CJ a mild, two-handed push and broke into laughter, echoed immediately by the coaches and players within earshot.

in paternal footsteps. Randy played football for New Rochelle, class of 1984, and then went on to play four years at Texas–El Paso. He knew that the earliest years of youth football could be definitive, that it was the beginning of children and parents reducing a more abstract concept ("you get hit playing football"), to a tangible one. ("This is how it *looks and feels* to get hit playing football.")

"Those first few years—ages 6, 7, 8—is when you'll see a lot of kids drop out. The hitting is not for everyone," says Randy. "As a coach what I'd tell parents is they have to understand that football is a little different. Running full-speed into another human being is not a natural act." Randy, who works for Avis, walks with a limp that's a result of injuries sustained on the field. "I had concussions when I played too. Several of them. I saw white light, got dizzy, everything got slow. You were just told to toughen up. Now these days that's different, people know more about it, they react differently and usually more considerately. That's good." Whatever the physical cost, Randy says he would very happily do it all again. "Football was everything to me."

Jonathan is listed at 5' 11" and 200 pounds and he is built thickly through the thighs and core. He says he has never in his 12-plus years of football suffered a concussion (and he swears he would admit it if he had). Nor has he had any serious injury, his latest foot trouble notwithstanding. "Lucky," he says. Forrest has the ability, at this high school level, to make a big play even when it appears that there is none to be made; the first tackler is rarely the tackler who brings Forrest to the ground. His particular attributes—that of a kid who can work reliably within a system, but also explode out of it as the flow of play demands—are a big part of what makes a high school player appealing to college recruiters.[4]

---

[4] Recruiters are also, of course, charmed by flat-out athletic ability and physical prowess, such as that of 6' 5" 290-pound Rasheem Green from Gardena, Calif., (who went to USC in 2015 and, at that size, runs the 40-yard dash in under 4.8 seconds) or 6' 4", 258-pound Byron Cowart from Seffner, Fla., (an Auburn selection with a vertical leap higher than 34 inches). But those kinds of players, in the scope of filling the sprawling rosters of more than 250 FBS and FCS football programs—we're talking close to 20,000 players—are exceedingly rare, a class of athlete unto themselves.

Forrest had been receiving recruiting letters and other college pitches in earnest since the spring of his 10th grade year—right after that state championship game. He is a solid student, attentive and dutiful if not enthusiastic, and by the time he arrived at Brookwood before his senior season he had received firm full-scholarship offers from Buffalo, Monmouth, Villanova and Army, with several other schools showing serious interest. No one else on the New Rochelle team had (at this point) received a firm scholarship offer from any college program. "The NFL is the dream, it always has been," said Forrest. "But right now I'm focused on getting into college and working through four years of that." Forrest's Twitter bio throughout his senior season read, "On a mission for a free tuition" and provided a link to his highlight reel.

All of Jonathan's offers had come from schools that operate outside—far outside—college football's most powerful conferences: the SEC, Big Ten, Big 12, Pac-12 and ACC. Both Army and Buffalo play at much less heralded levels within Division I's Football Bowl Subdivision (FBS), and both programs have extravagant decades-long traditions of losing. Monmouth and Villanova, meanwhile, compete at Division I's second tier, the Football Championship Subdivision or FCS.[5]

In other words, the Huguenots' best player was not being sought after by programs such as Alabama or Ohio State, Texas or Oregon, nor any other among those that dominate national college football and serve, for many players, as a place to get an apprenticeship to the pros. Kids from New Rochelle just don't get offered scholarships to football programs at that level. But that did not in any way dim Jonathan's NFL dream. All of the schools that offered him a scholarship *have* produced at least a few players drafted into the NFL after all, and the fact is, as Jonathan and every other aspirant at New Rochelle knows, it can be done. You

---

[5] For many years Division I schools were classified as I-A, the top level, or I-AA, a notch below. This was a far more intelligible naming convention for the casual fan; the current model of FBS and FCS serves mainly to confuse the un-immersed. The football universe (and many other sports') has long taken pleasure in its arcane and confusing nomenclature. Division I's current naming convention is another example of it.

can go from playing on this high school field, for this coach, against this suburban New York competition, to a college football program that will help to hone you and send you on to success in the hallowed NFL itself.

It can be done and it has been done. And when aspiring New Rochelle players look for something to sustain their conviction, they find it in one of their own—an undersized kid who ran the ball brilliantly in high school, then left the Huguenots in 2005 for Rutgers (at a time when Rutgers had not had a winning season in more than a decade) and then went on to the Baltimore Ravens and to the NFL Pro Bowl and to a Super Bowl title. Kids on the New Rochelle team have T-shirts with this NFL star's name on it, given to them on one of the special days that he came back to the school to teach some football, give some words of encouragement, talk about having confidence in yourself and reaching high. So, sure, Jonathan Forrest, the latest standout running back from New Rochelle, could make it to the NFL someday. Just look at Ray Rice.

CHAPTER 4

What We Do

FF THE field at Camp Brookwood, the New Rochelle coaches gently monitor the boys through the pockets of downtime and over the nights. An assistant stands sentry-like in the hallway as curfew kicks in, and might saunter over once again later for a walkthrough and a bed-glance before the staff turns in—but the coaches are hardly Draconian and they are well aware that things will go on among the boys that they will miss. They're O.K. with that. As much as coach DiRienzo and the staff want to keep close tabs, they believe too that allowing the boys a degree of freedom, in effect bestowing trust upon them, can, in the best scenario, be part of the secret sauce that leads a young person to follow, fully, where an elder would lead him.

In other words, with 40-odd teenage boys spending four days together at a football camp there is perpetually the chance that some out-of-bounds events may unfold in the wee, dark hours. And in Brookwood such events certainly did.

Throughout the camp, the bunkhouse closest to New Rochelle's—the two buildings were separated by a stretch of knobby, late-summer lawn, a short hill and a few small trees, about 60 yards in all—housed the football team from Brooklyn's Canarsie High School. This meant that there were plenty of opportunities for players on each team to encounter one another. One afternoon as a clutch of Huguenots walked back to the bunk from the lunchroom, they found themselves striding very near to a group of Canarsie players. Someone on one of the teams began snickering and needling at the other group. (As a soldier come back to earth from Lexington, Mass., 1775, might attest, it is often neither clear nor overly relevant which side fires the first shot.) Words were exchanged. Players made personal remarks, and both teams talked some tough-boy trash. For its street cred, Canarsie had the imprimatur of being a New York City school; for its field cred, New Rochelle had its recent state titles.

That night, returning from the bunkhouse lobby where much of the team had gathered to watch or participate in the advancing and increasingly raucous Madden video game tournament, one of the Huguenots leaders, tight end and defensive end Demetrius Rodriguez, found that the room he was sharing with two other seniors (Corey Holder and Justice Cowan) and a junior (Jayson Prince) had been "messed up." Clothes were strewn around, a mattress had been overturned and there seemed to be an odor of urine. The room next to that one had been similarly mistreated. Canarsie had struck.

Rodriguez, known also as Meat, was incensed; but rather than tell the coaching staff, he called the players together and resolved to get revenge. Later that night, well after the coaches were asleep (they were themselves worn from the long, hot hours on the shadeless field) a large pack of Huguenots stole over to the neighboring bunkhouse to confront the Canarsie team. Exactly what happened next is unclear (even to some of those involved), but there was a determined, if somewhat muted skirmish (the hush because neither team wanted to rouse its coaches) outside the bunk. At some point a special envoy of New Rochelle players broke away from the skirmish, stole inside and ransacked several of the momentarily unoccupied Canarsie rooms. Urine, allegedly, was sprayed: *You curs mark our territory? We'll mark yours.* The deed done, the New Rochelle kids stole back toward their rooms and the entire skirmish broke up.

"Then at like three o'clock in the morning some of them came over, outside our bunk, and they had these air guns. Honestly, it was kind of scary," Alex X recalled the next day. According to other New Rochelle players, the Canarsie players, who wore hoodies, "lit up our rooms" by firing pellets through the window screens. Some Huguenot players ran outside, managed to wrest away one of the air guns and to chase Canarsie away. Finally, with breakfast and then the long day of practice looming just a few hours away, the Huguenots, feeling both irate and nervous, closed their doors and went to sleep.

It so happened that the next day Canarsie and New Rochelle were, by previous agreement between their coaches, set to practice together. But when the teams saw each other on the field, players on both sides couldn't help but hurl more hot words at one another. Quickly, news of the previous night's renegading spilled out, leading DiRienzo and Canarsie coach Kyle Allen to abruptly cancel the joint practice.

DiRienzo, livid, made the Huguenots run and run. Then he stopped them and asked for the names of who had done what in the Canarsie incident and for more details about what had happened during the night. No one said a thing. "I will call your fuckin' mothers and your fuckin' fathers and tell them to come up here right now and pick you up from this fuckin' camp," DiRienzo screamed. "Should I do that? What the fuck is the matter with you?" Profanity is not uncommon from coach D, who'll use it to emphasize particular points in what he calls his "not-the-King's English," but rarely does it fly so forcefully. This was different, an unchained intensity.

"I have never seen Coach so angry," said Forrest weeks later. "We didn't know what he was going to do. We all felt it. It was like he wasn't just angry, he was disappointed. We had let him down and the season hadn't even started yet."

The team was told to run some more, again and again around the perimeter of the field, as the sun climbed higher into the August sky. Once again coach DiRienzo stopped the players and brought them together and once again he asked who had been responsible, and this time Demetrius Rodriguez stepped forward and put up his hand and said in a full voice, "It was me coach. I was the one who got us into this. I'm the reason we're running."

DiRienzo, silent, seething, looked at Rodriguez. Then he barked to the group, "O.K., and now you can all run some more. Thanks to Meat. Get the fuck on it. Move!"

Neither the whole team nor any of the kids involved were sent home. They were made to exchange apologies and handshakes with the Canarsie players and for many hours they were subject to a sheer, febrile tension coming off their coach. But before too long, by the end of that day, things at the football camp had pretty much settled back to the way they had been. The nighttime escapade and its discovery, each harrowing and exhilarating in its way, were left to be interpreted.

"We got in trouble, but that whole thing brought us closer together," junior defensive back Haitam Coughlin would later say. "We knew we had each other's back. We saw the way Demetrius responded—how he right away had the idea that no one would mess with us. None of us got hurt and if anyone had been in a bad spot all he would have had to do is yell and the team would have come running to help him. We saw that and it made us tight."

If Demetrius had in some ways won over and helped to unionize the hearts of his teammates, he had also, he knew, violated the trust of coach DiRienzo, a trust that he had fought to achieve, and not always with success. (Demetrius was a determined and dedicated All-County caliber player, but there had been a rules-breaking incident the season before.) Rodriguez is also an excellent wrestler, All-Section at New Rochelle and a leader on the wrestling squad. He comes from a racially mixed family and his older brother, Tyler Lilly, was a football captain for coach DiRienzo, and himself a fine New Rochelle wrestler. Tyler went on to wrestle and play football at SUNY Cortland, and Demetrius hoped to wrestle and play football in college one day too. DiRienzo believed he had the ability and the on-field drive to play Division II.

"When he came to see me later on at Brookwood, he started bawling so much," DiRienzo said. "There was snot coming out of his nose, the whole thing. He told me he was sorry and he told me how there had been air guns and water balloons and how he felt he had to do something, that he had to act. That was a mistake he made, and of course I know it was not only him. It couldn't have been. It takes a lot of guys for what happened that night to happen. He made a mistake, they made a mistake. But I decided we weren't going to give up on them and scrap the whole thing, the whole camp. If I had sent them home I might have lost them. I punished them, but I couldn't have it be them on one side and me on the other side. Better or worse, it had to be us. Together. That's pretty much what we are trying to do here."

––––––––––––

THE CANARSIE practice scotched, New Rochelle did run a short scrimmage against a high school team from New Jersey. This was just inside drills—7-on-7, nobody set up wide—which made it much easier for coaches on both teams to get concentrated, naked-eye looks at their blocking schemes and at individual players. Coaches stood on the field, often in the defensive or offensive backfields, and gave instruction while the rest of the team, the nearly two score players who were not in the scrimmage at the moment, stood on the sideline cheering each play as if it were a real game, and waiting, hoping, for their chance to be rotated in. The results of the ImPACT tests had returned and Justin Cossifos was cleared to play. X, however, was not. He hadn't scored close enough to his baseline and would, upon returning to New Rochelle, have to take the test again.

Before the scrimmage DiRienzo told the boys that he wanted them to employ their technique, to rely less on strength and speed and more on form. "And when the whistle blows, stop. We do not want anyone, not any of us and not any of them, to get unnecessarily hurt."

Among the Huguenot players in the first stages of the scrimmage was Shameek Miller, the once over-heavy senior now hoping to establish himself as an offensive lineman who could be counted on. The early snaps, though, did not go Shameek's way. He was beaten off the ball a few times, he missed a couple of blocking assignments and the opposing defensive linemen were getting through to Powell and the running backs and disrupting the New Rochelle offense. When Shameek got summoned off the field, he was visibly upset, pushing through his teammates to stand behind them on the sideline, bent with his hands on knees, breathing heavily and crying.

Teammates crowded around, telling him it was O.K., not to worry about a couple of plays, to keep his head up. Then someone remembered Shameek's asthma and everyone backed away to give him better air. "I'm O.K., I'm O.K.," Shameek spat out, and moved farther off, well back from the sideline where he knelt on one knee, his helmet off in the hot day, and quietly sobbed, his big body shaking until he could compose himself. Later, when the scrimmage ended and it was time for the players to take their packs off, Shameek was the last to do so. Coach DiRienzo had to remind him a few times.

They would practice again later in the day, while on the sideline the injured troops—three others were now out: Bryce Davis (hand), Haitam Coughlin (knee) and Jasper Baskerville (foot)—talked about girls and about their Regents exam, and about how the St. Louis Rams quarterback Sam Bradford was now out for the year and the Rams were really up the creek. They talked about the upcoming school year and all agreed that they really liked leaving the building in the middle of the day and walking over to the nearby McDonald's for lunch. The topic of Denver Broncos wide receiver Wes Welker came up, specifically the news that he was intent on returning to play even after having his third concussion in 10 months. "I don't know, bro," said Bryce Davis, a senior, "that doesn't seem too smart to me." Davis, a rather ornery defensive back and wide receiver, had missed coming to Brookwood the previous year after being concussed during a hell week tackling drill. The persistent dizziness and nausea of the following days was not a feeling he was at all eager to experience again.

The players continued with the practice sessions, the familiar drills, the sometimes-numbing repetition. They ran into the old tackling sleds that Brookwood provided and they drank cool water from the spigots draped on a metal hose tree by the field. They worked on offensive sets called Black Jack and Tiger 3 and many more, and they came inside to sit in on film sessions with their position coaches.[1]

At these very moments and all through the days, the danger and efficacy of high school football was being evaluated and argued across the country, a movement of recent times. Indeed, while the Brookwood retreat was unfolding, the Minnesota Department of Health and the Minnesota-based Institute of Athletic Medicine were polishing a report for publication. The report estimated, based on voluntary responses, that over the course of an academic year high school athletes in Minnesota had sustained nearly 3,000 concussions during games or practice, far more than previous evidence had suggested. Even in that ice-hockey-mad state, football, having the most participants, was the greatest contributor to that head-injury total with more than 1,350 Minnesota high schoolers having been concussed playing the game in one season. "A concussion," Bryce Davis was saying on the Brookwood bleachers, nursing what would turn out to be a torn ligament in his thumb, "that is the worst injury. Worse than any hand or leg thing you're going to get. With a concussion, you feel, like, helpless you know."

THE FINAL night at Brookwood provided what by general player consensus is the highlight of camp: The Rookie Show, an annual event of skits and routines put on by first-year varsity Huguenots for the entertainment of their teammates and the coaches. Rookies might be pressured to act out a specific scene, or to sing—and this year a skinny junior named Eric Stenroos belted out a Bruno Mars song, a cappella, carrying it off extremely well and winning whistles and shouts of approval from the older guys. But the heart of the show is the lampooning

[1] Classic stuff. The team watched, in groups, plays from the previous year's games or hastily cut sequences from the Brookwood scrimmage itself. The players got analysis and direction like this from coach Violante: "Jasper, see this, on this play you're just going vertical, right into him. There should be no hesitation. Just clean the guy's clock. Clean his clock. Now on this play here, though, you've got to be careful. You need some finesse. See how you stepped with your left foot first? You need to step with your right foot first or this guy in the gap here is going to move right around you."

of the coaching staff. Player after player did versions of coach D: fussing mad-scientist-like with the stopwatch hung around his neck; being alternatively irascible and inept; scolding a kid and then wrapping him in an embrace. The actors swung their arms and pitched forward as they paced the performance space; they pretended to lecture one another, speaking with great earnestness about obviously trivial matters. It was like a roast. DiRienzo and the rest of the coaches sat in the back of the big room eating popcorn and chips, grunting good-naturedly at times.

The assistants got made fun of too, their idiosyncrasies seized on. Greg Foster's gruffly bellowed instructions ("Punch it through! Punch it right through!") were delivered in falsetto voices; Violante was portrayed as dreaming about the lacrosse team on the sideline, arms rested upon his belly; Rich Tassello got it for the careful choirboy way he sometimes combs his hair; Keith Fagan, who does much of the filming for the team, and who is given to reminding the players of his success as a receiver at Western New England College, was depicted pointing a camera at his own large hands and marveling at them. Anyone was fair game.

"This is hilarious, but I'm sitting way back here because I do not want to have to go up there and do something," said Nigel Bailey, a junior and a rookie Huguenot. Bailey is of Caribbean descent. He wears his hair in dreadlocks. "Now that's something I'm scared of. I'm getting through this week O.K., being away from home and without my family and everything, but I am terrified of going on stage. I will just sit way back here and watch. For some of us, this team is a chance to play with the gods. Jonathan Forrest! Corey Holder! We've been watching them on the varsity the past two years and now we're on the same field as them? I'm serious—they are like gods to us. I'm not going up there to make a fool of myself in front of guys like that."

When the show was over, the songs and skits and mockery complete—all along the coaches had laughed as readily and collegially as the boys—the players were asked to cast ballots to elect the team captains. Forrest was returning as one of the four, so the players were told to anonymously list three teammates, in order of preference, on squares of loose-leaf paper that the coaches then collected. Though the players would not learn the results until a few days later, back in New Rochelle, the coaches all knew the outcome that night. The players had elected to the captaincy Quincy Mack, Corey Holder and Demetrius Rodriguez.

––––––––––

THE MORNING practice on the day the New Rochelle team bus would depart from Brookwood at noon was devoted in large part to replicating typical game-day preparations: An early walkthrough and then the pregame drills and stretches, exactly what the team would do when, as the coaches said, "the bullets are live."

Members of the Fieldston soccer team strode past—tall and lithe with their neon knee socks and neon shoes and Bieber haircuts. Scandinavian somehow. One of those Fieldston players, spotting coach D, capless under a cloudy sky and drumming home a point to his linebackers, pointed and said to a teammate, "Man, how old is that coach?"

The Huguenots stretched and did width-of–the field laps, the seniors peeling off from one sideline, underclassmen from the other. They did high-stepping drills and a mild tackling circuit. It was getting later in the day than the boys had imagined it would be and they were still on the field. Camp was coming to an end now. Over the days, in all the drills, in the camaraderie and the disagreements, in the physical toll, and in the satisfaction of getting things right, in all of that, so much of the football experience—as wide and varied as it can be on so many levels in so many places—had been distilled. Four days, one high school team, 46 kids. There had not been any real games played, of course, and the bright lights of the outside world had not shone in as they soon would, but in the scrimmages and even in the day-to-day intrateam showdowns, plays were made that would be remembered and talked about among the teammates for many months, important and image-building.

Very soon they would all be back in the Brookwood bunkhouse, collecting their last sundry items. Toothbrushes, headbands, phone chargers, a rare pair of clean socks, ankle tape, a baggie of weed never smoked, notebooks and books and magazines, combs, all getting packed into the boys' respective bags alongside their clothes and bed things. They packed quickly when they packed, hurrying to gather together in the lobby and wait for the bus and tear into the white boxes of pizza that the coaches had ordered for a send-off treat.

The boys were loose and free, laughing and poking at one another, pepperoni slices in hand. Watching them there like that and seeing the things they carried (one had a Peanuts sleeping bag he'd had passed down, another cradled a pillow in a pale blue case with his name stitched in) and the way some sat holding cushions on their laps, and knowing too that they came from all kinds of homes, some with fathers around and some without, some from a world where the mandate of schoolwork was drilled in every night and others from a world where expecting the grownups around them simply to stay sober was more than they could ask, it was all a reminder. Although they had engaged in manly things—battling one another physically again and again, heeding coaches' orders, leading their peers, working repetitively at something that at times they would rather not have—they were still unquestionably boys, some just a few years out from losing the last of their baby teeth, boys playing at something, trying on a certain kind of mask, standing in.

Earlier that day, when that simulated pregame prep had finally come to an end, DiRienzo had brought the team together. It was a slightly cooler morning—no sun, and you could feel a hint of autumn in the sporadic breeze—but the players were sweat-soaked and close to disheveled. Their uniforms, unwashed during the camp, showed heavy grass stains and some of their pant legs had had blood wiped on them. Forrest limped over, along with other injured players. One kid had a bad bruise on the side of his face. Two had their wrists in casts, and a couple of players, as they kneeled down, did so very gingerly as if they were workingmen in late middle age, and sought support on the shoulder of a teammate already down on one knee.

"Move in," said DiRienzo. "You guys there move in. Nigel move in. Mickey move in. Move in, all the way in, close as you can get." The players knew what was happening now, that they would hear words that coach D had become known for, words that even veterans like Forrest and Holder never minded hearing again. There were no other humans anywhere to be seen. All of the other football teams that had been at Brookwood had already gone home.

Coach D: "Now, I really need two more minutes of your time and then you're free for 24 hours. And I know you're tired right now, and I know today's practice was longer than it was last year. I need you to focus. And there's a reason that I'm asking you to get as tight as you can.

"Because this right here is the inner circle. And nothing and no one penetrates this circle. Nothing and no one penetrates the circle." He paused and closed his lips and breathed in deeply through his nose. "These are your brothers. You might have friends that you're closer to on the outside. And that's fine, that's all good. I've got friends on the outside. But when it comes to football these are my brothers"—he pointed at the assistant coaches. "Because when things are going good everybody's got a hug for you. But when things are going bad they're going to have something bad to say about you and you and you and me. You've got to keep that outside the circle. Because they have no idea what we do. How we do."

DiRienzo's voice rasped. He was strained and tired from the days of camp, from the nights of little sleep. At times he cracked with emotion, understanding what he was asking of the boys, and what he wanted to give them, hoping they would accept the offering. He believed it could make the difference in what happened on the team, how well the Huguenots performed in games, whether the team won or lost.

"Might even be your parents." He spoke slowly, deliberately, and the pauses were more frequent and part of the rhythm of the words. "And I'm not telling you to disrespect your parents. But they're not standing inside this circle. They want to have opinions about me then that's O.K. But they cannot penetrate the circle.

"I go back to Ray Rice, who is a three-time Pro Bowl player in the NFL. We lost to White Plains on Opening Day 2003, by a score of 7 to 6. Everybody on the outside, every security guard, people's brothers and parents, everybody had something to say to Ray because he had made a bad play at the end of the game. It brought him to tears. And if they can bring Ray Rice to tears, they can get into *your* head.

"But they can't now. Because we understand that we've got the circle. And nobody and no one gets inside the circle. Nobody and no one gets inside the circle.

"Take it down. You're home."

DiRienzo turned and walked away, long low strides, hearing the boys behind him as they stood and closed together, facing inward, raising their helmets and cheering together. He made his way down to the bunkhouse and into the empty lobby and then stood for a moment finding his thoughts. He still needed to wrap up a couple of last things with the Fiedlers. And he wanted to make sure the pizza had arrived.

CHAPTER 5

Opening Night

ART OF football's appeal for high school boys, and for the men that they become, is the feeling and the reality that to be part of a football team is to be part of a revered and exclusive club—a secret society with public heft. They are on the inside, everyone else is not, and there is comfort in that. "We all wear our football jerseys around school on Fridays," said Huguenots linebacker Justice Cowan. "It's not like we're celebrities or anything, but you do feel special. The first time, people look at you twice. Most of the other kids don't even know if I'm a star on the team or if I never play." (Cowan, a first-stringer most of the season, was vocal on the sidelines and solid on the field.) "It doesn't really matter. We're part of the team, so a lot of times everyone will be like, 'Yeah, go win for us!' Sometimes a kid will say to me, 'Yeah, I saw you out there last week man, I saw you on that one play where you did this thing and that thing.' And it wasn't even me! I don't say anything, though. I just smile."

Beyond the status—which other sports might also yield—football derives a particular fraternal power from its broad and living array of customs and rituals, the enduring shibboleths that shape the experience of the game. Consider specifically football's elaborate lexicon, so sprawling and nuanced it might fairly be called a language of the game: words, phrases, code words, code phrases, intonations and verbal cues that are all but unintelligible to those on the outside. Men and women on a small fishing vessel may talk of knotting their becket hitches and cleaning the livewell; car mechanics may banter with one another about ball joints and the overhead cam; doctors and lawyers have full-blown dictionaries to contain and explain their terms of art. Yet football provides unique linguistic adventures. The common language gets altered, evolving to fit each tribe, then each clan. Truly byzantine sentences are produced. This comes about partly because coaches and players don't want coaches and players on other teams to understand what they're saying. Football folk certainly like the idea that they are all speaking the same language—we are men, talking football!—but each clan tends to want to speak that language in its own way.

Watching a random practice a few days before a team's season-opening game (in this case a practice on the field at New Rochelle High), and listening to a random coach (in this case Lou DiRienzo) addressing his defense, you might hear something like this:

"So it's a zone read. They'll bucket step inside. When it's going to the Force I've got to scrape for skin and be inside-out on the quarterback. When it's going to the Dog it can't be a pull, so either Eagle's got to get me a gap or Will's got to get me a gap. Okay? Now where's the Dog?"

Moments later: "This would say to me Okie read, an Okie Front and then Fire or Blaze. Linebackers, no motion? Okay they're in Fire or Blaze, we've got to back out. Once they check for Sky I don't have to back out anymore. Regular Force linebacker we're in Cover One; it's odd.

"Now, if they come out unbalanced, whether it's Fire or Blaze it turns to Jam. I just have a regular anchor M. If it's Fire, the Sam linebacker is under, the strong safety is over. If it's Blaze, just the opposite."

It can go on like that all day.

That small and representative bit from DiRienzo is an amalgam of familiar and clearly intended words—the term Okie Front, for example, (usually) designates a standard defensive alignment with four players up front on the line and three linebackers in the area behind them. Any football player (and many fans) knows who the Sam and the Will linebackers are and many more might grasp the nuance of zone coverage that "Sky" describes. But when it comes to DiRienzo's use of "Fire" and "Blaze," say, or his "scrape for skin" metaphor, or his suggestion that the opposing team's play might be "going to the Dog," well, other coaches may employ a completely other set of terms to get their points across, markedly different verbal renderings for very similar concepts. Other coaches may say Rover instead of Dog. They may never ever use the expressions Fire or Blaze. They may go an entire coaching career without issuing the phrase, "Eagle's got to get me a gap."

Still, specific terminology aside, there's a discernible syntax to footballspeak, a way of rendering ideas with a swift intensity, the sound and pace of which is itself a signifier, part of what makes the language a language indeed, wherever it is used. It's a language that football players and coaches embrace as comfortable and familiar (if not always wholly precise) while most other human beings find it roughly as accessible as the patterned chirps and clicks exchanged among a pod of traveling dolphins.

To young players footballspeak can be puzzling, even intimidating, early on—a crash course in Chinese or Calculus—and on the New Rochelle junior varsity, in which DiRienzo's terminologies first get implemented, practice-field huddles are stocked with players displaying wrinkled brows and shaking their heads. Truth be told (and here is the downside to the appetite for the arcane) a lack of real understanding may last until a player reaches varsity and beyond. He may never quite comprehend all the things that get said, all the instructions that get barked out. Or if he is someone else, a Jonathan Forrest type, he may have the argot essentially down pat after a month or two of practice.[1]

---

[1] Inside jargon is found in many high school activities, in the chess, theater, tech and debate clubs just as in athletics. Teenagers adore it. The public high school in New Rochelle's neighboring Mamaroneck, N.Y., is home to the longest running high school Shakespeare program in the country. The Semi-Royal Shakespeare Company, as it's called, began putting on plays more than four decades ago, and the cast rehearses up to six days a week in the months before a show. Each year the student-actors, high on

The inside language greatly enhances the bonding, and the players love to fling it around among themselves. A couple of New Rochelle players waiting by the counter for their nuggets-and-fries plate at their beloved local dive, Chicken Joe's, could start talking like this: "I can't believe that play went to boundary. We thought it was goin' field."

"You were in a Cover One, right?"

"Cover Two, boy, and I was up looking A-gap. Then it went B-gap. And I got all thrown out."

"Yeah, just like that. Bingo, bingo in the slot and it's done."

They'll speak loud enough for others in the restaurant to hear—Chicken Joe's is perpetually filled with peers—and though the other kids might pretend they don't hear, they do, and most of them are impressed.

THE SUMMER heat was back for New Rochelle's opening game, on a Friday night in early September, at Clarkstown North, a high school about 25 miles northwest of New Rochelle, and over a commuter bridge, the Tappan Zee. Trying to get there on a Friday, late afternoon, could have meant snailing along in crippling suburban New York traffic, which is why the players, upon DiRienzo's petitioning, were all excused from school one period early, and why some of the players' parents set off from home at 3 p.m. for the 7 p.m. start. The heat and humidity was such that soon after the team came out to the field, a couple of hours before game time, the players' brows and cheeks were heavy with sweat.

"Seven months of practice all shows up tonight," said Robbie DeRocco, the New Rochelle field goal kicker, during the pregame stretch. DeRocco,

---

Shakes, raise money for a Company T-shirt adorned with a unique slogan. Things like "We're Making a Scene" or "Ruining Saturday Mornings since 1974." One recent year the T-shirt said: "The Semi-Royal Shakespeare Company: You Don't Know What We Are Saying. (And Neither Do We.)"

That's not entirely on point in this analogy of argots (how many activities, after all, have Early Modern English as a staple?) but it does relate and it was too delightful to leave out.

like his older brother before him, had been plucked off the soccer team by DiRienzo. A senior, Robbie had come on board just seven months earlier, in late January, and this was his first autumn in football after many seasons on the pitch. He said he liked football better than soccer because of the physical rigor, the weightlifting. He felt stronger than he had ever felt in his life. "I went the other way," DeRocco said. "I know kids from soccer tournaments, travel teams, who left football to come play soccer—a little less painful you know?" He laughed. "I went the other way. What I like about this team is the family feeling. It's different than soccer. We were a family there too, but this is more, I don't know, intense I guess. It doesn't leave you even when you aren't on the field. It never really leaves you. And you know that football is a big deal at New Rochelle, much bigger than soccer. It feels important."

Because he is a kicker, who rarely makes hard physical contact on the field and who needs to master only a fraction of the knowledge of the playbook and its nuances compared to what the other players must learn, DeRocco can at times feel like an outsider. Sometimes he's a target of disdain, often he's a figure of envy. Listed most generously at 5' 8" and 183 pounds, DeRocco is the one guy on the team not regularly being rammed into by other kids. At Brookwood, he spent a good portion of each day on the sidelines with the injured players, fetching water or equipment, sometimes doing specific leg stretches, or running short sprints, or kicking a football off a tee and into a net. After getting onto the field for a sequence of field goal or punting or kickoff drills, DeRocco tended to sit on the Brookwood bleachers and log the direction and results of his kicks into a worn spiral notebook. "What is the point of *that*?" Bryce Davis teased him. "You like doing homework or something?" DeRocco said he needed to show the log to his personal kicking coach back in New Rochelle. He was hoping to kick for a team in college, he said. He was hoping his one year on the football varsity could bring him some attention.

Now it was the first game of the season and DeRocco was on the field at Clarkstown North, wrapping up his backpedaling work. "It all starts tonight for us," he said. "It's finally here."

ABOUT 40 MINUTES before kickoff, the Huguenot players milled about in the Clarkstown North gym, many of them eating oranges, quarters of the fruit stuffed into their mouths as they made rind-full, big-eyed faces at one another. Players pulled on receiving gloves, adjusted headbands, took Advil, dabbed on unnecessary eye-black ("My war paint," said the defensive end and captain Corey Holder). The names of the starting players—offense, defense, special teams—were written on pieces of foolscap taped to a wall beneath a basketball hoop. Coach DiRienzo crouched near this wall while calling out to certain players to come over individually; when they did, he quietly passed along a few words about the night's assignment and tasks, about what he believed that particular player could do. The other coaches were around too, talking directly with players, reminding them of things, helping them get their equipment square.

DiRienzo and his assistants weren't yet sure what to think of the team, believing its character would be revealed only by the demands of the games ahead. There is a covered-dish quality to a high school football team; you don't really know what you've got until you've got it, until the real competition begins. As Keith Fagan said while surveying the high-step drill before the game that night, "They're not fully committed yet, you know, to all the details. We can't tell whether or not it's a continuation of last year, when the team never really came together like we wanted them to. Last year's team thought, 'Hey we're coming off a state title, we can win just by being New Rochelle.' They found out that that didn't work. That's never going to work. We've been talking together as coaches about how we're not sure if some of that attitude is still here, or whether they've actually learned some things and are just holding back, and will be ready when the lights go on. That could be. We have a good team, with a lot of potential. Our concern is that they take that for granted."

Now, with kickoff nearing, the players were summoned from the gym to be addressed for the first time of the season by Bishop Fetson Leak, a constant in the New Rochelle football experience. "I have been around this team for 40 years," he said. Bishop Leak leads services at Baptist congregations in Long Island, N.Y., and he also works as the civil service commissioner for New Rochelle, but he says that in the boys of the Huguenots football team he has found a calling. He was consecrated as a bishop only recently, in 2013 at the Shiloh Baptist Church, about a mile from New Rochelle High, and many around the team still refer to him by his prior title, Reverend.

Leak serves as a kind of spiritual adviser, a counselor at times, for the players and for the coaches and he is a vocal fan of both the game of football and of the team. He has closely cropped white hair and a thin, elegant moustache and he wears eyeglasses with half-moon, dark-plastic rims. Sometimes he sports a fedora. At his consecration ceremony Leak was described not only as a man of strong faith but also of courage, someone who will stand up when others sit down.

Bishop Leak waited on a small corner of lawn outside the entrance to the Clarkstown North gym as the boys came hurriedly out, some chatting, nerves clearly wound, and got down on one knee around him. A large rock rose up out of the ground, a boulder really, and Bishop Leak stood directly beside it on a small hillock. As the group assembled, some of the kids reached down and tightened the laces on their cleats. "That it?" Bishop Leak called. "We all here?"

"Hold on Reverend, one more," answered DiRienzo, as Corey Holder emerged through the gym doors pulling his jersey down over his head and shoulder pads. Corey is well-muscled at 6' 2" and 225 pounds, at once broad and lean, and is the team's most physically impressive player. "O.K.," said DiRienzo as Corey knelt into place, "we're good."

Bishop Leak stood quiet in the warm evening air, letting the boys' eyes settle upon him. In the little parking lot off to the side, a car pulled into a spot and a family got out—man, woman, a child of maybe 12—and walked together toward the field, taking this back way to avoid the crowd out in front of the school.

"Everybody learns from a child how to lace 'em up," Leak began. "Everybody learns from a child how to tie their shoes and lace 'em up. That's wonderful. I watched you all when you would just play with your laces and learn to tie them. This is a new theme tonight. This is a new journey. This time we go on this journey on this field and it is time to strap 'em up.

"What is it time for?"

Boys: "Strap 'em up!"

Leak: "What time is it?

Boys: "STRAP 'EM UP!"

(The distinction between strap 'em up and lace 'em up seemed evident to all.)

"Yes, strap 'em up," Leak went on, louder, now, sharper than when he began. "Today we see who the men are. Today I want to see the men. Today you become a man. You went up to the camp and all everything else. Today you become a man! Today you strap it up. Today is about manhood. Today is about getting after it. Gettin' after it. From the sound of the whistle you get after it! And when you do that you know that you're going to have success. As we pray . . . "

The boys bent their heads toward the ground. Most had taken another player's hand in his own, and there was a hush. You could hear a car moving nearby on the narrow residential streets and you could hear voices from the football field, out of sight. Leak led the team in the Lord's Prayer, and the boys murmured along, even the Muslim kids on the team, even the Jewish kids ("Why *not* pray with them?" Jack Stern, a broadly talented receiver and defensive back would explain to me later. "I figure that before a game we might as well get all the help we can get!")

> *"Our Father, who art in heaven,*
> *hallowed be thy name.*
> *Thy kingdom come,*
> *Thy will be done,*
> *on earth as it is in heaven.*
> *Give us this day our daily bread,*
> *and forgive us our trespasses,*
> *as we forgive those who trespass against us,*

and lead us not into temptation,
but deliver us from evil.
For thine is the kingdom,
and the power, and the glory,
for ever and ever.

With "Amen," the players burst to their feet, emitting shouts of "Let's go boys! Let's go!" They clapped and banged on their helmets, shouted "whoo-hoos!" into the air. In an eager procession, two-wide, the team clattered along the pavement next to the school, cleats clacking rhythmically on the concrete, and then up a short grassy hill, cresting it and emerging through the gate of a chain-link fence and out onto the football field where you could see the Clarkstown North players and the referees. The crowd was moving steadily into the bleachers. High floodlights shone moistly down, although the sky was still streaked by the day's last sunshine, bright pink against the belly of the clouds. In the lower rows of the home-team stands, the Clarkstown North band had begun to play. "Time to eat, fellas!" shouted Demetrius Rodriguez, up at the front of the line with the other captains. "It is time to eat!"

The Huguenots made their way across to the far sideline while the Clarkstown players assembled on their side of the field and the band, in first-game high school form—energetic, erratic—rose to a crescendo and then stopped. "Ladies and gentlemen, good evening and welcome to this kickoff classic between the New Rochelle Huguenots and your Clarkstown North Raaaams!" the game announcer called out over the P.A. Soon after, he introduced New Rochelle's starting defense by jersey number: "Number 1 Bryce Davis, Number 3 Keith Wheeler, Number 4 CJ Anthony, Number 9 Carmine Giordano. . . . " The New Rochelle coaches were announced as well and then the Clarkstown North offense and their coaches. Students and parents were still getting to their seats and the main parking lot was all but full. New Rochelle fans, mainly parents, sat in a smaller set of bleachers in back of the Huguenots sideline and the cheerleaders ran through some pregame cheers. A couple of guys from the field crew appeared and wheeled away a well-worn blocking sled that had been in the girls' way. The sled is a staple of the daily football practice, ever-daunting and emblazoned with words of caution: KEEP YOUR EYES UP. SEE WHAT YOU ARE HITTING and PLAY SMART: DO NOT LEAD WITH YOUR HEAD.

It was now just minutes before kickoff and the line at the hamburger-and-cokes food stand near the home bleachers had temporarily thinned. An ambulance quietly appeared and, backing in so that its rear double doors were closest to the field, parked just off the northern end zone. The announcer asked that the crowd rise for the national anthem, and DiRienzo called out to the Huguenots to get focused for it. "Everybody raise your helmet above your head with your right hand and find the flag," he called out. And the players did.

THERE WAS no questioning that New Rochelle was the better, more talented team on this opening night, though for much of the game, the scoreboard hardly showed it. The Huguenots moved the ball well on offense but they fumbled twice, and Bryce Davis, with the hand injury, his torn thumb still in a cast, dropped a punt. The team kept committing penalties: offside, illegal motion, holding, a hit from behind; one big gain after another was called back. There were eight New Rochelle penalties in the first 22 minutes of the game. It was awfully hot and humid and the team seemed fundamentally bedraggled. "We don't know if they're being less intense because they're like 'we got this' or if they're feeling nervous," coach Keith Fagan had said in his pregame assessment. "Like we keep reminding each other, we don't know this team yet."

The score remained 0–0 through to the final minutes of the half. For all the sloppiness on offense, the Huguenots defense was unyielding and often overpowering. Clarkstown North could barely get a first down and was repeatedly undone by big New Rochelle plays, including a series-ending sack by number 77, junior defensive tackle Dylan Cohen. Dylan was listed at 6' 2" and 227 pounds and his twin Tyler (6' 3", 182) also played on the team, mainly as a tight end. The brothers were on the varsity for the first time and although they were of markedly different body types—Dylan has competed as a shot putter, Tyler as a cross-country runner—it was not uncommon in the early season for their teammates to call each brother by the other's name. To simplify, and organize, some Huguenot players referred to the Cohens, who on high holidays attended Temple Israel a few miles from school, and to Jack Stern, as the Jew Crew. "The Jew Crew, makin' an impact!" shouted Alex X from the sideline after Dylan's sack against Clarkstown North.

The Cohens' father, Mike, is a retired Bronx police officer now working in security, and one of his favorite stories to tell about the twins is how Tyler was "supposed to be the first one out, but then Dylan pushed his way past and came out first and he hasn't stopped since. It is still like that." Tyler is the more athletically gifted of the two, softer hands for one thing, but it is Dylan's physical commitment that earned him playing time on both sides of the ball for DiRienzo.

Before the start of the 2014 season it wasn't clear that the Cohen brothers—who were also tagged, by the coaching staff, with the names Tweedledum and Tweedledee—would even play varsity football. Dylan had suffered a concussion as a freshman while playing pickup football, and the injury remained a source of trepidation for the boys' mother, Pam. ("Another concussion and you're done," she told Dylan. "That's it. One more and there's no more football.") Tyler was coming off a season in which he had needed stitches in his arm after getting cut during a tackling drill, and in which he had also suffered a fractured foot during an in-game pileup.

The twins had been playing football since middle school (Dylan joined the team in seventh grade, Tyler in eighth), and had for the most part enjoyed junior varsity, but neither was sure whether a commitment to the varsity, to the stresses, to the schedule and to DiRienzo's demands, made sense. Junior year with all its academic pressures was upon them, and they wanted to maintain their lifeguarding jobs to earn money to buy a car. They played lacrosse in the spring but football, in terms of what Dylan called "total life takeover," was different.

It had also happened that during a late-spring football camp at New

Rochelle, Mike Cohen had had a bit of a run-in with DiRienzo after seeing that there was no trainer supervising the mild contact drills. The team's trainer had abruptly quit, and the replacement had not yet arrived. When Mike complained, DiRienzo testily offered to refund the money for the camp, but Mike said it was not the money, but safety that concerned him, and that his boys would not play again until a trainer was there—which she was, the very next day. The matter blew over ("Looking back, Mike was right," DiRienzo would say) but still, the relationship between the Cohens and New Rochelle football was not all touchdowns and pom-poms.

"For a lot of reasons, we didn't think we were going to play," said Dylan. "A bunch of guys we had been with on jayvee had stopped playing. We talked with our parents and we decided we would go up to Brookwood, see what it was all about and make a decision afterward. Well that was pretty much it. The way we bonded with the team, there was no way we were going to quit and leave them. And Coach too, you could see the work and commitment he put in and how much he cared. You respected him and what he was doing. Yes, we ran till we felt like throwing up, and the practices where you are just hitting each other back to back to back are tougher than a game by far. But it was like we were all going through something together as a team and that made it O.K.—that made it good."

Plus, added Tyler, "We decided we wanted to try to get a ring, to win a championship before going away to college. We knew that with this coach and with this team we had a shot. It gave us something to reach for."

A FOURTH-DOWN completion from Greg Powell to CJ Anthony late in the second quarter against Clarkstown North, followed by Forrest's two-yard touchdown run, gave New Rochelle a 7–0 lead just before halftime. But the scoring drive did not in any way assuage the coaching staff. "There is an official running around out there with cerebral palsy," DiRienzo barked as he began his halftime talk. The players were on the grass behind the south end zone, sweating, and they were sitting as instructed with their backs against a chain-link fence and their helmets off. DiRienzo was not making some ill-advised joke—the afflicted official, though highly compromised in his gait, was working the secondary actively and very competently. When incomplete passes fell it was he who ran over to pick up the football for the next play. "There is an official running around out there with cerebral palsy," DiRienzo repeated, louder. "And he is in the same temperature that you are. Stop feeling sorry for yourselves. Stop giving in to fatigue, and let's stop talking, because we've been doing that all camp, but we ain't playing for a minute."

One of the coaches produced a greaseboard and held it for DiRienzo as some designed plays were reaffirmed. The coaches asked the kids what they were feeling and seeing out on the field and some had a few observations to contribute about the Clarkstown schemes. Coach Foster broke off from the team and assembled the linemen around him on a nearby plot of grass to talk about specific assignments. DiRienzo came over to reinforce: "Let me ask you, Coach," he said to Foster, "is everything in 40?"

Foster: "Yes"

DiRienzo: "Everything is in 40. Then any three or seven is opposite. Any three or seven pass protection is opposite. Any bootleg is either a deuce or the tackle has the B-gap. You understand what I'm saying?"

Foster, to the kids: "He is saying only with Backside Two do I want opposite."

In the second half, New Rochelle, with its continually stifling defense and the play of Powell, who would throw for 201 yards and run for a 20-yard touchdown, pulled out to a 17–0 win. There were casualties, though small, along the way. Demetrius Rodriguez was shaken up on a big hit, the air knocked out of him so that he lay for a while on the turf as a hush fell over the crowd. When Rodriguez rose and was escorted off the field by the Huguenots' rookie trainer, Rebecca Schwartzman, known to all as Becky, the P.A. announcer said, "And it is good to see he is back on his feet," and applause came out of the stands.

Rodriguez soon reentered the game but when Corey Holder had to come out there was no going back in. From his slot as an edge rusher off the right side, Holder had been beating his blockers and making tackles in the Clarkstown backfield all game long. He was prevailing despite being double teamed, sometimes triple teamed, and despite various three-stooges-like hijinks on the part of the Rams offensive line who grabbed and held him however they could. Corey, though, is a tempestuous sort, always has been, and after his arm got especially twisted during a scrum, he lashed out and threw a punch at Clarkstown North's right tackle, a senior named Josh Maurer. For this Holder was ejected, which meant that by District rule he was out not only for the rest of this game but for the Huguenots' next game as well.

"Man, he was pulling my arm like this and this," Corey complained as he came back to the sidelines, bending his arm backward to illustrate. "This is bullshit. Bullshit."

Holder had taken off his helmet and thrown it to the ground, then peeled off his jersey and his pack and thrown those down too. He has the talent to play Division I football—Holder's ability is on a level with Forrest's—but he doesn't have anything close to the grades. He'd had behavior issues on the team in years past, acting headstrong and sometimes uncooperative, aware that his superior talent gave him special privilege.

"For Corey it has often been his way or he won't do it all," says his mother Dawn, a community service officer with the New Rochelle Police Department. Dawn separated from Corey's father before Corey was born and the two of them live with Corey's two sisters on Lincoln Avenue in downtown New Rochelle. "But he was always a sweet kid, quiet. He wouldn't look you in the eye. Football is changing that. It is a place for Corey to get out his aggression and it gives him confidence. On the field, he has a whole different personality. I think he finally understands what an important part of his life football is, and with him being a senior now, in his last year and everything, I think that has grounded him."

"When Corey came to camp this year he was like a new kid," says Keith Fagan. "I don't know if Coach D finally got to him, or we all did, or if it was the game itself. But in Brookwood he was all 'Yes, Coach' and 'Whatever you need, Coach.' Incredible. The kids saw it too. That's why he got named captain, which was not something you would have predicted last season. I hope it lasts, we all hope it lasts."

Now Corey sat on the bench by himself, seething and moping, as teammates came by to slap his back, put a gentle headlock upon him—*We got you, man.* Shortly after Holder's ejection Powell ran in for his score to put New Rochelle ahead by two touchdowns, and then DeRocco kicked a field goal to lock down the win.

Holder was also visited on the bench by Bishop Leak, who spent all game, every game, on the sideline with the team. Leak leaned over and put a hand on each of Corey's shoulders and stared at him until Corey finally stopped looking away and met the gaze. "You have to be bigger than that. You have to turn the other cheek," said the Bishop. "You are going to get it worse than this. You are going to get spit on, poked in the eye, kicked in the balls. You've got to walk away from all of it, because you do no good for your team sitting on the bench. We need you in there." Corey grumbled and shook his head—"He had my arm like this," he said, demonstrating—but Bishop Leak didn't leave or break the gaze, not until he had gotten Corey to agree to go in front of the whole team at the next practice and apologize.

On the Clarkstown sideline, Josh Maurer had become something of a celebrity. He had taken a punch, and he had somehow done something to get the unstoppable Corey Holder out of the game. That meant the Rams offensive line could breathe at last. Josh, 6-foot and 200 pounds, is the older of two football-playing sons of Shari Maurer, a young-adult novelist, who says the question of whether or not the boys should be playing the sport is part of an ongoing discussion in their house. Her husband, Matthew, is a cardiologist. They met as teens at sleepaway camp. Josh takes AP and honors classes.

Throughout the boys' football careers—Eric, the younger son, was a freshman player in 2014—Shari and Matthew have seen broken fingers, sprained ankles, a broken collarbone, a ruptured disc. "They've been injured in other sports," says Shari, "but none of those sports are structured like football where tackling and hitting a guy is so much a part of the game. The fan culture, particularly through the parents, supports that. I stood next to a guy at a game last week who was screaming at his kid, 'I want you to hit someone on every play!'

"Our concern about football is 100% related to injury," she continued. "It's not broken bones we are worried about—we've had plenty of those—but head and spinal injuries. The ones where you don't get a do-over."

Shari also says that given the publicity around concussions and other head injuries in football other parents in her social circle often express disbelief that she allows her boys to play the sport. "They'll say, 'I would *never* let my kid play football,'" says Maurer. "Those people clearly believe they are better parents than us. About what other activity is it socially acceptable to say those things?"

In spite of that peer judgment and in spite of her own very real fears, Maurer says that she is glad that her sons play. She says that football helps Josh focus and get his schoolwork done, even if he is practicing with the team 24 hours a week. "There are so many positive aspects," Maurer says. "The camaraderie is unrivaled, and it is great for them to be part of a team and to feel like they have a place in school. They get exercise every day and they feel better physically during the season. They are happy to be playing and that bleeds into everything they do."

That is why Shari Maurer—who went to Duke as an undergraduate and to NYU for graduate school, and who spent six years developing productions of *Sesame Street* for Children's Television Workshop—says with complete conviction that "despite my worries, and on the hope that my sons are never injured in a way that I will regret it, I think football is a very positive thing for them. And it is a joy watching them play the game they love."

CHAPTER 6

A Homegoing

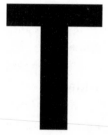HERE WAS always a coterie of onlookers at New Rochelle practices—afterschool students who stopped by to set down their backpacks and watch; members of the JV team when their own practice was done; guys who had coached in the district and were now retired; a former player here, a friend of coach D's there. Siblings and parents sometimes came by: Mike Cohen; Keith Wheeler's father, Keith; Dawn Holder once in a while; John Hinchey, the father of Chris, a strong 600-meter runner, who as a 150-pound junior was trying, in full-on *Rudy* fashion, to get off the New Rochelle bench. But the stalwarts of the practice audience, the every-afternooners in 2014, were a small group of fathers: Kirby Mack (dad of Quincy, a captain), Gary Powell (quarterback Greg) and Donald Baron, whose son Jared was the lone freshman on varsity. Jared, a compact and explosive running back, was recruited by several private high schools but chose to play in New Rochelle, where Donald himself had played in the 1970s, and where Jared had now emerged as Jonathan Forrest's heir apparent.

"People come by here and say to me, 'Aren't you going to get a hobby?'" said Kirby Mack one afternoon, leaning on the low metal fence overlooking the practice field. He works the 7 a.m. to 3 p.m. shift as a guard at the Westchester County jail, so by the time football practice rolls around he's free for the day. "I tell them that this *is* my hobby, watching Q and the team."

Quincy, thick and barrel-shaped at 5' 11", 220 pounds, and also the third baseman on the Huguenots baseball team, came to New Rochelle High School from nearby Mount Vernon ahead of his junior year. "It was a big move for the family," says his mother, Exzodia, a special needs teacher at the Fred S. Keller School in Yonkers. "We had been where we were for a long time. But you do what is right for your child." Quincy had begun playing baseball and football at age five; he grew up in the Mount Vernon programs. In the early years there, says Kirby, who coached Quincy's Mites team, "a lot of the boys couldn't tie their shoes yet. I mean, it was a good practice for us if every player's shoes were tied. But they could tackle!"

The football played at Mount Vernon High School, though, was not close to the caliber of New Rochelle's and, with a college scholarship looming as a possibility for Quincy, "We wanted to play under coach D," says Kirby. "If you had asked us to say which was Quincy's main sport while we were at Mount Vernon, we would have said baseball. Now it is definitely football." Quincy had been receiving interest from colleges such as Pace, Western Connecticut and Delaware State, and there was a thought that he might play both sports in college. Recruiters had only mild concern that Quincy had had a metal pin in his right hip ever since he was injured during a football game at age 12. Young Quincy, carrying the ball, had tried to pull free of a tackle but the tackler held on and Quincy's hipbone was wrenched out of its socket, leading to its being surgically repaired.

Jared Baron, Greg Powell and so many others on the New Rochelle team had come up through the town's competitive Youth Tackle League in what senior noseguard Jasper Baskerville calls a "rite of passage" for local football players. By the time they reach varsity, many Huguenots players have developed a bond over more than a decade of shared punishment and triumph on the field. (Even the lowest-level teams in New Rochelle are typically excellent and big winners.) Quincy arrived at the high school as an outsider—"He showed up from Mount Vernon and we were like, 'Yeah, what about this guy?' " says Jonathan Forrest—but he immediately established himself in practice as a ferocious tackler. He was unfailingly accommodating to the coaches, switching from fullback to tight end to linebacker without complaint. His production and execution made him a deserved two-way starter all along. Though not a hoot-and-holler type, Quincy was the rare player who took an interest in virtually all of his teammates. When little-used reserves got in for a few plays at the tail end of a lopsided game, made a tackle or two, Quincy would go to them on the sideline afterward and compliment them on their play.

He was tough on the field, steadying on the sideline, respectful and disciplined in street clothes, and when the players voted for their 2014 captains, Quincy, said coach Fagan, "was number one on just about every single ballot. No one else had close to that support."

Donald Baron, who works as the parts manager at a local Chrysler dealer, has instilled in Jared a similar discipline to that which Kirby has passed down to Quincy. Jared stays away from any tomfoolery on the field or the sideline and he greets people with a firm, confident handshake. He addresses adults as ma'am and sir. "He's an outstanding, highly respectful kid and, even better, he eats, sleeps, drinks, breathes football," says coach Greg Foster.

Jared is in superb condition and his running ability immediately stands out. He's fast and bullrushing and low to the ground and if not for Forrest, Jared would have been the team's primary ballcarrier even as a ninth-grader. Donald also sees New Rochelle as the conduit to the important next step in his son's football life; within the Baron family there have been not at all unrealistic discussions about Jared's one day going to play at Rutgers.

The quarterback Greg Powell, meantime, has made it clear, through his social media activity for one thing—and also by "constantly, constantly talking about it" says his father, Gary—that he plans to play in the NFL. "And if anyone can get themselves to do it, he can," Gary says. A longtime emergency medicine physician at a hospital, Gary attends and videotapes each of Greg's games. When Greg was eight and wanted to switch positions from defensive lineman to quarterback, Gary found a Pop Warner team in Brooklyn that needed a QB. To play there, Greg traveled 45 minutes each way from his home in New Rochelle, several times a week. Greg is a legend of sorts among students at the school, partly for having made junior varsity while still in eighth grade (Forrest did as well) and partly for making varsity as a sophomore QB (he was the backup) and also for innumerable playground and gym-class feats over the years. There was the time in eighth grade when, as the lone man still alive for his team in the class dodge ball championship, he caught three balls at once to eliminate the other team and win. Powell is quiet and determined, willing to take a hit, and one of the Huguenots players who tends to knock back a couple of Advil before games.

Greg's mom, Samantha, is a nurse and, much like Gary, she has seen her share of serious injuries caused by sports. Yet while Gary seems essentially unrattled by the potential of Greg's being injured playing football, Samantha is more squeamish. She does not come with Gary to watch Greg in practice and she rarely comes to see him play in games. Explains Gary, "She says that if her son gets hurt it will be all my fault."

Like many of the team dads, Gary Powell has an extremely high opinion of his son's abilities (he wasn't happy that Greg didn't get much playing time as a sophomore, for example, an opinion he made known to the coaches); but at the same time he strives to keep Greg's feet on the ground. Greg is a conscientious student because his parents have threatened with conviction to take football away if he does not maintain good grades in school. And when Gary learned that a media outlet had named Greg the region's high school offensive player of the week after his opening night performance against Clarkstown North (the 201 passing yards, the 55 more—and the touchdown—on the ground) he didn't immediately tell Greg, wanting to leaven the news with a caution against overconfidence. Often at the end of a New Rochelle football practice, Greg, helmet in hand, will come over to Gary standing by the fence that surrounds the field and Gary will quietly ask if Greg has had enough to eat, and how he is feeling and whether there is anything he needs.

The fathers' group of Mack, Baron and Powell was at the season's first practice—just as months later it would be at the season's last—and it was not long after that very first day, on a hot afternoon when there was sweat on every brow and the three men passed a bag of pistachios casually among themselves, that Kirby suddenly said to the others as they watched, "Hey, did you all hear about that kid in Staten Island who died? Died right on the field."

On the other side of the fence, between breaks in a series of running-formation drills, some of the players—X and Jasper, Quincy and Forrest and Stern—had been talking about the kid who died too.

THERE MUST have been 500 people in the Shiloh AME Zion Church, men, women and children squeezed into the long pews, or standing in the back looking down at their just-polished black shoes, murmuring quietly and embracing one another, waiting for things to begin. Shiloh is a low, redbrick church on the middle of a block on Henderson Avenue in the West Brighton section of Staten Island, N.Y. There's a tall white wooden cross on its front facade, and two smaller ones off to the side, and a row of narrow two-pane windows. The building is powerful for its simplicity and its modesty, and it has an architectural timelessness that seems apt. For more than a century—since 1907, long before the housing projects went up in West Brighton, and a time when the new immigrant Irishmen still played cricket on the neighborhood lawns—parishioners have come to the Shiloh AME Zion Church seeking solace in difficult times. The Saturday morning of September 13, 2014, was unquestionably one of those times. The little church was filled to its stained glass edges for the funeral of one of the community's own, Miles Kirkland-Thomas, a 16-year-old, 6' 2", 305-pound boy who had been preparing for his junior year as a lineman on the Curtis High School varsity football team when, just like that, in the middle of morning practice he collapsed and died.

Everyone who came into the church that day received a program outlining the schedule for MILES' HOMEGOING SERVICE. A large photograph of Miles in his crimson-and-white Curtis football uniform, number 54, dominated the cover of the program and beneath that photo were his life dates ("SUNRISE: MAY 1, 1998 — SUNSET: SEPTEMBER 1, 2014"). Additional pictures of Miles adorned the program's inside pages and in many of those he wore a football uniform too. In the pews his Curtis teammates sat together in their jerseys. The head coach and the school's athletic director were seated up front, with Miles's family.

Miles had arrived late to practice on the day he died—perhaps, his parents later thought, he had stopped off to see a girl—and so had been made to do some extra running. He had finished that running and had drunk some water and was breaking out to his position group for the rest of the practice when the coaches, as they would later describe it to Miles's father, Jamar Thomas, saw a strange wooziness pass over the boy's face. Suddenly, he dropped hard as a sack of bones to the earth. Miles tried to get up, a teammate said, but he could not. The ambulance came and took the boy to Richmond University Medical Center, two miles of city driving away, and when Jamar and Miles's mother, Tanza Kirkland, arrived they were met by the cold, hard everydayness of hospital life—they could see a defibrillator sitting there on a countertop and some knob at the desk had immediately mentioned there would be forms to fill out—as they learned that their youngest son had died of cardiac arrest.

At the Homegoing Service, Jamar got up and spoke, delivering a long and moving tribute full of anecdotes about Miles. You would not have known from his eloquence how nervous and how empty Jamar felt. He talked about what football had meant to Miles—how proud Miles was to have first made the varsity as a freshman—and also about what the sport meant to Miles's older brother Shawndell, who had himself been on the team at Curtis High and who was now playing at Bacone College, an NAIA school in Oklahoma. "There's one thing I've been remembering most in these days now," Jamar said as he stood there in the front of the church. He is a large man and he was taking care to stand up straight, to keep his shoulders back and his head high. "There was this one time a couple of years ago when I was watching Miles and the team practice. I looked over and I just happened to see him coming off the field and there was this look in his eyes and this smile on his face and I knew that he was truly happy and that right there playing football was where he wanted to be."

Around the high school, students had held vigils and ceremonies for Miles all that week, and the principal had brought in grief counselors. Near the Curtis football field a memorial site had sprung up where young people put candles and flowers and left notes of friendship and remembrance under a sign that said LONG LIVE 54. The Curtis team had gone ahead with playing its season-opening game the weekend after Miles's death, which is what the Kirkland-Thomas family had said that they wanted the school to do.

When the pastor spoke at the service he too brought in football, borrowing analogies and metaphors from the game and saying at one point without elaboration or explanation, that "God is sometimes more on the football field than he is in other places." One of Miles's Curtis High teammates spoke about how he and Miles had always pushed each other to succeed on the field, and then a congregant led the Shiloh choir in a beautiful, rousing, organ-accompanied version of the great gospel song, "Jesus You Are the Center of My Joy." The reverend returned to deliver the eulogy proper, and he reminded everyone, looking toward Tanza and Jamar in particular, that earth has no sorrow that heaven cannot heal.

Miles's death had made some national news, as such deaths always do. He had been the fifth child to die on a high school football field in a little more than three weeks, quite a high number even for a sport that is invariably dealt an annual toll.

In Douglasville, Ga., 17-year-old Zyrees Oliver had died after his football practice at Douglas County High from what was determined to be "exercise-associated hyponatremia." Trying to ward off thirst and muscle cramping, Oliver drank far too much liquid: two gallons of water, two gallons of Gatorade. The overhydration had caused severe swelling around the brain. He was a captain of the team and, at 6' 2", 220 pounds known to be in fine shape.

In Jackson, Miss., 17-year-old Walker Wilbanks of Jackson Prep had come off the field during a Friday night game against Oxford High not feeling well and was taken to the University of Mississippi Medical

Center where he later died. The doctor who treated Wilbanks, Joe Pressler, a pulmonologist and a specialist in the area of critical care, told *The Clarion-Ledger* that "a sodium-water imbalance" had caused Wilbanks's brain to swell, leading to his death. The loss of sodium, in Pressler's reported assessment was "caused by Wilbanks' sweating during the game. He lost more sodium than was being replenished as [he] tried to rehydrate on the sidelines."

In Lower Burrell, Pa., 16-year-old Noah Cornuet, a sophomore offensive tackle, collapsed after he had done his stretching and was simply walking over to take part in the first conditioning drills of Burrell High's preseason. It was an evening practice and about an hour after collapsing Cornuet was dead. He was found to have atrial myxoma, a noncancerous heart tumor.

In Starke, Fla., 14-year-old William Shogran Jr., a homeschooled boy playing his first season of football with Sebastian River High, felt ill and vomited during morning practice on the second day of a four-day team-building retreat—the equivalent to the Huguenots' Camp Brookwood. It was 85°, inland Florida, and the team had been practicing in full pads. One of the Sebastian River assistants called 911 and said, "I've got a football player at camp who's suffered from some heat issues." At the regional hospital, Shogran Jr.'s body temperature was measured at 107°; heat stroke was determined to be the cause of death.

You couldn't say that football alone had caused these deaths. Oliver's overhydration might have been avoided, and Cornuet's heart tumor, sadly, might have struck at some other time. Yet football was clear and present for all of them. These are what the National Center for Catastrophic Sports Injury Research (NCCSIR) classifies as "indirect fatalities", defined by the center as a fatality "caused by systemic failure as a result of exertion while participating in a football activity (e.g. heat stroke) or by a complication which was secondary to a non-fatal injury (e.g. infection)."

These events were not related to the most prevalent fear around football; in other words they were not part of the concerns about concussions, and head, neck and spinal trauma that sit at the center of the national debate and inquiry into the dangers of the sport. These indirect fatalities, often at least tangentially related to heat, and tending to occur in the late summer during preseason training or preseason games, were a grim side-casualty in the larger discussion. But a genuine issue they were and remain.[1]

From 1982–83 through 2012–13 (measuring academic years and using the most recent time frame as reported by the NCCSIR), there were a total of 222 known and reported indirect fatalities associated with high school football. Over that same 31-year span there were 180 known and reported indirect fatalities associated with the following high school sports *combined*: baseball, gymnastics, cross-country, soccer, field hockey, swimming, wrestling, volleyball, ice hockey, lacrosse, track, tennis and softball.

The raw total does not tell all of it—football, remember, has the largest participant population among those high school sports. Leveling for that, however, yields a similar conclusion: football's incidence rate of 0.53 indirect fatalities for every 100,000 participants (again as reported by the NCCSIR) is much, much higher than those other sports taken as a whole and also much higher than any specific sport that has a significant participation rate.[2] That 0.53 incidence rate translates to about one death for every 200,000 boys who play high school football. From a strict perspective of odds, that is about the same as the chances of someone drawing four-of-a-kind in seven-card stud. You would be about twice as likely to flip a coin 16 times and have it land on heads each time than to die by indirect fatality playing high school football. In other words, suffering an indirect fatality is quite unlikely, and the odds

---

[1] "Direct fatalities" are those that the NCCSIR defines as having "resulted from participation in the fundamental skills of football," and might be caused by those head and spinal injuries that tend to occur during the season itself, in actual games or full-bore practices. These are addressed later in the book.

[2] The only sports with higher incidence rates of indirect fatalities are boys' softball (2.66), water polo (0.94) and lacrosse (0.60). But each of those has such a low national participation rate that the incidence rate is unreliable. These are the indirect fatality totals in the 31-year span: two in boys softball, four in water polo and eight in lacrosse. A single fewer indirect fatality over 31 years in any of those sports would have dropped its incidence rate well below football's.

are of course further (and incalculably) impacted by factors such as the physical condition of the individual football player and the environmental conditions and circumstances in which the football is being played.

Yet, the chance of an indirect fatality in high school football, slim as it is, is not without statistical relevance. It is, after all, about 537 times more likely than the chances of a participant winning a typical state lottery jackpot. Or, think of it this way: Imagine the combined crowds at Darrell K. Royal Texas Memorial Stadium in Austin and at Bryant-Denny Stadium in Tuscaloosa on any given college football Saturday. That's 200,000 people right there. At an incidence rate akin to that of the indirect fatalities in high school football, one of the fans in those combined crowds would die each week. (Remember that at this point we're only considering "indirect" fatalities. Add in the direct fatalities and the football fatality incidence rate jumps to roughly one per every 100,000.)

The only high school sport with anything remotely close to football's number of indirect fatalities is basketball, with 138 such deaths over those 31 years.[3] One possible explanation for basketball's relatively high incidence rate is that indirect fatalities in all sports are sometimes related to heart conditions such as hypertrophic cardiomyopathy, a thickening of the heart muscle. Several studies, by the *Journal of the American College of Cardiology*, among others, have found that this condition seems to occur—or rather to go unrecognized and thus unaddressed—more commonly among African-American athletes, a group whose participation in basketball is higher than it is in many other high-school sports.

Hypertrophic cardiomyopathy is also what Miles Kirkland-Thomas, an African-American, was posthumously determined to have had. His condition, as those studies might have forewarned, was not detected during Miles's medical examination a month or so before his last Curtis High football season began. It will never be clear, in identifying the

---

[3] Basketball, however, has a truly tiny number of direct fatalities, just two over that 31-year time period. This is opposed to football's whopping 118 direct fatalities, also to be looked at later.

factors that contributed to Miles's death, just how his preexisting heart condition intersected with the environment of the day, other aspects of his physical fitness and with the running that he was made to do.

It was not Florida-hot in Staten Island on the day that Miles Kirkland-Thomas died, but it was hot, and sticky besides: about 80° with humidity close to 75%. Bylaws of the New York City Public School Athletic League say that, "When the temperature reaches 85° Fahrenheit and the humidity is **80%** or higher, **NO EXERCISE IS TO BE CONDUCTED**." (The emphasis here and throughout, both the bold type and the capitalization, is theirs.) PSAL rules also say that when the "humidity percent is between **50%** and **80%**, practice may be conducted but **EXTREME CAUTION MUST BE EXERCISED**." In other words, the weather conditions for varsity high school football practice that day, especially for a person of Miles's size, were permissible but far from ideal.

Had she known about Miles's heart condition, says his mother Tanza, she would have "done something to protect him" before letting him go back to play football; she would have never wanted him endangered. But to imagine doing it all again, to imagine having a child who is medically cleared as Miles was, who loves football the way Miles did, well, neither Tanza nor Jamar could say that they would forbid a son of theirs to play the game.

"We are a football family," Jamar said a few weeks after the funeral. This was not long after the community had planted a Chinese chestnut tree in Miles's honor on the corner of Richmond and Wall. "And we still are a football family. We will still follow Curtis football. You know, at homecoming just now they presented us with a banner."

Jamar said that because of the way his sons attached themselves to football, and how they identified with the sport, he used it as a way to talk to them about things that he wanted to talk to them about. "About how to be a man in the world and how to have honor." Jamar said that when they were watching football together and he saw a player's act of courage or selflessness he would always point it out.

When her sons started playing football so avidly, Tanza got herself involved too, although she knew little about the sport. She would come to watch Miles play as soon as her shifts as a nurse's assistant allowed. They live in the West Brighton Houses, a development built by New York City after World War II, and Tanza says that even on days when she felt sad or lost, when her circumstances seemed straitened, going over to see Miles playing football gave her renewed energy, a boost in her spirits. Tanza would cheer from the stands and often, given her merry ignorance of the rules, at inopportune times: after a handsome-looking Curtis run fell short of a crucial first down, say, or when a Curtis punt landed and bounced the wrong way. These slipups provided amusement and laughter for the family—*Mama's got no sense for football, boys*—and ran as an ongoing family joke, binding them all a little closer.

These sad-awful high school football-related deaths happen just about every year in late summer, and five such fatalities in a few weeks of 2014 was especially unsettling and so made for national news bites. You might have thought there would be cameras around at Miles's funeral, and at least a few reporters. But the reporting of that day, and throughout the aftermath of Miles's death, was done mainly by the local *Staten Island Advance*. And the only television truck on hand was from NY1, a local New York City cable channel.

Right behind the Shiloh AME Zion Church, behind some fencing and a stand of resilient city cedars, lie the playing fields of Corporal Thomson Park, where children of all ages play tackle football on Saturdays and grownups from the neighborhood come to watch. When the mourners spilled out from the Homegoing Service that day, lingering and talking soberly under the cloudy sky, you could hear children's voices shouting out from those fields, and the coaches, and then the deep, solid *boof* of someone punting the football.

They were playing football too, or preparing to, 30-some-odd miles away at New Rochelle High, where the Huguenots and their opponent, Ramapo, were at that moment running through pregame routines. Here, the media was plentiful. Trucks from the ABC, CBS and NBC affiliates, a half-dozen photographers or more, and several people ready to go on air, their hairdos sprayed stiff and foundation applied thick upon their faces. Word got around among the crowd that video from this New Rochelle game, or more specifically from the scene around it, would appear on CNN.

It wasn't that there was interest in the actual football matchup, the run-of-the-mill second game of a high school season that no one beyond town limits cared much about. The hoopla was stirring because New Rochelle football alumnus Ray Rice, all of sudden the most famous football player alive, and for all the worst reasons, would be in attendance, to see his alma mater play. He would be watching from the sideline, at the invitation of his old coach.

———

THERE MUST have been 700 people in the stands at William H. McKenna Field, side-by-side on the long metal rows. The crowd on this afternoon was larger than would have been expected given the steady drizzle falling on New Rochelle and the fact that the opponent, Ramapo, was a nonrival and without local ties. Fans wore rain-slickers or held small umbrellas or wore caps against the rain, and quite a number of them had on replica Baltimore Ravens jerseys—"Rice 27"—pulled over their sweatshirts and plain to see.

On the far side of the field, New Rochelle principal Reginald Richardson stood talking to reporters in a roped-off area designated for the media. Such a setup was unprecedented here, as was the school's hiring of a media consultant to help handle all of the day's interview requests, and to try to make sure that Richardson and DiRienzo, and anyone else at the school who was asked to talk, didn't say anything inflammatory or inappropriate. For everyone around New Rochelle High and the football program it had been a busy and trying week.

Five days before the Ramapo game a video had surfaced of Ray Rice assaulting his fiancée, Janay Palmer, with a short, brutally efficient left jab to her face that knocked her unconscious. The three-and-a-half minute clip, captured by camera in an elevator at an Atlantic City casino, had been viewed more than a million times, and, like that, the pride and inspiration of New Rochelle football had become an international pariah, a monster of sorts, the embodiment of ills in a sport and a society. Along with the violence of the punch, Rice's cold nonchalance as he tried to maneuver the body of his battered fiancée while she lay facedown and inert on the floor, had been galling.

Now principal Richardson was fielding questions from the reporters about the school's decision to remove a framed Ray Rice NFL jersey from the athletic "Wall of Fame" in the New Rochelle gymnasium, and also about DiRienzo's pronounced objections to that decision. The coach had complained publicly. Privately, he had hustled upstairs in the school building, bypassed the assistant seated at her desk in the anteroom, and burst into Richardson's office. DiRienzo was pissed. "They should have consulted me before doing anything," DiRienzo seethed to Richardson. "This is a time to stand by Ray. Do you understand the relationship here?" The mandate to remove the jersey had officially been issued by the school district's superintendent, but Richardson was in full support.

"Lou looks at this from the football program standpoint, and almost from a family standpoint," Richardson said later. He had come to New Rochelle High 14 months earlier, having previously held the principal's position at Performing Arts and Technology High in East New York, Brooklyn. "I look at it from an institutional standpoint, thinking, 'What do we want to say at a time like this?' It wasn't a complicated decision to take the jersey down. You think about why we display things in schools. Two reasons: First, we want to inspire kids to be like these individuals. And, second, we want to honor the contributions of the person to the school. That was the balance."

A Solomonic compromise was reached: While the Ravens jersey, as well as a recent photo of Rice, would come down from the Wall of Fame, Rice's New Rochelle jersey—a white 5 on the Huguenot purple—would stay up, allowing the school to honor, as Richardson put it, "what Ray did while he was here." There would be no reference to what he represented now: a Pro Bowl–level NFL running back, a frequent and vital contributor (in both money and deed) to New Rochelle's school and public service programs, and a 27-year old man suddenly synonymous with domestic violence. After the elevator video went public, Rice had been suspended indefinitely by the NFL and released, by the Ravens, from the last three years of a five-year, $35-million contract. All of his sponsors, including Nike, had quickly severed ties, and the sporting goods chain Modell's had removed its Ray Rice jerseys from the shelves.

You could not, on the morning or afternoon of Sept. 13, 2014, have picked up a newspaper or browsed a news site or tuned into a news show on television or radio without coming across discussion and dissection of what Rice had done, of the problems that it seemed to reveal about football and its culture, and of how the NFL, through erratic messaging, inconsistent discipline and its thick veneer of arrogance, had made such a further mess of it.[4]

---

[4] The elevator assault had happened in February 2014. Soon afterward, and long before the video of the actual punch came out on Sept. 8, a different video had gone viral, showing not the act of the assault itself, but only its disturbing aftermath in which Rice dragged the unconscious Janay out of the elevator. In light of that video, Rice had been charged in March by an Atlantic County grand jury with third-degree aggravated assault—though Janay had not pressed charges—and in May a New Jersey prosecutor had allowed him to avoid trial by entering an intervention program that would wipe the charge from his record after one year if he met certain requirements, including attending counseling sessions. (Rice did meet the requirements and on May 21, 2015, all charges were officially dropped.)

In July 2014, the NFL, after interviewing Rice and Janay jointly (a jarring and myopic choice by the league: in domestic violence cases, interviewing the victim and the alleged perpetrator separately is much more conducive to candid testimony and typically more revealing) and also conducting what it classified as an "investigation," had suspended Rice for two games. That meager punishment led to such fierce condemnation from the public and from advocacy groups that a blindsided NFL commissioner Roger Goodell wrote a letter to league owners saying, "I take responsibility both for the decision and for ensuring that our actions in the future properly reflect our values. I didn't get it right. Simply put, we have to do better. And we will."

However, until that second elevator video emerged in September showing the fist to the face, the unhappy Ray Rice situation had seemed destined to sink further out of sight, into the thick muck of NFL player criminality (dozens of active players, at any given time, have histories that include an arrest for assault or other violence) and that after the two-game ban, Rice, scathed but unbowed, likely would simply return to the Ravens' backfield. The firestorm of publicity around the caught-on-camera punch changed everything.

Was it true, principal Richardson was now being asked on the damp grass alongside the New Rochelle field, that Rice would be on hand for today's game against Ramapo, thus making his first public appearance since the second video went public? Richardson said that he didn't know for sure and at that moment he did not. When DiRienzo had taken it upon himself to invite Rice to this week's game, over Richardson's strong objections, even Rice had been surprised—"Coach, I can't show up there now," he said.

"Yes, Ray, you can show up at our game, and that is what we are going to do," DiRienzo responded. There was, for the coach, an important point to be made.

As Richardson stood in the media area and the New Rochelle players came off the field after their last backpedalling drills and gathered on the sideline with kickoff just minutes away, a noise came out of the stands. Neither a roar nor a murmur quite, but more of an awakening, as Rice, with a sizable group around him, emerged from the school building, out through the football doors, striding past the side lawn and over the running track to merge onto the New Rochelle sideline. Janay, now his wife (they got married the month after the assault), walked right beside him with their two-year-old daughter, Rayven, and also in the group were Janay's mother and Ray's sister, and others from the inner circle of his life. Rice wore a black ball cap, a black V-neck T-shirt, a black jacket and black pants.

"It's right that he's here," said Shameek Miller, who with his teammates watched from the New Rochelle sideline as Rice came in. "It's good. This team is where he belongs. Ray means a lot to us. He's taken time with me, and with other guys. We know what he did was wrong, but we are not going to go away from him now."

It was time for Shameek and the other Huguenots players to line up and lift their helmets high in their right hands. The P.A. announcer had asked everyone to stand, as a New Rochelle cheerleader named Dymond readied to sing the national anthem. Rice did not have a helmet to raise but he took off his cap, and held it over his heart and turned to face the U.S. flag. It had been a little less than 10 years since he had played his final down as a Huguenot. The field environment was not much changed and the flag was where it had always been. There was still purple everywhere and the people in the stands still called out his name, and for a brief moment as Dymond sang the words, Ray Rice, standing on the sideline with all those high school players not far off and with the familiar smell of that particular damp field at such a particular time of day, 1 o'clock on a Saturday, had a familiar sensation. He felt much the same way he had felt when he was about to play a football game for New Rochelle High School back in the day.

CHAPTER 7

Ray Rice Is Here

AYMELL RICE—AS he was captioned in the high school yearbooks and referred to in local clippings after yet another game day when he'd torn it up on the field—grew up in a public housing project in New Rochelle known as The Hollow Courts. These are two large brick buildings on a citified stretch of the Boston Post Road. There is an old Getty gas station down the street, and a Taco Bell by the traffic light and, across the busy boulevard, the beige brick buildings of the for-profit Monroe College. The Hollow, as the residents all call it, is about two-and-a-half miles from New Rochelle High. The Rices lived in a corner apartment on the sixth floor.

Ray's life was blown off course when he was a year old, in 1988. His father, Calvin, was killed in a drive-by shooting while walking on a sidewalk in the neighboring city of Mount Vernon. Upon conviction years later, the man who shot him said that Calvin had been an innocent bystander, an unintended victim.

Ray would become the eldest of four siblings—his brothers Markell who is three years younger than Ray, and Durell, seven years younger, would also go on to play football at New Rochelle High—and their mother,

Janet, held several jobs. She looked after kids at a day-care center for a while and later worked as a special-needs aide at Isaac Young Middle School. The family relied on public assistance as well, food stamps for groceries, and Ray worked odd jobs from as young as age eight.

By then the Rices also had a young man living with them, Myshaun Rice-Nichols, a cousin who was 10 years older than Ray. It was Myshaun who, as Ray would say, "took me for that walk in the park, and did things with me." The things, he meant, "that a father would do. [And] he was the one who told me I could be someone if I set goals. He kept me focused."

Myshaun taught Ray to play basketball on the outdoor court at the Hollow and to do pull-ups on the water pipes in the basement of one of the buildings. He also introduced him to football, and Ray—who, Janet says, "had muscles when he was five"—took to the sport immediately. The boys who lived there played games in the concrete courtyard at the Hollow and crowds would gather, calling out, huzzahing and smoking blunts, and urging the players to test one another. Large planters with hip-high cement sides were within the field of play and the physical games in this environment, as Ray told ESPN in 2011, "made me tough."

Myshaun was also a rap artist who performed under the acronym S.U.P.E., which stood for Spiritually Uplifting People Everywhere. He rapped about God and family and having purpose, and he secured a recording contract. "He was the one guy in our family," as Ray recalls, "who actually went out there and made it."

The recording contract led Myshaun to move to Los Angeles when Ray was 10. Soon after the move, though, Myshaun was killed in an automobile accident. Ray did not attend the funeral or watch the coverage on the regional news programs. He knew even then that it would be more than he could bear. A few months later, Ray, who had not flirted with such trouble before, was caught in school carrying a pellet gun in his backpack. He was suspended for a week and given 100 hours of community service. In stories and documentaries about Rice that appeared during the years when he was a rising NFL star and before he punched Janay in that elevator—that is, when he was viewed as an inspiring example of perseverance and success—this pellet-gun incident is described, by Ray himself and by others, as a turning point. It was the pellet-gun punishment he received, along with seeing the pain and tears that the whole messy episode caused his mother Janet, Ray says, that led him to fly right. He did not get into disciplinary trouble again.

He was powerful on the football field, dedicated and ferocious as he made his way through New Rochelle's Youth Tackle League. He was never tall, but he was thick, shot through with muscle, incredibly balanced and astoundingly strong. (Calvin had been an avid bodybuilder, and Ray was a young gym rat.) Although he was always a ballcarrier, Ray also at times played nosetackle on defense, and invariably overwhelmed the opponent's offensive line. In at least one game Ray was so dominant, crashing into the backfield even against older and much larger boys to deliver bone-jarring hits, that the referee made him leave the game, fearing for player safety.

Although he also played basketball, football had become the focus and center of his life, the milieu in which he lived and in which he set goals and worked to achieve them. In the eighth grade Rice played junior varsity at New Rochelle and by year's end he was being recruited by area private schools. But he knew Lou DiRienzo, and he knew a coaching staff that included Ray Rhett, then the varsity running backs coach. He regarded them as solid and important men, he loved the town where he lived and the particular football culture within it, and he says, "Growing up where I had grown up, going to private school wasn't right for me. I was a New Rochelle public school kid." Neither Rice nor Janet ever thought about him going to school anywhere else.

Rice embraced DiRienzo as a father figure and he embraced the coach's standards and expectations. In addition to being New Rochelle's best player, Ray remained the team's hardest worker, and a direct leader of his peers. He played four years on varsity and while other people sang his praises and "told me how great I was," he liked it that DiRienzo did not dote on him in this way. "He made me feel like the rest of the players,"

Rice says. "He was not a coach to let star players off the handle. You had to do your schoolwork and you had to follow what the team was doing just like everybody else.

"When I was in ninth grade I went to this golf outing with coach D," Rice went on. "All these alums had come back for it. He had that kind of hold on them. At the golf outing coach D said something to me that I will never forget. He said: 'You are coming to me as a boy, but you will leave me as a man.' And that was true; he was all about responsibility and discipline and doing things in a respectful way. That was how he defined being a man and that is what he expected. It wasn't just me, it was everyone who played for him."

As a player, though, Ray was unquestionably special—conspicuously skilled and dauntingly strong; he was able, even at his diminutive size, to squat 450 pounds and to bench-press 295. He played both defensive back and running back for the Huguenots and everyone on both teams and everyone in the stands knew when Ray was in the game.[1]

As a junior, in 2003, Raymell Rice—and now it was not a local outlet but *USA Today* describing him—ran for 167 yards and two touchdowns to help lead New Rochelle to a 32–6 win in the Class AA state final.[2] As a senior, a season during which he ran for 462 yards in one game, Ray took New Rochelle back to the final where it lost to Christian Brothers Academy, 41–35, in a matchup that more than a decade later is regarded by many as perhaps the best game ever played in the state. That Rice doesn't appear among New York State's career high school rushing leaders is due in large measure to the fact that when New Rochelle had a big lead, which it most often did, DiRienzo would rest Ray in the second half of games. "That's another lesson I'm grateful for," says Rice now. "It showed us two

---

[1] Rice was also the team's incorrigible jokester, unpretentious and unabashed: On rookie show night at the preseason football camp retreat he came out wearing only a diaper.

[2] Courtney Greene, who would go on to appear in 30 NFL games, also starred on that New Rochelle team as a running back and he scored three touchdowns to win MVP honors for the game. Greene and Rice are the only New Rochelle football alums to reach the NFL in the past 25 years.

things, that no one was bigger than the game and that he had such respect for the other coaches."

Coach DiRienzo guided Ray as he was recruited for college ball, supporting the belief that he could play running back in Division I, and not focus on being a defensive back as most interested colleges wanted. There weren't a lot of offers in any case—Rice was still so small—and it was DiRienzo who helped Ray get an offer to Syracuse, and then, after a sudden coaching change there, to move instead to Rutgers. There Rice rushed for a Scarlet Knights record 4,926 yards in three seasons, and, along with coach Greg Schiano, transformed Rutgers into a team with a national presence. Despite his full-grown height—listed at 5' 8" he is closer to 5' 7", even in cleats. "My fault," says Janet, who is 4' 11"—but there was no longer any doubt that Ray was a serious NFL prospect.

The Ravens selected him in the second round of the 2008 NFL draft, the seventh running back taken. Soon he had leaped to the top of the Baltimore depth chart and by '09 he was the mainstay of the offense. Rice was a favorite of the casual football fan, the triumphant little guy with particularly eye-pleasing skills. Few could slash and slither away from tacklers as Rice could, a brave North-South runner with just enough East-West jitter when he needed it. He was the top pick of the fantasy football world—catching an average of more than 70 passes a year and, in 2011, generating a league-best 2,068 yards from scrimmage. Rice broke off long, creative runs that reminded football men of the great Hall of Fame back Barry Sanders.

He had become a leader not just on the field for the Ravens, but in the Baltimore community as well. He visited hospitals as part of team events and then came back again on his own. He went to schools and into troubled neighborhoods. He spent long hours with fans who were ill or somehow down on their luck. Rice was hardly the only do-gooder in the NFL—the league was and remains thick with players who devote their private time and resources to helping those in need—but he was especially committed, and seemed to have an uncommon intent and sincerity. Teammates knew that when their phone rang on an off day it might be Ray summoning them to come down to appear at some medical clinic somewhere. When

Rice was asked why he did these kinds of things, he allowed that he had been through certain difficult times in his life, and that now he wanted to be remembered "as a guy who made it and gave back."

Most of all Rice was beloved back home in New Rochelle and around the football program there. You might have come across him, some random afternoon, pressing the heaviest dumbbells in the high school gym. When New Rochelle won the state title in 2012 Rice bought Beats headphones for every player. The Huguenots coaching staff had a standing invitation and free passes to Ray's Ravens games, and in '13 Rice brought DiRienzo to New Orleans to see Baltimore play in the Super Bowl. The Ravens won, and he gave the helmet he wore in the game to DiRienzo. "I wanted him to have something real from me, something I sweat in, something that reminded me of us," says Rice. "Having him there to see me in the game, that was a bucket list thing for me."

He also put New Rochelle assistant Rich Tassello in charge of designing and implementing a withering off-season conditioning program for him. They ran stairs and did push-ups, flipped tractor tires, swung sledgehammers, wore weighted vests, sprinted on the beach. Tassello helped Ray build a body more commanding than it had ever been, a body meant to protect and empower Rice amid the violence of the football field, and also to be cruel in its deliverance. The conditioning program was tremendously taxing and deeply bonding and when Rayven was born in 2012, Ray and Janay asked Tassello to be the girl's godfather.

Rice was always showing up back at the Hollow, to give impromptu clinics or host a barbecue on the community grills, or pass out flyers for educational and civic programs or just to shoot the breeze on the steps. When he saw a kid like Shameek Miller, who lives in those buildings, he would ask whether Shameek was listening to his mother, whether he was keeping up with his schoolwork and thinking about learning a trade, and whether he was getting into shape and making strides on the football field. At one point a large, city-approved sign was installed near an entrance to the Hollow, reading, in white letters on a purple background: *"When people told me that I wouldn't be able to accomplish something, it just made me work harder to prove them wrong."* —Ray Rice, 2011

Six hundred kids or more would show up to an annual "Ray Rice Day" at New Rochelle High. There were football clinics and games of two-hand touch, and a fair amount of messaging. Ray always took a microphone and spoke at the event—as he also did at the parade in New Rochelle after the Ravens won the Super Bowl, and as he did as well on the day his number 5 Huguenots jersey was officially retired, and as he did on other visits on other days. Rice had themes that he liked to impart, explicitly those regarding the fragility of success. "One thing I know about dreams is you can live them," Rice said more than once. "But the other side about dreams is that you make one bad decision and a dream can become a total nightmare."

That, of course, was said before the spring and summer of 2014, before everyone saw what Ray did to Janay that night. Back in those years, 2011, '12, '13, saying the name Ray Rice in a public setting conveyed something completely different than what it would come to convey. The day the elevator video went viral, a pall wrapped itself around the New Rochelle practice. Lugubrious men and boys doing half-hearted things. Coach Tassello looked devastated, distraught, and he was short with the kids. DiRienzo hardly spoke at all. Nor did Fagan. Between drills, the boys didn't banter on the sidelines the way they usually liked to do.

Still, the team went grimly through its business. Mistakes that had been made in the Clarkstown North opener were addressed, and work that needed to get done got done. Afterward DiRienzo took the time he had set aside to talk one-on-one with Tyler Cohen, to encourage him to apply himself more in practice. "There is an opportunity for you here that you do not want to miss," DiRienzo said in their meeting. "I need to see what I was seeing from you two weeks ago in practice. I need to see that every day."

The coaches' evening session after practice, however, the hours when they come back to the football space after a quick dinner to break down film of the upcoming opponent and to tune their playbook—those added hours that are a staple of DiRienzo's and so many other football coaches' regimens—that would not happen on this night, or rather it would happen without DiRienzo. He and Tassello were getting on a train to Baltimore to go see Ray. Lou had been down there after the first video had surfaced and at other times as well. He had known Ray for better than a decade now, and he had known Janay nearly that long. He knew both of their moms.

It was long after dark by the time that train arrived in Baltimore. Ray had come out to pick up DiRienzo and Tassello at the station. In the car, Rice looked at DiRienzo with his face bereft, an expression, DiRienzo would say, that showed "shame and fear and helplessness. I was really worried for him." No one said anything for a few moments as they embraced, and then Ray pulled back and looked right at DiRienzo and said, "Coach, what are we going to do now?"

THE RAY RICE video, the assault itself and then the case around it, were the most prominent inciters of what became, in stunningly short order, a series of news stories and developments that tainted the NFL's image, opened a window into the workings and priorities of the league's operations and delivered an ugly, perhaps lasting mark to the sport:

• First, Rice's updated ban refocused media attention on an ongoing but largely underreported situation in which Greg Hardy, a Pro Bowl–caliber defensive lineman for the Carolina Panthers was continuing to play in games while appealing his conviction for threatening and assaulting a female. Amid the heightened, post-Rice scrutiny, the Panthers removed Hardy from their active roster and put him on the commissioner's exempt list.

• Three days after the Rice video went public, Minnesota Vikings running back Adrian Peterson was indicted for causing "reckless or negligent injury" to his four-year-old son, whom he had whipped on the hindquarters with a switch, damaging the boy's upper thighs and testicles. Minnesota deactivated Peterson, its best player, then reinstated him. Then, following heavy pressure from team sponsors—including the Radisson Hotel chain, which pulled its advertising support altogether—deactivated him again. Peterson pleaded guilty to a misdemeanor charge of reckless assault.

• A few days after that Peterson indictment, Cardinals backup running back Jonathan Dwyer was arrested, and later charged with assaulting his wife (allegedly breaking her nose with a head-butt) in a pair of incidents over the summer. He was placed on an inactive list by the team. Dwyer pleaded guilty to a lesser change of misdemeanor disrderly conduct.

• It was around this time that wider public attention also fell on 49ers defensive lineman Ray McDonald, who in late August had been arrested and released after an altercation with his fiancée that police said left bruises on the woman's arm. The Niners allowed McDonald, who was an essential part of their defense, to continue playing. (Three months later, in December of 2014, McDonald was investigated on a separate sexual assault charge; this time the 49ers, by then shuffling toward a disappointing .500 season, terminated his contract. McDonald pled not guilty in both cases.)

Each of the cases was different in its circumstances and its particulars and yet they were predictably, and understandably, lumped together and even conflated in the public's hasty reckoning. Judging by the breathless news analysis programs and the high-pitched discussions across all media channels, it was as if the NFL had become a refuge for violent criminals. The league was strafed for its inconsistencies in discipline—remember that, along with the Vikings' vacillations on Peterson, Rice's two-game NFL suspension had been abruptly changed to an indefinite ban and a contract termination, even though nothing about his actual, horrific actions had changed, save for what the public saw of it. Those inconsistencies leant an ad hoc sense, in the public mind, to the league's and teams' decision-making and their approach to player punishment. The inexpert handling of the Rice case appeared cynical and narrowly driven (that is, guided by a determination on how best to protect the brand and its vast moneymaking apparatus) and the NFL's series of actions and inactions were debated within and without the world of sports media. Editorials from coast to coast decried the NFL's hubris, including, conspicuously, commissioner Roger Goodell's own, and many wondered whether the commissioner would survive his missteps and the firestorm.

For all of that, there were layers of the discussion that raised questions with much deeper implications than whether Goodell, a man with a $44 million salary standing astride a $10 billion industry, might lose his job. Armchair analysis turned to the nature of NFL players: Did football breed violence in the men who played it or did the sport simply attract and keep men predisposed to violence? Does spending one's professional life in an arena where violence settles all tests—as football players do—lead to the imposing of that value in one's personal life as well? Does the prevalence of steroids, painkillers and other drugs among pro football players lead to more violent off-field behavior? All of the above? None of it?

Such topics, which had been explored by academics over the years without much result, were now being addressed in 800-word columns and four-minute video segments, as well as on the sidelines and in the stands of football fields everywhere. When New Rochelle principal Reginald Richardson was interviewed on NPR radio about six weeks after the Rice case broke open, he spoke in part about how the school had a standing relationship with My Sisters' Place, an organization dedicated to ending domestic violence. "They're working specifically with our athletics teams," Richardson said, "so we can help them become the best people they can be, so they can make good decisions."

The musings and the discussions, inevitably inconclusive, were wide-ranging and, for those in the league office or otherwise involved in the business of football, they seemed interminable. On the field the NFL rolled on, the beauty and high spectacle of the sport on some levels untouched, but away from the games the talk and the mood quickly darkened. "Football is tough to cover right now," the managing editor of *Sports Illustrated*, Chris Stone, confided about 10 days after the Rice video came out. "There's a black cloud over it. You have to be careful of the message you send."

Despite the rash of proximal events, however, the awareness and monitoring of violent crimes in football was not a new or sudden reality. A database maintained by *USA Today* showed more than 700 NFL-player arrests between the 2000 season and September 2014. That's more than 50 a year. (The rate has not slowed since.) A majority of those arrests were related to nonviolent drunk driving and drug offenses, but scores were on charges of violent crimes, spousal and child abuse and various other charges of assault. At the website fivethirtyeight.com, the writer and analyst Benjamin Morris put the information in that database to work. Even while acknowledging that those arrest rates may for various reasons be underinflated,[3] Morris determined that NFL players commit violent crime significantly *less* frequently than do men in their mid-to-late-20s across society at large. That holds true even when adjusting for the NFL players' generally higher income bracket and lower incidence of alcohol and drug dependency as compared to the greater population. Professional football players, in other words, are not the scourge of society that, in the fall of '14, they seemed to be. Remember that databases on the crime rates of, say, hedge fund managers, police officers, dentists, journalists or virtually any other career-category subset you can think of are not available.

Even so, the number of arrests among NFL players can be startling, and stands out next to the comparatively clean rap sheets of athletes in other prominent pro sports such as Major League Baseball. In 2014, the rash of incidents tended to cast all NFL players as guilty by proximity. "You can see people looking at us differently," Jets guard Willie Colon, who has never been associated with violent crime, said during the wave of domestic abuse cases. "It's embarrassing."

That sense of embarrassment was felt on every rung of the football ladder. As Laura Bittelman Procops, the mother of two football-playing high schoolers in Roslyn, N.Y., said, "It's not like a mom now thinks that playing football will turn her son into a violent criminal. But all of those things in the news made football more difficult to talk about. These were terrible, high-profile acts and the one thing they all had in common was football. Even your kids start to feel aware of it. It leaves a bad taste."

---

[3] The *USA Today* database relies on media reports and some arrests may have gone unreported. Also NFL players, in positions of relative privilege and power, and with team influence behind them, may be more likely to escape arrest than other people who commit violent crime. So it is likely there were more arrests and arrestable offenses than the database could capture.

As public outcry continued, the NFL scrambled to abruptly put women in internal organizational roles of greater power and discipline. The Ravens invited fans to come to M&T Bank Stadium and exchange officially licensed Ray Rice jerseys for those of other players (thousands did so). But in the end there was no immediate measurable impact on the sport's bottom line. Television ratings continued to dominate other programming, stadium attendance held strong, more people signed up for NFL fantasy leagues each day. And in an unexpected, almost cruelly ironic sense, the miscreant behavior provided a kind of cover for the league, a distraction from the larger issues that threatened it.

AMONG THE ways that it produced football content during this time, *Sports Illustrated* (whose parent company, Time Inc., is the publisher of this book) revealed results from a wide-ranging poll of more than 500 NFL fans. The poll determined, among many other things, that 38% of those polled believed Goodell should lose his job over his erratic discipline and communication. More than half of the respondents said that player-violence incidents had "worsened" their opinion of the NFL and 46% felt that NFL players were "not good role models."

But when it came to the issue at the core of football's existential troubles—head trauma—the league and the sport still had a level of insulation. Nearly two thirds of those polled through *Sports Illustrated* said that information about the long-term health risks of head injuries to football players had "no effect" on their high interest level in the games. And, in response to the question, "If your son wanted to play tackle football, would you let him?" the huge majority, 85%, said yes.

The stories about Rice and Peterson and Hardy and Dwyer and McDonald were frothier, and had greater legs in the media than the ostensibly earth-shifting news that also came out, first in *The New York Times*, right in the heart of this tumultuous September. In court proceedings between the NFL and the 5,000 former players suing the league for allegedly having failed to reveal evidence about the potential impact of concussions, the league made a staggering admission. As the

Times related, the NFL said in these federal papers that it "expects nearly a third of retired players to develop long-term cognitive problems and that the conditions are likely to emerge at 'notably younger ages' than in the general population."

Nearly a third. In each NFL game, 92 players suit up and are eligible to play. By the calculation above, 30 of them may spend years or decades of their lives with a significantly diminished intellectual capacity, a significantly diminished physical functionality, an incalculably diminished life. That, as all sides of the debate now seemed to agree, is simply the price of doing business in the NFL.

There was other similarly portentous news during that September of 2014, news both particular and general: Autopsy results revealed publicly that Jovan Belcher, the Kansas City Chiefs linebacker who in 2012 shot and killed his girlfriend and then, standing in front of Chiefs' front office officials, shot and killed himself, had shown clear signs of chronic traumatic encephalopathy, or CTE. That degenerative brain disease, caused by extended head trauma, had also been found in other NFL players, including Junior Seau and Dave Duerson, both of whom had also committed suicide. Each shot himself in the chest, so as to preserve his brain for scientific research.

On the heels of the Belcher revelation, the Department of Veterans Affairs brain bank in Bedford, Mass., working with the Boston University CTE center, revealed through a report on the PBS news magazine *Frontline* that the brains of 76 out of 79 deceased football players who had autopsies showed signs of CTE. This was something of a preselected group: such examinations can only be conducted posthumously and in these cases there was often some suspicion of brain damage based on the player's symptoms before death. Even so a 96% positive rate over a sample size of 79 players is no random happening. This was not a theory anymore, this was fact: NFL players are at very high risk for developing this deadly brain disease. And some might develop it at a startlingly young age. Jovan Belcher was only 25 years old.

Also jarring, and immediately relevant in households everywhere, was this: the results of an additional 49 autopsies were also revealed at this time by the VA/BU group, these being of men and boys who had played football only on the college, semi-professional or high school level. Twenty-five of those 49 brains, or 51%, were found to have CTE. "You do not like to see numbers like that, you do not like to see them at all," said DiRienzo one September afternoon after practice. "Like I always say, this is not the same game that gets played on Sundays in big, sold-out stadiums. It isn't anything like that fast or that physical or that unrelenting. But these kids are playing football and you want them to play hard, and we have to find a way to protect them."

It was at this time as well, mid September of 2014, that the career of John Abraham—a splendid defensive end with the Arizona Cardinals, a player who had made five Pro Bowls and who was the NFL's active leader in quarterback sacks—came to an end. Abraham had suffered a serious concussion in the Cardinals' season-opening *Monday Night Football* game against the Chargers. He became despondent, and in the days afterward he volleyed back and forth between retiring and staying in the game. Arizona coach Bruce Arians referred to the event as Abraham's "first concussion," but other players essentially scoffed and rolled their eyes at that. As Cardinals linebacker Lorenzo Alexander said, "Playing this game, everybody's had multiple concussions. Whether or not they're diagnosed is something totally different. I'm pretty sure [Abraham] has had multiple concussions throughout his career like we all have." A report by ESPN football reporter Adam Schefter suggested that Abraham had been beset by memory loss for more than a year.

Eight days after the game against the Chargers, Abraham failed to pass a concussion protocol. Two days later he failed again. The Cardinals put him on injured reserve, meaning he would miss the entire season. As it turned out, Abraham had played his last career down.

"ARE WE even going to be playing football in 15 years?" Steve Young, the New Rochelle athletic director, was asking. Rain still fell continuously on the field, and the Huguenots had taken an early lead in the game against Ramapo. Kids from the Youth Tackle League were scampering about the sodden running track, splashing into puddles, and occasionally darting over and, quite literally, tugging on Ray Rice's sleeve. A little goofing, to everyone's delight.

"All the stuff that has been going on," Young continued, "and the things you hear from parents, it makes you think." He was wearing a dark blue slicker and standing among the loose thicket of men on the New Rochelle sideline, about 20 yards away from Rice. Young kept glancing over to where the media was corralled across the field. "We're definitely seeing participation start to drop—that's the thing we talk about most at our AD conferences. Some districts are fine, going strong even. Here in New Rochelle we're down a little, at the younger levels, but we're hanging in pretty good. But a lot of other districts across the state and the country, especially in more affluent neighborhoods, they're really feeling it in terms of numbers. Football is getting to be a hard sell."[4]

---

[4] The drop in Pop Warner football participation by an alarming 9.5% between 2010 and '12 was the largest decline since the organization began tracking its number of participants. That may be part of a wider trend: A report by the Sports and Fitness Industry Association showed a decline in several sports, specifically football, basketball, baseball and soccer, among children ages 6 to 17 from 2007 through '12, with football down 5.4%. A similar finding by the group, spanning '08 to '13, showed a starker drop in younger participants, with football down close to 29% in the 6 to 11 age group. The numbers may be traceable to greater athletic options for kids (sports such as ice hockey and lacrosse saw participation increase during that time); to the fact that, in the 6–17 group, more teenagers have begun concentrating on one sport and eliminating others; and also, of course, to the likelihood that social media and various forms of video entertainment are drawing some children away from organized athletics altogether. At the high school level, though, participation across all sports has increased steadily, and is up 3.6% from 2008–09 through 2014–15. That's why it rings significant that participation in 11-man football, still the most popular boys sports by an enormous margin, has *fallen* by 2.5% during that time. The statistics come from the National Federation of State High School Associations, and some of the most striking changes are regional. In New York, for example, the number of high school football players dropped by 8.3% from the 2008 through '14 seasons, while in both Texas and Florida participation rose by about 1.8% in that time. Other states with significant participation numbers have shown even more dramatic changes: Boys' high school football participation in Ohio has plunged 23.2% since 2008. In Alabama that number has shot upward by 41.2%.

Young, who had spent 2002 through '12 as the high school athletic director in the tonier Westchester school district of Chappaqua (it's a high-income nest; the Clintons live there), now straddled lines and perspectives at New Rochelle. He maneuvered his budget carefully within the program's emphasis on football and he advocated for the importance of certain safety protocols even when at odds with the teams' other goals. Young is devoted to education through sports (his official title was Director of Health, Physical Education and Athletics at New Rochelle) and although neither of his sons played high school football—both were undersized, as is Young himself—he loves the game. An old photo on a shelf behind the cluttered desk in his office shows his now-grown son Danny at age four in a three-point stance wearing a way oversized Pee Wee football uniform and an oversized helmet. Young also has a small sign in his office that reads: DOING THE RIGHT THING MAY BE HARD BUT IT CERTAINLY ISN'T COMPLICATED.

Young supports DiRienzo, trusts him and his values, and he is impressed by DiRienzo's dedication and methods. "Lou's special," he says. "I've been around a lot of coaches. Lou's special." But the Rice situation presented a source of discomfort, a strain. Although Young had gotten to know Rice a bit himself, and had seen first-hand the benefits Rice provided for the community and the program, the tenor of the response to Rice's assault and predicament unnerved him. Young operated very close to this football family, but he was not quite in it. When he heard that New Rochelle's Bishop Feston Leak had organized a so-called "Night of Prayer for Redemption and Restoration for Ray Rice, His Family and Friends," to be held at the St. Catherine AME Zion Church in New Rochelle, Young all but gulped.

"Okay, I get it. It's fine, I understand he needs prayer and the people here are behind him," said Young. "But what about the victim? That's what gets me. What about the victim? You look around here, you listen to what everyone is talking about, about what Ray did and what he has meant, and what happens now. No one is talking about the victim. Honestly that's true on TV and in the papers too. Nobody is really talking about what she went through and is going through. It was an actual, real woman on that videotape, Janay. Not some anonymous person. Not a statistic. They are going to be praying for Ray, but do they think about having a prayer service for Janay?"

From where Young stood you could see a child of maybe five years old, fair-skinned and red-haired, wearing a Ray Rice Ravens jersey and tossing a football to himself through the raindrops, paying no attention to the game. Rice and his family were still there, weather be damned, actively watching and reacting to the play on the field. The Huguenots were having a time of it: They'd gone ahead immediately when Keith Wheeler returned the opening kickoff for a touchdown. Then Greg Powell had thrown a scoring pass to Forrest, and another to Tyler Cohen, the tight end who'd gotten the talking-to from DiRienzo about raising his effort. Then Demetrius Rodriguez recovered a fumble in the end zone. The Ramapo football program had been wrecked by budget cuts in recent years and had nearly been shut down. There was no junior varsity team, there were few resources. By midway through the second quarter New Rochelle had put in its second-string players and led the game by a score of 34–0.

DiRienzo was coaching from his usual vantage point: staring into the heart of the line of scrimmage from the very edge of the field, in a hands-on-knees crouch, headphones on his ears, when he suddenly stood up straight and called out: "Ray! Hey Ray, come over here." Rice was jiggling Rayven on his shoulders but he immediately lifted her off and gave her to Janay to hold, and jogged briskly to where DiRienzo stood. "You needed me, Coach?"

"You know what Ray," DiRienzo said quietly, leaning over, "It is a good thing the score of this game is the way it is so I don't have to worry so much about the plays. I can think about what I'm going to say when the media asks me about you at halftime." Rice laughed and nodded—*You ain't lying about that, Coach*—and DiRienzo chuckled too and gave Rice a playful tap on the belly before breaking back away to the game. It was this very moment, this interaction between the two of them, that a photographer from the *New York Post* caught from across the field. The photo would run the next day as the cover of the

Sunday *Post* under the big block headline "BIG MEANIE ON CAMPUS."[5]

DiRienzo did indeed speak to the media at halftime, standing out on the football field surrounded by boom mikes and handhelds and recorders and cameras and notebooks and, all in all, more than two dozen people gathered around him. Because he was out there and not in the locker room, DiRienzo had to entrust the midgame breakdowns and adjustments to his assistants—possible, the coach said, only because the game was so lopsided. DiRienzo talked to the reporters about how Ray had made a terrible mistake but said that he knew "the character of the man and he will rise from this . . . . Success is not in never falling," coach D emphasized, "it is in rising again after you fall."

He explained that these were the kinds of things he had been talking about with his players in recent days, along with other lessons to be learned from what had happened with Ray. "That they need to think before they act," DiRienzo said. And that when it came to making a mistake the most crucial response lay in, "admitting it, not repeating it, and learning from it." He also told the team that the Ray Rice situation proved that whatever you have done and accomplished in your life, it can be "ruined in 20 seconds."

"I respect New Rochelle for having Ray Rice at that game," said Garland Allen later. Allen was a longtime athletic director at Greenwich High in Connecticut (15 miles north of New Rochelle) and a member of the board at NYU's ethics-based Sports and Society program. Other high school administrators and coaches in the area echoed Allen's view and were, as a majority, in support. "Some schools would have distanced themselves from it, but New Rochelle had a strong coach who recognized the big picture. This was absolutely a teachable moment, and those are precious. If you banish Ray, the window on that teachable moment gets a lot narrower."

---

[5] For long stretches of the game, I shadowed DiRienzo and, to some extent, Rice. And so it was that I wound up in this particular *New York Post* photograph too, just behind and between the two men, looking on as they broadly grinned. "That *Post* cover," DiRienzo said to me later in the week, "did you stick it up on your wall and throw darts at it?"

The most lasting of the lessons that DiRienzo preached during that time, the big takeaway that really stayed with the kids, that, as Jonathan Forrest said, "brought us together even more" and that in many ways tapped into the essence and allure of football's draw upon so many young men, was something else he said at that halftime address, and said again in postgame interviews and reiterated in the days that followed. "New Rochelle is a very proud program, and once you're a member, you're a member for life," DiRienzo said. "Even though Ray made a mistake doesn't mean we throw him out of the house. Ray's one of my sons in my football family and we'd never throw him out of the house."

In other words, said Forrest, "He let us know that once you make a commitment to New Rochelle football, New Rochelle football will make a commitment to you. Coach D will always have your back."

CHAPTER 8

The Stand

ERE WAS the football game in the balance, right here at the edge of the New Rochelle end zone, the big boys from John Jay-East Fishkill in possession of the ball and with four downs to score. This was the first really good opponent the Huguenots had faced this season and, truth was, they might not face a better one. Each team had two wins and no losses and New Rochelle led this one 14–6, and there were seven minutes left in the game.

They were playing in New Rochelle, not at the high school itself, but rather a couple of miles away on a snappy green turf field with built-in bleachers on both sides and a permanently installed place to buy hot dogs, French fries and sweet drinks, all within a complex of athletic fields known as City Park. It was a Friday night, late September, and big bright floodlights shone down illuminating the field. The bleachers were close to full. John Jay had come from 60 miles upstate, arriving hours early in three buses. They had a lot more players on the team than New Rochelle did; a lot bigger players too. "This is a huge game for our team," said Steve Young, the New Rochelle athletic director, shortly before kickoff. "You could see it in the players during the day, their excitement. But overall there wasn't much buzz around school. There's just too much else going on. We have an art museum event there tonight."

Football linemen, on both offense and defense, are the lifeblood of every team at every level and have been for as long as the game has been played. These are the players who, snap after snap, engage in the most fundamental tests of strength and will. They crack helmets on every play, their fingers tend to get swollen and battered from the grappling. The battle among opposing linemen controls how much time a quarterback has to throw the ball, and how much space a ballcarrier has to run. In football, that's pretty much the heart of everything. This is why steady dominance by an offensive line is what most often leads to a team dominating a game as a whole, and why a big stand by the defensive line, a denial as it were, can raise a team's spirits like nothing else short of a scoring play.

John Jay's offensive line had more players than usual on it now and they were all lined up tight together in short-yardage formation, with the ball inside the three-yard line. John Jay hadn't been able to run effectively on New Rochelle all night, but they were going to try to run it again now. The Huguenots had stacked their defensive line in response—no safeties, just a couple of cornerbacks on the outskirts of a front wall that went, end-to-end, like this: Demetrius Rodriguez, Garrett Noake, Dylan Cohen, Jasper Baskerville, Corey Holder. Four others, nominally linebackers were up close behind them: Jonathan Forrest, Quincy Mack, Justice Cowan and CJ Anthony.

During the week DiRienzo and his staff had studied film of John Jay's goal-line tendencies from previous years. It was still too early to have anything from this season go on. They were not entirely sure what to expect.

First Down. John Jay ran right into the middle, off left tackle. Jasper and Dylan led the defensive push, CJ and Justice surged in to make the stop. The play gained a yard and half. Now John Jay had second down at about the one. "That was O.K.," DiRienzo would say later, watching the film. "We knew we had a little something to give. Because of what Jasper and Dylan did pushing back those linemen, that runner had nowhere to go but right to where CJ and Justice were coming to knock him down."

The players knew who had done the heavy lifting on the play and when Jasper, a senior, and Dylan, a junior, got up off the pile, they quietly slapped hands and nodded to one another. Both are thickly built, Jasper at 5' 10" and 236 pounds the shorter and stockier of the two. He has skin the color of bittersweet chocolate, a round face with a broad smile, good-looking despite an unfortunate attempt at facial hair. At practice Jasper likes to do a thing with the younger players in which he lets them take a running start into him and then holds his ground, doesn't budge. "Like a brick wall," says Alex X. Jasper has a girlfriend, Cynthia, a pretty cheerleader, and by the start of Jasper's senior season they had been dating for well over a year, an eternity to the high school set. Cynthia has black hair and light olive skin and they are very handsome as a pair. They'll post photos of themselves together on social media and a Twitter shot of them kissing inspires students to respond with tweets like, "This is what Martin Luther King Jr. died for!"

Dylan is quieter than Jasper, not that kind of team leader, and in school he runs with a less jolly hallway crowd. But both players carry themselves with a similar quiet strength, a straightforward reliability.[1] Dylan and Jasper are both the kind of kids (and kids are surely not all this way) who will bring their big bags of chips to the sideline to share. Dylan is seen as an important anchor for the team and a prospective leader after seniors such as Jasper are gone.

"One big reason I'm glad I stayed with football isn't just the game itself; it's also some of these guys," Dylan said. "Before the season I didn't even think I'd like these kids, but then they become like your closest friends. A guy like Jasper, I'm out there battling with him on just about every down"—both play on the offensive line as well as the defensive—"and I've learned a lot from him. How he is on the team. How he handles it when he gets poked or kicked. He's like calm and confident and you

---

[1] These traits help explain why Jasper is often called "grandpa" by teammates. Dylan, you may recall, is half of Tweedledum and Tweedledee with his twin brother Tyler. The nicknames, in feel and sense within the context of the team, are not so dissimilar.

respect that. Jasper's this great kid and we wouldn't even know each other if it weren't for football."

Second Down. John Jay ran the ball again and this time it was Jonathan Forrest and Quincy Mack who came together for the tackle. The play gained two feet, 10 inches; John Jay was still a nose short of the goal line. Again, New Rochelle's stop was traceable to others in addition to the tacklers. Garrett Noake, getting low and leveraging, moved a much larger tight end off the play, creating space for Forrest and Mack to close in. Thus far the two defensive plays at the goal line had directly involved seven different defensive players. Indirectly, more. "You have to do one-eleventh of the job when you're out there," coach D likes to tell the players. "If everyone does his one-eleventh right, the whole job gets done. I don't need players doing two-elevenths. Do your part and we work."

Noake, a senior, is the ruddiest in complexion of the many-toned Huguenots, with bright orange hair and cheeks that easily redden. He almost always has a serious expression when he is on the football field, and during the third quarter against John Jay, Noake was especially ticked. "We should be up 35–6 not 14–6," he said on the sideline. "It's the stupid penalties that kill us." Noake plays center on offense, and one of the half-dozen penalties the Huguenots were called for in the first half had been his fault. It's rare for Noake to get penalized and when he does he does not forgive himself. His closely-cropped side hair and his short but pronounced apricot bangs give his skull a squared-off look. He is 6' 2" and weighs close to 210 pounds.

"I could see him playing football at a NESCAC school," DiRienzo said, referring to the competitive, academically proud Division III New England Small College Athletic Conference. "He's disciplined out there. Good mentality." There are currently 11 football teams in NESCAC and since the conference's official formation in 1971, a total of four of its players have ascended to the NFL. By comparison, more than 50 players from the Division I Southeastern Conference might get drafted into the NFL in a single year.

Noake's older brother Griffin also used to play center for New Rochelle, as a starter on the 2012 state championship team. He and Garrett look a lot alike and Griffin has gone on to play football at SUNY Cortland. Griffin was also an excellent tennis player, and Garrett played tennis for a time too, though the brothers were always loath to talk about this with their peers. "You could tell they found it too embarrassing," one of the school's newspaper editors told me. When it comes to macho and street cred at New Rochelle High (yea, in America at large), tennis is to football what the Coast Guard is to the Marines.

The stands at City Park were alive now, with the ball so close to the end zone and third down coming up. New Rochelle's cheerleaders jiggered and pom-pommed with full effort ("N-E-W. R-O. New Ro!"), encouraging another big play by the defense. The sky was dark and starless above the floodlights and the evening air felt moist and already sharply cool, the true autumn announcing itself. Everywhere around the field young boys, football players themselves and wearing their purple jerseys, scampered around: Eight-, nine-, ten-, eleven-year-olds thrilled to be out on a Friday night. Their parents and caretakers stood leaning against the fence by the end zone, plastic cups in hand, watching the game.

City Park is where the Youth Tackle League hosts its home games and on a wall of the building that houses the snack shop hang large placards covered with long columns of names. The heading reads: FORMER YOUTH TACKLE LEAGUE OF NEW ROCHELLE PLAYERS WHO PARTICIPATED IN COLLEGE ATHLETICS, and beside each name is the sport the player competed in during college and then the name of the college itself. Ray Rice and Courtney Greene are on the list, with FOOTBALL and RUTGERS UNIVERSITY by their names, and so is New Rochelle assistant Greg Foster, who played at Albany and whose own son was scheduled to play in a YTL game the very next day. The lists, many years in the making, have hundreds of names on them and the catalog of colleges is also long and varied: SUNY Farmingdale, Concordia, University of Miami, Army, Columbia, Texas A&M, Iona, Monroe College, Nassau Community College, Middlebury, Michigan, Southern Connecticut, and on and on and on.

The list is meant to be aspirational. Given its prominent display at the field and the way you see so many kids, in their YTL jerseys, chewing

Skittles and stopping to read through the lists, to find and point out names they recognize—fathers, uncles, big brothers, cousins, neighborhood legends—you have to believe that aspirational is exactly what it is. "My kids know my name is up there because I went to college and because I played football in college," says Foster. "And they know that that is not a given. You work for that."

Third Down. Just before the snap, DiRienzo and his staff saw that a couple of players on the edge of the defensive formation were misaligned, and started waving frantically. Forrest, predictably, noticed this formation issue and began to yell and point for Demetrius Rodriguez and CJ Anthony to adjust their positioning, which they did. (As a captain and signal-caller, Forrest regularly makes late adjustments like this, and the other players trust him completely.) And then, the play: Again Jasper Baskerville helped tie up the middle of John Jay's offensive line and through a slender gap in the bodies, Quincy Mack charged through into the backfield and drilled the ballcarrier chest high, stopping him cold. Loss of a yard. The crowd erupted. Only fourth down remained.

It is often the case that DiRienzo's defense behaves so aggressively that it essentially dictates the play, so that the opposing offense is trying to react to what New Rochelle's defense is doing rather than the other way around. That's far from unheard of in football, with its play-by-play chess matches and reactive moves on both sides, but for a defense to be so routinely in charge is not particularly common either. Not on any level. New Rochelle's D, a mix of a 3–4 and a 5–2 alignment, which DiRienzo continually shapes, sharpens and alters as players come and go through the program, is known and discussed countywide.

High up in the bleachers, Exzodia and Kirby Mack were cheering on their son, delighted by the hit Quincy had just delivered. They had come to the game early, and staked their spot in the stands by the time the first of the team buses had arrived from New Rochelle High. The Macks were in particularly good football moods because just the night before Kirby had fielded calls from several college coaches with an interest in Quincy. "Football has been very good for him," Exzodia had said before the game. "For Quincy to be where he is at in his life because of this game . . . I am so proud of him. He is confident and he's strong and he has an idea of where he wants to go in his life. We see a lot of kids at his same age who just don't have that kind of direction at all. Quincy's got it and football has meant so much to that."

Now, Kirby and Exzodia were standing, applauding Quincy's big tackle-for-a-loss, along with Quincy's sister beside them and just about everybody else in the densely packed stands. During the excitement of this sequence of downs, the crowd had become so increasingly animated that it almost seemed enlarged. That was true as well on the New Rochelle sideline. Numerous coaches, some with long-standing but tenuous links to the team—former assistants, long time residents, retired coaches from other schools—had come to the game and kept calling out random instructions and exhortations to the players, telling them they *hadda do this* and *hadda do that*.[2]

The sidelines were crowded as well with former New Rochelle players, some one year out of the program, some 20 years out, and many in-between. Members of the family as it were. Every New Ro game is a reunion, and that is especially true on a Friday night. Two alums, the twins Chris and Courtland Cargill, who had graduated three years earlier ("great program kids" Foster calls them), had assumed an interesting responsibility during the game. They stayed near to DiRienzo, and when the coach would forgetfully step out onto the field between plays, shouting directions to his team—a technically illegal and potentially penalty-drawing wandering that DiRienzo is prone to—one of the Cargills would quickly call him back before a referee threw a

---

[2] An array of hangers-on and sycophants populates the sidelines at all levels of football. Take a look at a major college sideline some Saturday afternoon and ask yourself, "Are all those men really needed down there?" The answer is definitely "No." Having so many vassals, though, is part of the cultural agenda and provides a circular benefit: They are happy and proud to be there, close to the action and feeling in the know, while at the same time their presence elevates the apparent importance of the mission at hand—the attempt to win the game—as well as the stature of the coaches who are doing the actual work. Said Steve Young good-naturedly during the John Jay game, "Hmmm, I think we have just about all of our 47 assistant coaches here tonight."

flag. Now the crowd was loud and DiRienzo had his headset on when the Cargill brothers suddenly saw that he had advanced some 15, 20 feet onto the playing turf. He had something he wanted to convey to his defense. New Rochelle assistant Keith Fagan, watching the game from a small booth at the top of the stands, had picked up a detail in the John Jay lineup that made him believe they were going to run a quarterback sneak, and DiRienzo very much wanted to communicate that to his players in the few seconds before the play began. John Jay had only this one last shot at the end zone.

A referee eyed the frantic DiRienzo on the field, called out a warning that coach D could not possibly have heard and seemed on the verge of levying what would have been a well-deserved but extremely costly penalty on the New Rochelle coach. The Cargills, though, dashed out and grabbed DiRienzo, one brother at his shoulders the other at his hips, and pulled and tugged him backward all the way to the sideline. It was a remarkable sight, and loud "whoas" went up from those who saw it. Fourth down, less than two yards to the goal line. A sense of pitch and moment, of a controlled mayhem, had the whole place in its grip.

Fourth Down. John Jay, desperately trying something different to solve the Huguenots defense and reluctant to pass from in so close, did indeed run a quarterback sneak. New Rochelle was right on it, crashing in. Corey Holder, working his pressure from the far right side seemed to topple not one but three members of the John Jay line with a push toward the middle. It was Dylan Cohen who met the quarterback—a talented, big-armed kid named Ryan Schumacher—and turned him back. Cohen, that is, and the army he rode in with.

The Cargills did not try to stop DiRienzo this time, no point and no desire, as he ran out onto the field, pumping his right fist. The defense came racing off, leaping into coach D, leaping into one another, reaching the sideline for a mobbing and a mammoth embrace while over the loudspeaker the play-caller announced, "No gain! No gain! New Rochelle takes over on downs!"

They had stood together, played through a genuine test against one of the toughest teams around, and that particular battle at that particular goal line had been won. Though the defense had made its mistakes through the sequence (DiRienzo and the staff would unearth and grumble about several of them as they watched the film), it had done the hard collaborative work it needed to do to succeed. A certain feeling washed through the team in the days after that goal line stand, a sense that the stand had been representative—representative of what disciplined, committed work could yield, and of how things talked about could evolve into action, and of how different people could come together as one functioning, interdependent unit. In short, there was a sense that that series of defensive plays represented the essence of what a football team was meant to be about.

It was as if by looking at the one thing under glass you might see something much larger and much broader, you might see it all. Much like a class of children in early grade school watching a seedling sprout in a plastic cup; or the researcher in her boots observing day after day from the tall grass the nesting behavior of a single, tagged bird; or the biologists looking through microscopes at single cells, and by the examination of these discrete little things engendering the conception of the double-helix, a theory of life.

In the weeks that followed the goal line stand, DiRienzo would show the team film of the best, sweetest parts of the effort and he would talk about it again and again. The players—kids from the projects, kids from the condos, kids from the five-bedroom homes in the North End—all knew they had done something difficult and painful and that none of them could have done it alone. When football goes right like that, says DiRienzo, "It makes it a whole lot easier to get them to buy in to what you are selling."

THE GAME against John Jay-East Fishkill did not in fact end with that momentous goal line stand. John Jay came back, behind quarterback Schumacher (who kept connecting with his older brother, Robbie) and tied the game 14–14 on a touchdown pass and then a two-point conversion in the final seconds. It would be in overtime that Forrest would run for his third touchdown of the game, and that the Huguenots defense would hold firm and a 21–14 victory would be sealed.

Noake had been right that New Rochelle could have won the game by more. The Huguenots controlled the action physically against John Jay, despite their deficit in size, and it was early-game evidence of this that had led DiRienzo to have such confidence when he had gathered the team for a few words during halftime. The score at this point was 7–6 in New Rochelle's favor. In the background the school band pounded out reconfigured Beatles songs and the cheerleaders hurtled through the air. There are no locker rooms at City Park, and the Huguenots were assembled outside, in the far end zone, away from the crowd, away from everyone but themselves.

"Like I said before," DiRienzo began, loud and energized, as halftime neared its end. "These are moments we live for. But I'll tell you what. This ain't gonna get done with your mouth . . . it's gonna get done with your shoulder pads. . . . And I know this: If we use our face and we use our shoulder pads on both sides of the ball, we're going to be able to dance a little bit tonight!" There was a big swell of yeeaaaaaaaa! from the team—Jack Stern was especially wide-eyed and stoked by the little soliloquy—as they took off back toward the sideline.

"You'd think that kind of stuff, those words, don't matter much to a player, but they do you know." Louis DiRienzo Jr., coach D's elder son, was speaking. He was a linebacker in his senior season at Southern Connecticut State, and the reason New Rochelle had several night games on its 2014 schedule was so that Lou Sr. could be free to go to watch Lou Jr.'s games on Saturdays. (When you have the stature DiRienzo has, other coaches and section officials will bend for your schedule.) But now Lou Jr. was injured, he'd needed surgery to repair the medial collateral ligament in his right knee and was out for several weeks, perhaps the year, and so would not be playing the next day. He had traveled the 60 miles to come to his dad's game.

The resemblance between father and son is striking—their shoulders have a similar slope, their heads are equally and entirely shaved, their gaits are unmistakably D. "Oh man, my brother is like the spitting image of my dad," says Andrew DiRienzo, Lou and Carol's youngest son. "When he was in eighth grade and I was in sixth grade, he was already about my dad's size. One day me and him are at home and he puts on my dad's coaching clothes, the sweatshirt and pants, the whistle, everything. He's going back in forth in front of the mirror making fun of dad, saying all the things my dad says, and I'm cracking up. And guess what? Dad came home early and he walked right in on it! There was nothing he could say about it, though—my brother was just so spot-on."

Both boys had been around New Rochelle football all their ambulatory lives, and both played varsity for DiRienzo, and both were now preparing themselves for a life in coaching. "Football," says Louis Jr., "is my passion. It's my life. I'd like to play the game forever but I'm not 6' 3". I don't run a 4.4. I can become a coach though. And that's what I'm going to do." At Southern Connecticut, Louis Jr. is majoring in exercise education. He dips Skoal just like his dad—spitting image indeed.

After Forrest had crossed the goal line for the winning score, and the defense had made that score stand up, and the players and coaches had shaken hands, and the Huguenots players had run over for quick hugs from parents and siblings and girlfriends, and the buzzing crowd was thinning out into the parking lot, the team came together around coach D one more time. They were near the center of the field and although just moments before the players had been rowdy, jumping around giddily from the win, now a silence had come upon them as they waited to hear what Coach would say. He did not say anything for quite a number of seconds, though. He just kept his arms by his side and, it appeared, studied something on the ground in front of him with great intent.

Louis Jr. was standing off to one side and suddenly a look of recognition shot over his face. "Watch this," he whispered, staring at his father.

"I have been waiting for this for a long time," coach D said finally and quietly. And then he thrust his arms straight into the air and shouted: "Way to go, boys!"

How the players whooped wildly at that—lifted by the confirmation that they had done well, that the game had mattered and they had acquitted themselves. As Louis Jr. and the current players know, coach

D saves that "Way to go, boys!" response for only the most satisfying and honorable wins.

The Huguenots, all aglow, moved off then, into the Friday night, knowing there would be no practice the next day, and that a diner cheeseburger or a six-pack of beer or a party somewhere awaited them as conquering heroes. And all the boys on the team—not just Jasper and Dylan and Forrest and Noake and Quincy, but every last one of these players wearing that New Rochelle uniform, on that New Rochelle team—could feel for this moment as if he were standing right on top of the world.

CHAPTER 9

Once and Always a Huguenot

HROUGHOUT THE game against John Jay-East Fishkill, Corey Holder kept coming abruptly off the field, visibly agitated and grabbing his right shoulder. He would shuck his helmet to the turf, and stand writhing demonstratively on the sideline. Becky, the New Rochelle trainer, would come over and talk with him, gently touch and examine his upper arm and back, have him sit down on the bench. Corey would miss a few plays, shaking his head and complaining of the pain. Then he would say he was O.K., go back in and for several consecutive downs dominate the blockers opposite him. A version of these events happened three or four times and because of Holder's general temperament and behavioral past—the kid could really act out—it wasn't clear just how injured he was. After the game Corey went over and met his mother, Dawn, on a grassy area near the fence that encircled the field. He peeled off his jersey and stood there shirtless and bending forward, bright white light from a lamp-post shining down. The crowd dispersed around them and a clutch of girls passing by called out Corey's name, giggling and uh-huhing. A few moments later another small group of girls passed by and did the

same thing. "It really hurts, Ma," Corey said, "but I'll be O.K. I'll be O.K." And Dawn said they should go home and put some ice on it, and Corey, who wasn't smiling, nodded to say O.K., that made sense to him.

"Partially torn labrum and a fracture of his right shoulder," said Keith Fagan shaking his head and kneading a football as he watched Holder practice six days later. "You know, before this if you'd asked me to name the toughest guy on our team I would have said Jonny Forrest. Maybe Demetrius. Maybe Quincy. But right now ahead of this game against North Rockland I'll say Corey Holder, the way he has been practicing through this—and practicing hard."

When Corey had finally gone to see Sergai DeLaMora, the orthopedist who services the players on the team, DeLaMora clucked. "If he's been playing all week with this, and he wants to keep playing," the doctor said to the coaching staff, "then he is one tough son of a bitch." It was said quite admiringly and word of this medical assessment got around among Corey's teammates.

The win over John Jay had vaulted New Rochelle from a national high school football ranking of 3,982 to 2,881 and from No. 76 in New York State to No. 49.[1] Now, at 3–0, the Huguenots would play their most relevant rival, North Rockland. From 1999 through 2012 either North Rockland or New Rochelle had won the Section 1 Class AA title, and in 2013 North Rockland had knocked New Rochelle from the playoffs. "If you're talking about champions in Class AA football in Section 1, the discussion begins and ends with New Rochelle vs. North Rockland," declared a local blog in a runup to the game. "Their large enrollments and strong feeder systems and coaching staffs have made them the very best for a very, very long time." Fractured shoulder, torn whatever, there was no way that Corey Holder, in his senior year, was going to miss the North Rockland game.

---

[1] The rankings point up that while the Huguenots could be seen as a veritable blue whale in their particular pond of Westchester County, N.Y.—Section 1, Class AA—within the wide sea of all U.S. high school football programs New Rochelle remains little more than a slender grey sole.

Because of the history between the teams, the North Rockland matchup was another that would draw considerable attention from New Rochelle alumni. The ledger of players who remain connected to the school, and to DiRienzo in particular, is too long and widespread to count—"Once you're New Ro, you're New Ro forever," Chris Cargill had declared on the sideline during the win over John Jay—and the life experience of these alums, both from back then and to now covers a tremendous range. A look at two of them begins to describe the reach of the program and the variety in the lives it has touched.

Fred Campbell came up through the New Rochelle football system and played three years at varsity, from 2002 to 2004—that is, the title-winning years of Ray Rice and Courtney Greene. Campbell was a tight end and a fullback on offense and a dangerous edge rusher on defense. "Fred was just a whole other type of kid," says DiRienzo. "Special. Now he's a grown man and he's still special."

Campbell was not only an All-State football player, he was also an All-State violinist, poised and tender in concert, as well as a superior student. He was known among the coaches and his teammates for his wide and intelligent view of the world, an ability to lend perspective to the things they did on the field each day. He loved tackle football, most especially, he says, the act of delivering a big hit, and he had played the game since he was in the third grade.

Campbell's parents, Marvin and Mary had met while undergraduates at Brown, and Mary, a cultural anthropologist, had gone on to get her Ph.D. from Stanford. In the summer before Fred's senior year of high school, DiRienzo encouraged him to follow his desire and go out to a Stanford football camp, even though Fred had not been one of the prospects expressly invited. Campbell went to the camp, and the impression he made there, along with his continued athletic and academic success at New Rochelle (he was named to New York's All-State Scholastic team as well), earned him a scholarship to the school. At Stanford, along with playing linebacker for the Cardinal, Campbell undertook a major in Mathematics and Computational Science.

Fred's mother, Mary, was of direct Inupiaq Eskimo descent and was raised in northern Alaska—Fred himself was born in Fairbanks, while Mary was teaching at the University of Alaska, and Mary's doctoral dissertation had centered on issues of education among native Alaskans. In New Rochelle she was a vibrant and avid member of the community, serving on the PTA and caring actively about local issues, even into the fall of 2005. By then, Mary, just 45 years old, was battling an advanced stage of cancer, and Fred delayed his start at Stanford to be near her. While at home in New Rochelle he would come to the high school to use the weight room, and here and there he'd spend a little time sitting on a weight bench talking about things with coach DiRienzo. Mary died in late November that year and, honoring Inupiaq tradition, Fred and the family traveled to Alaska to help dig her grave in the frozen Alaskan earth.

Fred attended Stanford, and played his first games as a Cardinal in 2006, primarily as a backup inside linebacker and on special teams. He made some big plays and stood out for his commitment, and by the start of the next season Fred had so impressed new Stanford coach Jim Harbaugh that he had won the starting middle linebacker position. During those years, when Campbell came back to New Rochelle on school breaks, he would bring game and practice tapes with him and go over to the football space at the high school where he and coach D would sit in those familiar chairs taking apart the film together.

"I wanted to show him what I was learning and also to see what he was doing," Campbell recalls. "He had shared and given so much to me and I would always share with him. I had great coaches at Stanford, but there was still something about talking football with coach D: he saw things in a way that I could relate to. He knew me. He got me. We would spend a long time watching film together, sometimes at night just the two of us there, and I always knew I would walk away having learned something."

"If I tell you that I learned more from Fred than he ever learned from me, I'm not making that up to be friendly," says DiRienzo. "He had a great mind—for football, which was our glue, but also for all the other things we talked about."

In the first half of the second game of Stanford's 2007 season, a home game against San Jose State, Campbell was defending an ordinary screen pass, charging in to make a tackle, when his head collided awkwardly with the ballcarrier or with a teammate who was also coming in hard on the play. The pain was sharp and intense, but Campbell, playing in a packed Stanford Stadium, wearing the Cardinal red in his second game as an anointed starter for a major college football program, went back to the huddle and stayed in the game. He swallowed some Tylenol at halftime, and then he played the third and fourth quarters. "My neck had locked up, my muscles couldn't really move, I was in a lot of pain," he recalls. "But you know, it's football. You deal with it."

Over the next two days, though, the pain hardly subsided, and so Campbell went to Stanford Medical Center to be examined. Upon reviewing the X-rays, Campbell's physician turned to him with a strange expression. Campbell had fractured the C1, or Atlas, vertebra at the top of his spine; the vertebra had in fact been split in two. Another hit to that area could have paralyzed Campbell. It could have killed him. His neck was immobilized right there in the doctor's office, and he was immediately wheeled in for surgery. His father Marvin took the next flight out to California from New York. Fred's football career was over. "Football ends for everyone," Campbell says now. "If I think about what could have happened to me, I feel lucky. I'm pretty much fine now, except for a little lack of mobility and a numb patch on the back of my neck."

Campbell is now, at 26, working toward a Ph.D. in statistics at Rice University. He likes to climb mountains and cliffs. He's been up Kilimanjaro. He has scaled the luminous Grand Wall in Squamish, B.C. Campbell still has family in New Rochelle, sisters in the school system, and while it has been difficult for him to attend Huguenots games during the fall, he keeps careful tabs on the team. And when Fred comes home around Christmas, he goes and talks with coach D at the high school, and he will take some time to see some of the guys. "We all really enjoyed playing at New Rochelle, and most of us who were teammates are still in touch. I'm always interested in how the current team is doing and I bet I always will be. I care about it.

"I learned an incredible amount playing football, things that are going to help me for the rest of my life," says Campbell. "The standards and the level of effort and enthusiasm that coach D had is a big part of it. I know how to work hard and how to prepare, and that applies to anything you do. You come to understand that for successful people so much work goes into what you are doing that other people don't see. And I know that whatever my work ends up being for my career, I want to be a part of a team. Football gave me that. And playing at New Rochelle gave me that maybe most of all."

Aside from the fact that they both adored playing football, and found their years on the New Rochelle high school team to be among the most enriching and impactful years of their lives, there has been and remains little in common in the life experiences of Fred Campbell and Mantey Boahene. Mantey played for coach D in the late 1990s and through the turn of the millennium. He played several positions, on both sides of the ball, but he most enjoyed defense, especially linebacker, because as he says, he liked to hit people hard. He liked to "take someone's heart."

Mantey is not tall but he is burly and solid as a fire hydrant and through weightlifting he became exceptionally strong for a high school player. Mantey stood out on the field, a true force, and a true leader on a team that went to the state title game in 2000.

"Football is the one sport—well, football and boxing—where if you have a lot of frustration you can get very physical with people and not get in trouble for it," says Boahene. "And I was someone who had a lot of frustration."

Boahene says he did not grow up with any strong parental guidance. "I never had a dad around in my life and my mom was involved with drugs. Coach D knew my situation, right from the start," he says. "Football helped keep me anchored. It gave me structure and purpose, and when there was no football I would start to drift."

Mantey ran with a violent gang called the LA Boyz, named for New Rochelle's Lincoln Avenue, a downtown thoroughfare on which many of those gang members lived and on which Corey Holder and others on the current New Rochelle roster live today. There were incidents. In the summer of 2000 Mantey was present at a scene in which a member of a rival gang from Mount Vernon was shot and killed. Mantey was not charged in that case, but in another, unrelated event he was sentenced to jail for possession of a handgun. He himself has been shot at least twice—in the hip and in the arm. When, in 2014, someone in his presence described Boahene as a "former gunrunner," Boahene responded with a somber nod.

Mantey says that he would have never graduated high school had it not been for DiRienzo's attention, helping him get to class, pushing him to study afterward, teaching him to see the things that he needed to get done and empowering him to do them. "Coach D gave me a place to stay, let me sleep at his house when I needed it. He came to see me in prison. He'd get me a pair of cleats," Boahene says. "He was there. I look back, I was vulnerable you know. Really vulnerable. And coach D was just there. So I felt like, you know, that I had to be there for him. That meant trying to be responsible. I tried to be a responsible individual, tried really hard."

Some of Mantey's gang-related trouble occurred while he was in high school and some occurred in the years afterward but the cord between him and coach D and the football program did not break when he took off his purple playing jersey for the last time. Just as DiRienzo visited Mantey in prison, he went to visit him afterward too; he would seek him out. "Coach would say to me, 'Come on down and we'll lift together in the gym tonight,' or he'd ask me to come to the games. He gave me something that stayed like a constant in my life that pulled me through some things. As I get older I keep thinking how it's amazing that something like that existed for me in my life."

Over the years Mantey has come back to DiRienzo to deliver any bits of big, good news in his life—when his son Bryce was born, for example, and when Bryce started playing organized football, and when Mantey got a steady job as an ironworker. When he heard that coach D had had ulcer surgery he came over to the school to see if DiRienzo was "mentally and spiritually all right, and to share a little time together." Bryce, age 10, plays in the Youth Tackle League and Mantey helps to coach the team. He already anticipates the day when Bryce too will be part of the New Rochelle varsity experience. Mantey has a smooth, rounded, handsome and boyish face and is still extremely muscular; and he has always possessed a certain energy as an orator, able to rouse a group. Before New Rochelle's Section 1 rivalry game against North Rockland, Mantey Boahene, proud to be raising a son and proud of his skill as an ironworker, and following a life path that he hopes is now at last straightened out for good, was entrusted by coach DiRienzo to deliver to the team a pregame speech.

The Huguenot players were inside the school, in the football class-room, and there were 18 minutes to go before the Saturday afternoon kickoff. They were all in full uniform, though they held their helmets in their hands or had set them down on small desks. Because the day was unseasonably hot, the pregame warmups had left a thick sheen of sweat on most of the boys. A few sat in chairs, although most of them stood, and Boahene started speak:

"All right, pay attention," he began. "Listen to these words: In the real world there only a few people that respect what you do, what you are doing on that field. There are only a few people who respect what it is that you do. But there are a lot of people who *don't* respect what you do. They don't. That's why this is not business today. It ain't business. This is personal.

"Hear me when I tell you this: Make your moment memorable. This, all of this, is a memory for me. My palms are sweating. I could barely breathe, I'm ready to cry. I'm ready to hurt. But now this is your moment. In a few weeks, a few days, a couple of hours, you could look back at this day and wish what you coulda did better, wish what you shoulda did. There ain't no time for that. You play this like you need to play to survive. You do your better *right now*."

Boahene had them all leaning in, watching him. His voice was strong and determined. "I can tell you this, I was never the fastest. I probably ran a 5.2, I'll be honest with you. I didn't jump high, nothing like that. But I'll tell you what I had. I had something in me that God gave me. I had a vicious attitude about myself. What God gave me was a will. I didn't care how fast you was. I didn't care how high you jumped. It didn't matter to me. When you got the ball I was coming for you. You could run a 4.1, it didn't matter to me. I'll tell you why. I will take this with me until the day that I die: If your will is stronger than the skill, you'll get him. I was determined every play to make a play. If the will is stronger than the skill. . . ."

Mantey paused and waited a few beats. "This is the Number 1 rivalry that is going down with you and that other team, right? So, you've got two options. Either you dig down or you lay down. Me, my memory when I thought about it—when we played this team, you know what happened? We made them *quit*! In the fourth quarter with three minutes left, they just quit. They had enough. Now it is your turn. Now, you make your moment memorable!"

The team was murmuring excitedly as Bishop Leak stepped forward. He put a hand on Mantey's back and asked the players to get down on one knee. They pushed the chairs aside, and bent their heads and said in unison the Lord's Prayer.

New Rochelle would beat North Rockland by a score of 35–7 that day. It was a beautiful sunny afternoon and the stands were about half full. Greg Powell threw an early touchdown to Tyler Cohen, and overall Powell completed 13 of his 15 passes. Demetrius Rodriguez caught four of them for 63 yards. Jonathan Forrest ran for three touchdowns, at times dragging defenders along behind him. Robbie DeRocco kicked every extra point. Bryce Davis and Corey Holder, fracture be damned, made interceptions and the New Rochelle defense was wholly dominant. The score was 28–0 at halftime and the backups were in for nearly all of the second half.

The New Rochelle coaches had known beforehand that this year's North Rockland team was not up to its usual standard, did not have the line strength to truly compete. But the staff never let that on to the players. All week the Huguenots prepared for the game "as if," as Steve Young observed, "we were going to play the 1961 Green Bay Packers. That's always how Lou prepares."

Yet the dominating win, on the heels of beating John Jay, seemed to announce the 2015 team and its potential. New Rochelle was now 4–0 and already people in the stands—Keith Wheeler's dad, Kirby Mack, John

Hinchey—were talking about how maybe this was, as Louis DiRienzo Jr., had put it, a "special year." There was this sensation all through the New Rochelle football community, felt by pregame motivator Mantey Boahene as he play-boxed with his son Bryce on the winning sideline, and felt by Fred Campbell on the campus at Rice, as he got the latest New Ro football result 1,600 miles away: Maybe this would be one of those seasons that would take New Rochelle deep into the playoffs, and that this team with its robust and high performing seniors, with Forrest and Holder and Rodriguez and all, would be one that carried them to the place the team always wants to go, the Carrier Dome in Syracuse where each year the state title game is played. "You have to make your hotel reservations early," Randy Forrest cautioned another team parent with a grin that afternoon as the players came off the field.

DiRienzo kept his postgame address very short: "It's Saturday, it's hot as hell and we gotta play our next game on Thursday night. You guys gotta take care of your bodies over the weekend, hear me? Take care of your bodies. Monday we're back and we follow our Tuesday schedule and we start to get ourselves ready to go Thursday night. All right, enjoy your weekend."

What DiRienzo did not say was that as pleased as he was with the convincing win, and to have seen some growth in Powell and in Tyler Cohen, and to have seen the toughness of Corey Holder, and to have incorporated players—Alex Gaudio, Alex X, Chris Hinchey—who would not have been given playing time in a close game, the result against North Rockland in some ways unsettled him. "Too easy," is what DiRienzo said a couple of hours later. Rather than being exultant, he seemed a bit concerned. "I try telling them but it doesn't always sink in. I hope these kids know. Winning is not really supposed to be so easy like that."

CHAPTER 10

Elephant in the Locker Room

HE ACADEMIC, clinical and even experimental study of concussions—how and why they occur, how to avoid and treat them, what their consequences are and so on—has become an industry in itself. "These are very relevant, topical issues and that's where the funding is these days," says Barry Jordan. "So people will tend toward it." Jordan's title is Director, Memory Evaluation and Treatment at the expansive Burke Rehabilitation Center in White Plains, N.Y.—about eight miles from New Rochelle High. He is also chief medical officer of the New York State Athletic Commission and a team physician for U.S.A. Boxing, and over his extensive career he has seen all kinds of head injuries sustained by all kinds of athletes at every level. Jordan has evaluated players coming off the field at New York Giants games on an NFL Sunday, he has tended to boxers out cold at Madison Square Garden, and he has advised countless high school and college athletes, among them Andrew DiRienzo, Lou DiRienzo's youngest son who suffered multiple concussions, two whoppers in particular, which ultimately led him to stop playing football after his second year at Division III Springfield College.

"My first big concussion was against Troy in a state semifinal game during high school. It was a running play and I was blocking," says Andrew. "I went to hit someone but he hit me harder." Andrew, who came off the field right away after that collision, says he has no memory at all of what he did or what happened around him for the rest of that day. Teammates, though, told him that while sitting on the bench late in the Troy game he began singing lustily, almost drunkenly, and as if to the heavens, the R. Kelly song, "I Believe I Can Fly."

Andrew says he is also without any recollection of the entire next day after the concussion. He does recall that he remained groggy "for two weeks" and that during that time his "head hurt a lot in class." But he was a gutsy, determined kid. To play football in the first place, Andrew had overcome a pronounced limp, severe back and neck pain, and other physical limitations caused by a chronic arthritic condition called juvenile spondyloarthropathy. In the aftermath of the Troy game (the team's last of the 2010 season), he did not complain much about his concussion symptoms; once they had diminished over time and a reevaluation by Jordan had cleared him, Andrew returned to football in time to play his senior season for his dad at New Rochelle.

Then, during his second year at Springfield College, Andrew absorbed what he calls a "pretty major hit" in the open field. The days and weeks afterward were again marked by a general fogginess and this time also by an uncharacteristic tendency to anger. "Even just talking to him on the phone he was like a different person," Lou DiRienzo recalls. "I knew something was up." An abrupt or irrational change in mood or demeanor is a common manifestation of ongoing head trauma.

Andrew tried on several occasions to come back and play, but says that he "could not take even a regular hit in practice without getting a headache." He traveled to White Plains and met again with Dr. Jordan. Then, finally, with his prognosis neither bright nor dim but predictably unclear, Andrew decided to stop playing football for good and to move into coaching like his father and his older brother. It was not that he *couldn't* have returned to playing the game once those symptoms disappeared (which they eventually did), or that he would have necessarily been putting himself in great danger if he had. It was more that he had become intimately familiar with some of the risks and potential outcomes of sustaining a concussion. While it is possible that Andrew is particularly susceptible to concussions, that is not an identifiable trait; he might have played two more seasons at Springfield entirely without incident. On the other hand, something very unpleasant, and with lasting effect, could have happened.

"A lot of times, when you are not dealing with an extreme case, the decision about whether or not to keep playing becomes very personal," says Jordan. "We can do evaluations and give recommendations, but even when a patient is symptom-free we don't know 100% whether he [or she] is O.K., and we don't really know what might happen if he goes back in a game. Our assessments are stronger and much better educated than they might have been years ago, but there is by nature more uncertainty in concussions and head trauma than with many other athletic injuries. Each patient has to weigh the risk without knowing exactly what the parameters of that risk are."

Jordan is an important figure in concussion treatment (he arrived to it long before the rush of funding for research) and has a valuable and uncommon breadth of experience as pertains to assessing the potential long-term effects of head trauma. Under Jordan's close direction, Burke Rehabilitation runs two related but distinct departments: the Retired Athletes Cognitive Evaluation Center (RACE) and the Memory Evaluation and Treatment Service. In other words Jordan is exposed to cognitive decline in patients who have suffered repeated head trauma through contact sports (there is an image of a faceless football player in a generic college uniform on the cover of a RACE informational pamphlet) as well as an analogous decline, often through aging, in patients who have not had those kinds of injuries. That honed expertise, and an ability to recognize and interpret subtle differences in symptoms and behavior, help Jordan begin to determine whether a former athlete's decline is in fact related to concussions or not—that is, to try to assess whether the patient is suffering from chronic traumatic encephalopathy (CTE) or is instead being affected by cognitive diminishment independently associated with aging or other psychological or physical factors.

"Basically, you need to be well-versed in doing memory evaluations," Jordan says. "And you need experience in examining not only athletes, but also patients who come to you with complacent cognitive impairment. We use the same protocol with impaired athletes who come in that we use in the memory evaluation treatment services. We draw blood, make sure there's no metabolic reason why they're having cognitive issues. We get neuroimaging to make sure there's nothing structural that's causing anything. There are a hundred reasons why somebody can have memory problems.

"What I see happening more now is that someone who used to play football will develop neurocognitive problems and will automatically assume it is from playing football," he continues. "That may be the reason, but maybe not. Something else could be causing it. Sometimes they can just be depressed, and that can cause cognitive impairment. That can cause the fogginess.

"So, I'm evaluating these athletes who participate or participated in contact-collision sports. It might be someone in their 20s or it might be someone in his 60s who played high school and college football 45 years ago. I try to get different types of imaging done and to diagnose reasons for their cognitive or behavioral problems. If you don't find any obvious reasons, then you have to base your evaluation on the pattern of cognitive impairment. The pattern helps you decide what type of dementia it might be. Could this be Alzheimer's disease or frontotemporal dementia or is it CTE?"

For all that careful work, what inevitably results is an imperfect assessment, a best guess as Jordan says. Yet given that the only way to definitively determine if a person had been afflicted by CTE is by a posthumous examination of the brain, Jordan's evaluations can be very helpful to patients, as well as very useful to the shared knowledge in a growing field.

A giant in this general area of research is Robert Cantu, the neurologist and clinical professor associated primarily with the Boston University School of Medicine and its groundbreaking Center for the

Study of Traumatic Encephalopathy (CSTE).[1] Cantu is the preeminent authority on head trauma as relates to youth and high school sports in the United States and his 2013 paperback *Concussions and Our Kids* belongs in the handbags and briefcases of everyone who knows and loves a child who is thinking of getting into high-impact sports. The book, cowritten with Mark Hyman, discusses different grades of concussions, how concussions are most likely to occur, the best protocol for recognizing and treating them, and numerous other issues relating to head-trauma prevention and player safety. The book imparts a good deal of information from current research and draws as well from a body of shared intelligence gained over many years.

That's why it rings strange when an early chapter of *Concussions and Our Kids*, titled "Collision Sports," begins with a quote from Buzz Bissinger, the writer of the great Texas high school football book *Friday Night Lights*. Bissinger's endlessly compelling book came out in 1990 and, after first spawning a decent movie, begat the best television series of its time. Bissinger writes: "Any parent who has let their child play football in the past fifty years and claimed never to have understood the risks involved was either kidding himself or an idiot."

That statement encapsulates a strain of attitude sometimes found among seasoned football folks—an in-the-know perspective that "we've been aware of this concussion stuff forever. The only thing that's changed is that now it's getting hyped up and sensationalized." Not only is it odd for such a view to be billboarded in a book as rich in discovery as *Concussions and Our Kids*, the sentiment is also largely false. It is precisely the fact that so many of the risks involved were *not* understood for many years that has made the work of people like Cantu, Jordan and many others

---

[1] The pathological research done through the center's brain (and spinal cord) repository has been perhaps the single most powerful driving force in the field, eliciting change in concussion protocol in football at the professional and to some degree amateur levels. It was the CTE center, for example, that in 2014 presented (along with the Veterans Administration) those stark numbers cited earlier: that the brains of 101 of 128 former football players showed signs of CTE, including 76 of the 79 players who had reached the NFL.

so pertinent and valuable. Never mind the past 50 years, what we have learned in the past *15* years of fertile concussion research has transformed the views about (and in some cases the rules of) impact sports.

Certainly people have understood that football is *dangerous* ever since men first lined up. Watching a game at field level—a century ago, just as today—or perhaps playing a few downs oneself, presents an immediate sense of that danger and of the sheer violence of the sport. The injury and death rates on college fields were so alarming in the early years that in 1905 President Theodore Roosevelt had direct involvement in a reform campaign that made intercollegiate football safer. One year later, still more than a century ago, the National Collegiate Athletic Association was formed with a safety-first agenda. And, yes, it is certainly true that on sun-choked fields in Texas and Oklahoma, in Pennsylvania and Alabama—indeed, on fields from the redwood forests to the shores of the Gulf Stream waters—football players have pretty much always gotten their heads conked, seen colorful stars and staggered around in confusion (along with breaking bones, tearing ligaments and otherwise mucking themselves up in both mundane and spectacular ways). We as a society have certainly known for many, many decades that playing football is an invitation to, as the argot has it, get your bell rung. Louder than Big Ben at midnight.

But there were many things we did not know for most of the last half century. We did not, for example, understand that (as Cantu and others have conveyed) a concussion can alter brain chemistry to the point that the damage remains even long after symptoms have ceased. We also did not know that the full range of those symptoms could sometimes include marked changes in a concussed person's emotional, intellectual and behavioral well-being. Nor was it commonly acknowledged (although it may have been intuited) that many of the most severe concussions are caused not only by hits directly to the head but also by hits to the body that cause the neck to snap, and create a whiplash effect.

Until a few years ago we were not aware—and this development is hugely important to those at the college and high school level—that even a series of *sub*concussive hits can have a significant impact on brain function. Subconcussive means head blows not severe enough to cause concussions (those that might lead to just a little dinging rather than an all-out ringing of the proverbial bell); that is, the kind of routine knock that a football player gets on most plays. Those minor skullings typically do not (and could not, from a practical standpoint) inspire medical treatment, but they can, over the course of just one season of competition, have a measurable and deleterious impact on the brain.[2]

"Imagine whaling someone across the head with a pillow as hard as you can," said Cantu during one of our talks. "That won't cause a concussion, but it will cause a minor brain injury. Do it one time and it may not be so serious. But do it 1,000 times—which is a reasonable estimate of the number of subconcussive hits for a player to absorb over the course of a high school football season—and those pillow-whackings are going to add up and make an impact."

We also did not know, as we are now told by the league itself, that one third of NFL players are destined to wind up with long-term brain damage. Most people didn't know, although some doctors might have

---

[2] Multiple studies have demonstrated this, including a paper funded by the National Institute of Health and the National Operating Committee on Standards for Athletic Equipment and written by Thomas W. McAllister of Indiana University School of Medicine. The study tested 80 football and hockey players at Dartmouth College, comparing changes in their cognitive function to that of 79 athletes in noncontact sports such as track. McAllister said: "We found differences in the white matter of the brain in these college contact-sport athletes compared to noncontact sport varsity athletes." White matter is what transmits signals within the brain. Added Dr. McAllister, " . . . there was a group of contact sports athletes who didn't do as well as predicted on tests of learning and memory at the end of the season." And these, remember, are players who apparently went without a concussion. As the paper concluded, the study "suggests a relationship between head impact exposure . . . and cognition over the course of a single season, even in the absence of diagnosed concussion."

Another study, this one by the University of Rochester Medical Center and the Cleveland Clinic and funded by the National Institute of Neurological Disorders and Stroke, looked at 67 college football players in Division III. Through comparisons of pregame and postgame blood sampling the researchers found elevated levels of a particular protein in players who had received a greater number of hits (albeit still entirely nonconcussive). That protein, known as S100B, has been suggested as a possible early indicator of Alzheimer's disease and brain swelling.

suspected this, that head injuries pose an especially unnerving threat to younger kids (up to and including high schoolers) because children tend to have less myelin protection in their brains than adults do (as well as weaker necks and disproportionately large, heavy heads—"like bobblehead dolls," says Cantu). Similarly, we weren't aware that high school players may, as a study by the National Academy of Sciences implies, be far more likely than college players to sustain a concussion. And for so many decades, we in the general public were most definitely not educated about the awful hazard of second-impact syndrome—a phenomenon in which suffering even a mild head trauma before the damage from a previous concussion has healed can lead to severe brain swelling and even death.

All of these specifics—along with innumerable others—add up to the fact that if you were a football player or a football player's parent 10, 15, 25 or 50 years ago, you were not aware of an essential bottom-line possibility that we are now just about ready to take for granted: Sustaining multiple head injuries early in life may significantly compromise a person later on.

And while we understand much, much more than ever before about the risks of concussions, and how those risks apply to children and young men playing football, that does not exclude the truth that there is also so much that remains unknown. Even today there isn't any comprehensive quantitative measurement of those risks, and even today many experts respond to in-depth questions about the nature and impact of head injuries by saying, "We have not determined that yet." Even today, you couldn't quite be called an "idiot" for not understanding the risks involved. A 2014 survey of football players from 11 Florida high schools, for example, found that nearly half of them were unaware that such basic symptoms as nausea and neck pain could be caused by concussions. The majority didn't know about such symptoms as irritability or anxiousness. Twenty-five percent of those students said they had received no education about head trauma at all.

"Concussion" in this time of awareness has become, as coach DiRienzo says, "a four-letter word." And in most high school football locker rooms it's a word far more attention-getting than even the most graphic multi-cuss obscenity you could think of. "That's because a lot of kids are kind of afraid of concussions, it's like a dark unknown sitting out there, so they don't want to mention it. Like out of superstition or something," says Bryce Davis, the New Rochelle senior whose concussion during tackling drills in the summer of 2013 forced him to the sidelines during that year's preseason trip to Brookwood.

There is, however, one thing that everyone who has been a victim of head trauma or who has studied it in any fashion does understand, and has indeed understood at anytime during the last 50 years: Getting walloped upside the head on a football field is no fun at all, an experience without reward. As Cantu likes to say: "No head trauma is good head trauma."

EACH AUTUMN day in high schools everywhere, boys (sometimes with parents and coaches in their ears) make choices about whether or not to play football: Do they join up? Do they stick with it? Do they turn away? Coaches often have judgments to make about whether or not to use a recently concussed player in a particular game or practice. The wave of concussion information in recent years, and the tempest of publicity around it, has a real bearing on both player and coach. So do certain gone-viral comments, such as Hall of Fame tight end Mike Ditka saying, as he did in an interview on HBO, that he would not want his young son [if he had one] to play football. (This sentiment has also been expressed publicly in some manner or other by NFL players Terry Bradshaw and Brett Favre and Troy Aikman and Drew Brees and Bart Scott as well as the NBA's LeBron James and . . . .)

Most of the decisions to play or not to play, particularly a high school player's bowing out of the sport or a coach ordering a sit-down, go pretty much unnoticed outside of a player's family and the immediate community around the team. (An exception in the fall of 2014: The team at Caro High in Michigan drew widespread attention when it ended its football season in midstream after a series of player concussions weakened its already undermanned roster.) But when such decisions are made at the college level, where more than 80,000 young men play a game that is as close to the high school version as it is to the NFL's—they do tend to get noticed, especially in these charged times. In a few-week span of that roiling autumn of 2014, three concussion-related personnel incidents not only made national news and sent ripples through the team at New Rochelle, but also illuminated the environment of concussion sensitivity as it is today.

In late September, David Ash, the 22-year-old starting quarterback for the University of Texas—a position that has long occupied near royal status in college football—announced he had played his final game. Raised in central Texas, where the sun never sets on football, Ash had set a Longhorns record by throwing four touchdowns in a season as a true freshman in 2011. He was named offensive MVP of that season's Holiday Bowl and then played well throughout 2012, leading the team to a 9–4 record. At 6' 3" and 230 pounds, Ash was a clear NFL prospect.

But in the second game of his junior season in 2013, playing against BYU, Ash suffered a concussion. According to Ash and his former coach at Belton High, Rodney Southern, he had never been concussed in high school. Yet his post-BYU symptoms forced him to miss the next game, and when he returned to play two weeks later against Kansas State, he lasted only one half—throwing for 166 yards and a touchdown, but also absorbing several hard hits—before those symptoms returned. That was the last game Ash played in 2013, and he was so openly sensitive to lingering symptoms that doctors told Ash not to even attend Texas games as a spectator, fearing that the noisy stadium and the bright lights could exacerbate his condition.

Ash returned for spring football in 2014 and on Aug. 30 was the Texas starter for its season opener against North Texas. "The real deal about the North Texas game," Ash would say in his retirement press conference a few weeks later, "is that I really didn't get hit. I didn't get a vicious blow."

Yet Ash's head ached for more than week after the game, and when watching film of his play—he completed 19 passes for 190 yards—he had this strange sensation that he was watching someone other than himself. Although he'd had no pre-college concussion history, Ash's physical reaction to the head injury and the way the even milder symptoms spooked him, led the Texas coaching and medical staff to give him their complete public support when he decided to step away. With Ash out, Texas finished 6–7, just its second losing record in 17 years.

The same month of Ash's retirement came the sudden announcement that Casey Cochran, the University of Connecticut's star quarterback, who grew up less than 50 miles north of New Rochelle, was also retiring from football. Cochran's father, Jack, was an extremely successful and controversial high school football coach. He had won multiple state titles at multiple Connecticut schools but had also run into various rules violations, had been cited for drastically running up the score on inferior teams and had allegedly punched a rival coach in the face. Casey liked to say that he first started handling a football while still wearing onesies and he eventually developed into arguably the best high school quarterback in the state's history, winning player of the year awards in 2010 and '11 and setting all-time state records for passing yards and completions. The day he chose to attend UConn rather than follow one of numerous offers to play at a more prestigious program out of state, was a proud day for Connecticut football.

Throughout that high school career, however, Cochran had also sustained what he later estimated as nine concussions, most of which went undisclosed at the time they occurred. Upon his retirement at age 20, he told *The Hartford Courant* that he had seen a doctor for concussion treatment in eighth grade and from then on understood how to identify one. "After that," he told the *Courant*, "I could tell when I'd get one, but I kind of just tried to hide them." With football at the center of his life, and the prospect of playing for his father in high school, and then a potential college and even a pro career ahead of him, Casey Cochran did not want to take himself off the field.

At UConn, Casey started four games as a freshman and then at the start of the next season he took a big hit in a game, which, he later said, was the third concussion he had sustained in his short college career. (This, said those who covered the team, was news to them.) In a discomforting and unintended pun, Cochran described his decision to stop playing football as "a no-brainer." He has since gone on to work as an active advocate for increased concussion education in high school.[3]

A third incident in that stretch of 2014 involved the University of Michigan. During a game against Minnesota, quarterback Shane Morris took a hard, helmet-to-facemask hit from Gophers defensive end Theiren Cockran. Morris was obviously and seriously dazed, staggering on the field and clutching onto a teammate for support, yet Michigan coach Brady Hoke left him in the game for another play. Then Hoke briefly pulled Morris off the field. Then he put him back in.

Hoke came under withering criticism—from the television commentators at the time, and from society at large afterward—for so blatantly jeopardizing Morris's health. There were immediate calls for Hoke's firing. With the Morris incident a touchstone for Michigan fans' larger frustrations with the team's poor performance on the field and a perception that the student body was becoming increasingly alienated from the football program, both Hoke (fired) and athletic director Dave Brandon (resigned) were indeed gone by season's end.

It's hard to imagine that kind of public outrage in a previous era. What, a coach expected to remove a player from a game just because he looked woozy as a midnight drunk? Ridiculous. Men did not strap on their football pads to be mollycoddled. ("You got your bell rung, you shook it off and held yourself together, and you stayed on the field," says the Hall of Fame NFL linebacker Harry Carson, who did not miss a game during his four-year college career at South Carolina State in the 1970s.) That tough-it-out approach was then, however, and this was now, and Hoke was roundly mocked for being out of

---

[3] Cochran's run of concussions, while certainly high, is neither uncommon nor abnormal. According to a 2014 report assembled by the National Athletic Trainer's Association, high school football players who have sustained a concussion are "nearly 3 times more likely to sustain another injury." Other reports suggest that players who have had two or more concussions are increasingly susceptible to recurrence. Whether this is because an individual has a predisposed vulnerability to concussion or whether it is because the concussions themselves cause the added vulnerability has not yet been fully sussed out in the medical world.

touch when he explained why he kept Morris in the game: "I don't know if he had a concussion or not. I don't know that," Hoke said. "Shane's a pretty competitive, tough kid. And Shane wanted to be the quarterback, and so, believe me, if he didn't want to be, he would've come to the sideline or stayed down."

Hoke's startlingly antiquated leave-it-up-to-the player attitude (Morris, as the eye-test overwhelmingly indicated, had indeed been concussed), along with the circumstances around Ash, who was active in addressing his concussion symptoms, and Cochran, who for many years was secretive about them, underscores a central issue in concussion treatments and why the obstacles to that treatment are greater in football than in any other sport. Cognitive testing procedures notwithstanding, head trauma, perhaps more than any other common injury relies on the self-reporting of the patient—both at the time of occurrence and in the aftermath.

"When you break a bone, the gold standard for diagnoses is the X-ray," says Barry Jordan. "You can see where and in what manner the bone was broken and how it is healing. For concussions, the gold standard is clinical. I describe a concussion as primarily a functional disturbance. For the most part it's not a structural injury. There's nothing we can see grossly. Some people have started to suspect there may be some sorts of microscopic physical changes we may be able to see. But that's not really well worked out yet."

In other words, adds Jordan, "To really understand the impact of a concussion—the symptoms of disorientation and confusion, the loss of cognitive abilities, nausea—for a lot of that you are ultimately reliant on how forthcoming the patient is."

ON THE New Rochelle sideline in 2014—as on every football sideline everywhere—players occasionally came off the field in an uncertain state. "My head is literally ringing after that one," Manny Walker said quietly as he pulled off his helmet during a midseason game. He had just returned to the sideline after crashing helmets with an opposing player during a kickoff return.[4] His helmet in one hand and kneading his forehead with the other, Manny walked away from his teammates, far down the sideline, toward an end zone. Then he turned slowly back around and rolled his neck a few times. He stood still and squeezed his eyes shut and then abruptly opened them. He walked a few more steps, carefully and deliberately, and then strode more quickly as he neared his teammates and said, to anyone who might have heard, "O.K. I'm fine." When the next kickoff came around Manny got back out there.

On the sideline during another game, the senior linebacker Justice Cowan suddenly sank down onto his right knee, his left elbow on his left thigh and rested his forehead in his left hand as he looked down at the grass. "You O.K., bro?" a teammate asked. Justice turned and looked upward and smiled somewhat dreamily. "Yeah, just a little lightheaded," he said in a voice higher than it usually was. He seemed in a detached state, almost zenlike. "I'm gonna be all right," he said grinning. The teammate gave him a reassuring slap on the back and a little while later Cowan stood up slowly, steadied himself with his hand on a teammate's back for a minute or so, and soon began his customary loud cheering, seemingly good as new and ready for his number to get called. He played just fine the rest of the game.

Such mind-rattling incidents were not exactly common during the Huguenots' season, but they were hardly white-tiger rare. Players come off the field that way during games every season and with the coaches absorbed in running the game and the trainer, Becky in this case, often tending to another player—icing a shoulder, stretching a hamstring—it is easy for the fact of a shaken or disoriented player to go unnoticed. A change in demeanor can be exceedingly subtle and players are usually not inclined to draw attention to themselves. (Why risk having to come

---

4 Because of the large area of open field and the fact that potential tacklers get up to high speeds as they hurtle downfield, kickoff returns are regarded as among the most dangerous events in football. A few years ago, in an attempt to minimize injury, the NFL outlawed one of the long time staples of the return game, wedge blocking, in which multiple players join together or stand side-by-side, to form a kind of moving wall or "wedge" in front of the returner. It was a smart, welcome move, but not one that greatly minimizes the inherent physical perils of the play.

out of the game? Why risk looking soft?) Neither is a teammate likely to inform a coach or trainer that something may be amiss. That would be ratting him out. When Walker and Cowan had those unsettled interludes ("It was noisy in there," said Walker pointing to his temple and describing his incident a few days afterward. "Just kind of foggy for a while," said Cowan describing his), New Rochelle's coaches—unlike Michigan's Brady Hoke—were completely unaware.

Of the many aspects that make football the most dangerous high school sport from a concussion perspective, perhaps most salient is this: When a kid suffers a potentially concussive blow in another sport it is almost always—not always but almost always—apparent to anyone watching that he or she needs to be attended to. A batter gets hit in the head by a pitch; a hockey player gets checked helmet-first into the boards; two soccer players collide skull to skull while going up to head a ball. Those are events everyone sees. But in football, 12 or 15 or more of the 22 players on the field are involved in some kind of collision on every play. Someone gets his brain rattled a bit and there is often no way for an outside observer to know.

Self-reporting, the most crucial aspect to concussion treatment, is most crucial of all when it comes to football. "There may be as many concussions that go unrecognized as go recognized on the football field," says Dr. Cantu. "There's no other sport you can say that about."[5]

---

[5] One constant about concussion rates in high school sports is that the rates are higher in girls' sports than in their corresponding boys' sports. Perhaps counter-intuitively given the speed at which the respective games are played, a much higher percentage of concussions have been found in girls' soccer than in boys' soccer, in girls' basketball than in boys' basketball and so on. Neck strength, which tends to be stronger in boys than in girls, probably plays a small role in this. The stronger your neck, the more stabilized your head and the better protected you are against head trauma. But neck strength only comes into play when you're braced to receive a blow to the head; if you are unsuspecting and your neck is slack when you get hit, it doesn't matter if you have a neck as thick as Bluto's or as thin as Olive Oyl's. The wider reason for the consistently higher numbers among female high school athletes is this: Girls are more forthcoming than boys are about having sustained a head blow and feeling symptoms. Much more forthcoming. And much more descriptive. In concussion reporting, as in life, girls tend to be better, more honest communicators than boys.

THE EFFORT to monitor concussions in high school football, and to combat the "don't tell" culture and reality of the game, has mainly relied on increased concussion awareness and education, some of it legislated into protocol by school districts. Those efforts, along with the greater publicity that attends head trauma issues in this era, and also the more widespread acceptance of head injury reporting and treatment guidelines, explains why the documented rate of high school football concussions has more than doubled over the past decade, from .23 per 1,000 "athlete exposures" (meaning a practice or a game), to .51 per 1,000 exposures. Even so, the problem of underreporting—either from a player's (or coach's) willful deception or because a player simply didn't recognize that he had sustained a potential concussion—remains enormous. That's partly what has led to an important technological development which seeks to more definitively monitor head blows and to minimize reliance on self-reporting: helmets outfitted with impact sensors. A chip embedded in a helmet's padding, ear flap, chin strap or mouth guard, records the impact of hits to the head, measuring them in terms of gravitational force (or g-force). The results, often signaled by small lights flashing on a panel attached to the helmet, can be seen more or less immediately by medical and coaching staffs, who might then evaluate a player who received a high-impact blow to determine if he needs to be taken out of a practice or game.

A few high schools and about two dozen colleges use some kind of helmet-sensor technology. (Virginia Tech players have worn them since 2003, and the school has leveraged the data to develop a helmet-safety rating system.) Sensors have also been tested, though not yet approved for use, by the NFL. Resistance to the technology, at all levels of the game, comes in predictable objections: that the sensors create false positives; that they measure only the impact and not the direction or specific location of a hit; that they may give players (and parents) a false sense of security; and that implementing and maintaining the technology for, say, 100 varsity and junior varsity players is, at this point in development anyway, quite expensive.[6]

However successful the sensor technology may become as it gets refined and enriched over time, and even should it at some point become standard (it's quite possible to imagine that one day it will), the sensors only gauge impact as an objective recording. They don't diagnose or treat concussions, of course, and certainly won't *prevent* head injuries or lessen their frequency. That mission, to reduce the number of concussions, has been at the heart of helmet manufacturing for years now, the impetus behind alterations and alleged improvements too numerous to list in their entirety and variety.

Many helmets now have thicker or more shock-absorbing padding, There are helmets designed with flexible outer shells so that there is a kind of "give" upon impact. Top-tier helmets now get tested with an awareness of rotational forces (meaning from an angle) as well as linear (straight on) forces. A Virginia Commonwealth University neuroscientist has proposed using a helmet with a magnet inside it to act as a "repulsive force" against concussion-level impact. There are even helmets with airbags in them. Essentially all of the helmet enhancements aim to in some way diffuse the impact of hits to the head, and this crusade—to produce impact-lessening headgear and accessories as a means of helping the sport, and with an eye toward reaping profit—has been furious. Football's gigantic equipment industry has moved from being a performance-based platform to being a platform based on safety and protection standards. "There is not a week that passes

---

6 Impact sensors have a role in several well-funded and long-range studies on how to better monitor concussion occurrence and how to predict the consequences of head injuries. The NFL and the National Institutes of Health are in partnership on several such studies, and there's also a three-year research project that's being run jointly by the NCAA and the U.S. Department of Defense. (There's significant common ground in terms of head injuries suffered in football and those suffered in combat or other military activity.) That latter project includes the baseline examination of more than 35,000 college athletes and utilizes research coming from helmet sensors. Of this latter project, NCAA chief medical officer Brian Hainline says, "I believe this will be the game-changer."

that I don't see a new device," said Kevin Guskiewicz, a University of North Carolina sports medicine expert who sits on NFL committees related to head injuries.

Given the time, energy, money and innovative thinking that goes into research and development on this front, it would seem only a matter of time before the emergence of a helmet that can truly and significantly deter concussions. Right? "No," says Barry Jordan, "you cannot build a helmet that really lessens concussion—at least there has been nothing we have seen to suggest that it could be done."

The football helmets used by the team at New Rochelle, as at many schools, get retested by the manufacturer after each season to make sure that they still meet safety specifications. There are a variety of models in the Huguenots' equipment room. Each year the seniors and A-team get first dibs on the ones they want, and a helmet might last 10 years with annual recertification. They have several models of the Riddell helmet: the classic "360" (it runs about $365 and is described by the company as using "energy managing materials and a face mask attachment system that disperses energy of frontal impacts"); the "Revolution Speed" ("A cool, aggressive shell design and comfortable anti-microbial overliner"); and the popular "Speedflex." ("Flexibility engineered into the helmet's shell, face mask and face mask attachment system with hinge clips to help reduce impact force transfer to the athlete.") These and other helmets marketed to youth come with disclaimers saying that they cannot prevent serious head injuries. The implication that the expensive headgear will better protect you, however, is clear.

Helmets obviously do protect players from superficial face and skull injuries, but, "When it comes to preventing head trauma, the difference in efficiency between a mid-level, up-to-code helmet and the most advanced one is negligible. Neither can do it," says Cantu. "The only way you might be able to prevent concussions is with a helmet that completely solidified the neck and kept it from moving, maybe with a belllike contraption. But think about that. You can't exactly play football without moving your neck."

For all the innovative work being done, and however much money parents and school districts spend on the best helmets, concussion rates appear to be impervious to it all. "The way I think about it," says Lou DiRienzo, "is I think about when you go to a carnival or a fair and you win a big balloon that has a teddy bear inside it. The balloon is your skull and the teddy bear is your brain. You can put any helmet you want on the balloon but when you slap that thing real hard, what is going to happen? The teddy bear is going to bounce against the inside of the balloon."

CHAPTER 11

A Death Too Close to Home

UST AS concussion rates in football are so much higher than in other high school sports, so too—as players and parents are grimly reminded each fall—are the death rates. Over the 20-year period from 1995 through 2014, an average of nearly 12 boys a year died playing high school football in America. With participation typically around 1.2 million during that time, that is about one death per every 100,000 players. Roughly one third of those are classified by the National Center for Catastrophic Sports Injury Research as "direct fatalities," meaning as a result of impact sustained on the field. As opposed to the "indirect fatalities" discussed earlier (deaths caused by such things as heat stroke during practice), direct fatalities typically come about due to head trauma, or severe neck or spine injury. With boxing out of the high school equation, football, in the unhappy matter of such deaths, is in a class of one.[1]

---

[1] The National Center for Catastrophic Sports Injury Research issues annual reports reporting and analyzing the deaths and serious injuries sustained across a range of both collision and noncollision high school sports. Football is the only sport that also merits its own, individualized, annual report.

The years of 2013 and '14 were particularly heavy in their toll, with 29 overall deaths including 13 direct fatalities. One of the boys who died was Chad Stover, a 16-year-old who played for Tipton High School in Missouri, and who sustained a head injury (or injuries) during a game on Oct. 31, 2013. In the second quarter, Chad, a defensive back, collided helmet-to-helmet with an opposing player, a collision that was noted but did not result in his leaving the game. Then, in the fourth quarter with about seven minutes remaining, Chad went in for a tackle and his head slammed into the ballcarrier's thigh. It was a thoroughly routine play, a crash common to the game. Moments after that tackle, though, Chad suddenly collapsed unconscious on the field. He was quickly taken to the hospital where he never regained consciousness. Chad spent nearly two weeks on life support, often with his mother Ann beside his bed, singing to him gently. He died of what was classified as "blunt force injury to the cranium." Whether this was an instance of second-impact syndrome was not established. The details surrounding Chad's last game and last weeks of life appeared in the Sept. 29, 2014, issue of *Time* magazine, which featured on its cover a photograph of Chad in his red-on-white Tipton Cardinal uniform. Two big-type headlines accompanied that image: HE DIED PLAYING THIS GAME and IS FOOTBALL WORTH IT?

(A copy of the magazine found its way, inevitably but briefly, into the football space at New Rochelle and although several of the coaches read or thumbed through the story, its content was not a topic they dwelled on then, nor one they brought up to the players.)

Chad Stover's tale is awful and heartbreaking; it badly shook the football-crazy town of Tipton *(pop. 3,100)* and it tore an irreparable hole in the lives of his parents, his sister and his two brothers. "We talk about him every day," Chad's brother, Kenton, said in the *Time* article. A memorial has gone up to Chad at the high school and his death lingers powerfully in Tipton's sports and high school community. Chad's death is also a reminder to all of us that, tragically, he is not alone—that it could have been a kid in your state or even your county or town who died during an ordinary football game, and that for all the advancements in safety and head-injury education it is not crazy to fear that one of these days such a death could hit a little too close to home.

"ABOUT TWO weeks ago I got a concussion in practice," Michael Cascio was saying before New Rochelle's Thursday night game at Ossining. The game was being played on a Thursday to accommodate Yom Kippur, which would begin on Friday evening and extend through Saturday. Cascio, a senior, had impressed the coaching staff through the early season. Despite this being his first and only year on varsity—he had not played football since middle school—and despite suffering a thumb injury at Brookwood that required a cast, Cascio, showing notable discipline, had worked his way to the point that he was rotating in regularly as an offensive guard. At 5' 10" and 212 pounds there was a valuable heft to Cascio, and he learned the blocking schemes quickly. Cascio was not, however, permitted to dress for this game in Ossining. He was on the sideline wearing his jersey and ordinary pants.

"Yeah, it was like two weeks ago and when I got home from practice that night I was pretty foggy, like dreaming almost," Cascio went on. "My mother was looking at me and she asked, 'Are you hungry?' I said no, but then a few minutes later I realized I was standing there holding the fridge door open and looking around inside it. Then my mom said, 'I'll make you hot dogs.' But I was like 'No thanks, I don't want any.' But then a little while after that I was standing at the stove cooking hot dogs. It's like I kept forgetting things. I didn't know what I had said, or what I was doing. I didn't even really know if I was hungry or I wasn't hungry.

"So I went to practice the next day and did everything I normally do. It was a full contact practice. And when I came home that night I felt *weird*. I fell right down on the couch. I was just totally out. The next day we found out I had gotten a concussion—and I took that ImPACT test. It wasn't that I had gotten a really big hit or anything that I know of. Nothing special. It was just the constant hitting. When you are hitting your head in practice like that it can happen. It's happened to other guys.

"I had to sit out last week's game," Cascio continued, referring to Week 4 and New Rochelle's win over North Rockland, "but then I passed the ImPACT test and got cleared. I felt fine and yesterday I practiced in full gear for the first time since the concussion. I felt good after that. When I went to school today I thought I was going to play tonight.

"But then I was sitting there in class and a security guy came into the room and called me down to the nurse's office. I thought I was going to have to fill out a form or something so that I could play again. But while I was in the nurse's office, she walked in—Dr. Weiss. [Adrienne Weiss, the New Rochelle school district's director of health services.] I called her Mrs. Weiss, but that was obviously offensive. She corrected me, like, '*Doctor!*' like she was making a point of it. And then she said that she was not going to be able to let me play tonight. I would have to sit out again.

"I said 'Awwww, no!' and I started to try to argue with her. But then she goes, 'Did you hear about the kid on Long Island?' I said no, because at that point I hadn't heard about it yet. Dr. Weiss said, 'He died from a head injury playing football.' After that I didn't argue anymore. What are you supposed to say to that?"

THE EARLY-OCTOBER football death of Tom Cutinella of Shoreham-Wading River High School occurred roughly as far from New Rochelle (less than an hour's drive), as did the early September football death of Staten Island's Miles Kirkland-Thomas. Cutinella's death, though, sent even fiercer ripples through New Rochelle's high school community, particularly among the athletes and football players. Partly this was because of when the news of the death landed—in the middle of the season, on the day of a game—and partly because of the random, inexplicable nature of it. (No extreme heat or prior heart issues were involved.) Also, Shoreham-Wading River was having a strong season, its best in years, and though the team plays in a different suburban county and district than New Rochelle does, results and news items about the two schools occasionally mingle on the same area football blogs. Most salient of all, there were kids at New Rochelle who had a direct connection to Tom Cutinella.[2]

A junior linebacker and offensive guard in football, Cutinella also played lacrosse, the prestige sport at Shoreham-Wading River High and throughout that area of Long Island. A few top lacrosse players at New Rochelle had competed against Cutinella, among them the football team's Haitam Coughlin, the vociferous junior. Coughlin, like some others on the Huguenots, had learned of Cutinella's death through a tweet by Kevin Devaney, an area sports reporter who often posts about New Rochelle and other local teams, and who is followed by many players. Coughlin immediately remembered Cutinella's name, and then, when he saw it, his face. They weren't friends, but they had played against one another in tournaments. They had jostled each other while running down loose balls. They had slapped one another's hands in postgame lineups. There is an intimacy to that kind of thing.

And so, for New Rochelle's football game against Ossining, Coughlin decided to wear a headband on which he wrote "RIP T.C." and "54", Cutinella's jersey number.[3] "It just kind of hit me when I found out he

---

[2] Like Miles Kirkland-Thomas's, Cutinella's death received some additional national attention because of surrounding events: He was the third high school football player to die of a head injury that week. Demario Harris Jr. of Charles Henderson High in Alabama, and Isaiah Langston of Rolesville High in North Carolina, were both 17 years old. Harris Jr., a cornerback, had made a routine tackle, then collapsed on the field. Although the official cause of death was not disclosed, his father attributed it to a "brain hemorrhage." Langston collapsed during pregame warmups two days after sustaining a blow in practice. He had complained of a headache, and an autopsy determined he died of "complications of vertebral artery dissection due to blunt force injury of the head and neck."

Coincidentally, Langston's death came two weeks after NFL commissioner Roger Goodell had been in North Carolina's Wake County—where Rolesville High is located—promoting "Heads Up Football." The program, which Wake County schools had adopted a few months earlier, was developed by USA Football and includes education on "concussion recognition and response," equipment use, and tackling and blocking methods. That all helps, but only to a degree. One might, at this point, note that you can smoke cigarettes that are low in tar and nicotine, and that are affixed with a cooling filter. But even then you are still smoking.

[3] It's a somewhat eerie coincidence that Miles Kirkland-Thomas also wore 54.

had died like that," said Coughlin. "You see a lot of kids when you play sports and this reminds you that something could happen to anyone. You have to respect the game. You have to respect what you are doing. It can be a little scary sometimes playing football. Not every kid will admit they feel that. But pretty much everybody does."

At 16, Cutinella stood 6-feet and weighed 180 pounds, and although he was not overly gifted as an athlete, he made a large impact on the teams he played on. "Never the best player, but always the smartest, the hardest worker and the toughest," his father Frank would say at the funeral. Tommy was a leader on the team, even as a junior, and along with excelling at linebacker he had moved quickly into his role at left guard, a crucial position to the offense and one demanding selflessness and a commitment to often drudging work. A guard, remember, does not throw the football, or catch the football, or run with the football. He does not score touchdowns. He does not make it onto highlight films. The left guard's job is to protect the quarterback and the running backs, to put his body in front of an onrushing opponent, to knock defenders out of the way. (*If you're playing baseball and the leftfielder misses the ball, it isn't going to hit the rightfielder in the face. Miss your assignment in football. . . .*) Of the many millions of people who watch NFL games each week, maybe 10%, probably less, could name even three NFL guards. "Tom," says coach Matt Millheiser, "was always all about the team."

It had been an ordinary play, in the third quarter of a Wednesday afternoon away game at John Glenn High School. Shoreham-Wading River had possession of the ball and on the snap Cutinella pulled to his right to block for the running back. The play unfolded in a predictable manner, with a gain of a couple of yards, though Cutinella had been leveled in a collision and knocked to the ground near the line of scrimmage. He then sat up but did not immediately stand. "I saw Tommy was down but it looked like he was about to get up," says coach Millheiser. "I went to go to my quarterback to give him the next play, and that's when I saw in my peripheral vision that someone was really helping Tommy up. It didn't look right. It wasn't just a helping hand, it was a lot more assistance than usual. That's when my focus went from calling the play to 'O.K., let's see what's going on here.' " Cutinella stood, but he was wobbly as he tried to walk and in a moment he dropped back down. By the time Millheiser reached him, seconds later, the player was no longer able to respond. An ambulance was called (there was none on hand) and the teams were sent to opposite end zones. As far as anyone knows, Tommy never became conscious and responsive again.

He had wanted to go to West Point, and he had made that clear time and again to everyone who knew him. And if not West Point then to Annapolis. And if not there then to an ROTC program somewhere, anywhere. Tommy believed the most worthy thing a person could do with his life was serve his country. He did not have favorite professional sports teams nor did he hang posters of athletes on his bedroom wall, but he did idolize a man named Michael Murphy who, like Tommy, had been raised in Suffolk County, Long Island, and who had gone on to receive the Medal of Honor as a Navy SEAL. Murphy had died in combat, and was a principal figure in Tommy's favorite film, *Lone Survivor*. That Cutinella was attracted to military life jibed with his suitability to football: He thrived in a disciplined environment, those near to him said, and he believed with full conviction in the power of collective effort.

He was the eldest of four children and his father Frank was a Suffolk County police officer (he'd been with the NYPD before that) and this partly explains why so many police cars were parked on the side of Route 25A in Wading River on the day of Tom Cutinella's funeral, ushering traffic, and why, when it came time for the procession itself to make its way to St. John the Baptist Roman Catholic Church, 18 police officers on motorcycles led the way.

It was a beautiful autumn morning, a bright yellow sun in a bare blue sky, and bright yellow leaves on the canopy of trees all around. Many of the hundreds who attended the funeral parked two miles off at the Wading River elementary school and were shuttled over in small buses. Near the church entrance milled friends, relatives, some local intimates and scores of students. Shoreham-Wading River had canceled classes for the day—in effect, the whole high school was there. Farther away from the church doors, roped off into the back half of the parking lot, stood hundreds of others—most of them not personally close to Tommy, but who had come out of respect and with a kind of spiritual connection akin to what Haitam Coughlin felt. Some wore formal clothes, but others, teenagers especially, had on their football jerseys from nearby schools: Rocky Point and Miller Place, Port Jefferson and John Glenn. There were NFL jerseys in the crowd too: Brady, Manning, Luck. Coaches from other high schools, from all over the area, had shown up, and some parents had taken the day off from work. This was a collection of people paying tribute to a life and also, in a sense, to a game and to a culture. It was a Tuesday and as the people waited outside for the procession to arrive and for the service begin, some talked among themselves about how the Seahawks had put away the Redskins on *Monday Night Football*, and also about the University of Mississippi's thrilling comeback win over Alabama, and how the Mississippi goal posts had been torn down afterward in jubilation.

This stretch of communal time outside the church went on for quite a while, an hour or more. Shuttle buses kept arriving from the elementary school, and people spilled out to join the parking lot crowd, or the closer group by the front of the church. Trees stood thick on the neighboring roads and a few bicyclists went by, as well as two middle-aged women wearing workout pants and nice sneakers and walking quickly, accompanied by a dog on a leash. These were not the cramped city streets—the cheek-by-jowl parking, the old city-apartment homes—that surround the Shiloh AME Zion Church where Miles Kirkland-Thomas's funeral had been held a month earlier. Approaching the church in Wading River, cars passed a cider stand and a corn maze, as well as hand-painted signs hung outside private shingled houses that said things like "FRESH EGGS: $2 FOR A ½ DOZEN. HELP YOURSELF (IN COOLER)." A candlelight vigil for Tommy earlier in the week had been held on the grounds of a local farm.

You could hear the bagpiping well before the procession arrived—the steady, overlaying harmonics coming invisibly, as if from a distant magic land, through the strange sunlit day—and when the sounds began, the people outside waiting grew quiet and turned in that direction to look. First the police 'cycles, and then a flatbed truck laden high with fresh cut flowers, some of them woven into a huge 54. After that, strode the bagpipers themselves, kilted, and part of the Suffolk County Police Pipe Band, some 30 players in all, on the bagpipes and banging in slowsteady fashion on big, echoing bass drums, the *boom, ba-boom, boom, boom* describing the solemnity of the day. And right behind the pipers traveled the hearse with Tommy's coffin inside, and the Cutinellas: Frank and Kelli and their children, Kevin, William and Carlie.

"Nothing meant more to Thomas than family," said Frank once people had filed inside the church and found a seat on the overflowing pews and the service was under way. "He was one exceptional kid." Kelli stood beside him, stoic. Frank talked about all the ways in which Tom had helped people and the things he had accomplished in school and his love for the military and the volunteer work he had done and the award he had gotten a few years back from the New York State Attorney General for his "commitment and character." Tommy was running for junior class president and, looking at the rows and rows of stricken classmates before him, Frank pointed out that Tommy was a kid who had a lot of friends in different walks of life and that he had an "ability to open people's hearts." He said that the day Tommy was born was the first best day of his and Kelli's lives and that the day Tommy died would always be the worst. There was not much talk about football or sports by Frank, not much at all. Though when the pastor spoke, he said by way of prayer, "May the joy that Thomas found in playing football foreshadow the joy that he finds in heaven."

The funeral mass lasted two full hours and every word from the lectern was broadcast into the parking lot to the gathered crowd. When the family stepped out from the church, the lot was still full, and people were still standing there in the sunshine, or seeking shade from the trees by the sidewall, wearing their jerseys, their dark suits, their long plain-colored dresses. Mothers had tears streaked down their cheeks and fathers stood grimly, and the teenagers were quiet and shifted uncomfortably from side to side.

The Shoreham-Wading River students and the coaching staff all climbed into yellow school buses and drove off to the cemetery, and soon after that the procession departed just as it had come, the police motorcycles first and then the pipe band (having struck up again) and then that flatbed truck with the flowers and the 54, and then, in the black car, the Cutinellas. Frank had rolled down the backseat window, as if making himself ready to face the world, and he sat looking out, silent and still, as the car passed the many, many people who had come to honor his son.

Tommy died on a grass field, soft and dotted with clover, at John Glenn High School, maybe 35 miles from his home. There are no permanent lights around the John Glenn field and the bleachers are made of long metal pews. A running track encircles the field, just as one does at Shoreham-Wading River, just as one does at New Rochelle, and sand pits have been built in for the broad jumpers. Neighborhood homes abut the John Glenn school property all around, and wherever in an American suburb you live, or have visited or simply poked around, you have seen such a field as this. A blue storage shed off to the side has John Glenn's team nickname, "Knights," painted in white upon it.

Here, on this field, on the early afternoon of Oct. 7, 2014, at about the time that Tom Cutinella was being laid to rest at the Holy Sepulchre Cemetery, a gym class was in progress with high school kids playing a kind of football game. No equipment and no tackling, just the classmates, boys and girls, tossing the ball around and laughing and joke-deking one another and spiking the ball dramatically and calling out each other's names. There was a gym teacher there, presiding, and a security guard who the week before had been at the Shoreham-Wading River vs. John Glenn game in which Cutinella absorbed his fatal hit. "It was just a normal run-blocking play," the security guard said, gesturing. "I was right there as a spectator and if you saw it you would not have thought anything of it."

Things would happen for the Shoreham-Wading River football team that season in the weeks and then months after Cutinella's death. Things that seemed almost surreal. The Wildcats won their first game after the funeral 54–0—Tom's number again—and they did not stop winning after that. They won game after game after game. They beat John Glenn for the first Suffolk County title in Shoreham-Wading River history and then, finally, in the big college stadium at Stony Brook University on the last day of November, the Wildcats did another thing the team had never done or even seriously dreamed of doing: They won the Long Island Class IV championship, beating the team from Roosevelt High, 47–13. Shoreham-Wading River finished its season with a record of 12–0.

When the title game had ended, the whole team went by bus to Cutinella's gravesite and left there a championship plaque and the game ball. One of the Shoreham-Wading River kids, continuing a hijinks tradition, had stolen a pylon from the stadium end zone, and every Wildcats player, and every coach, signed his name on the pylon and they left that at Tommy's gravesite as well.

Weeks later when coach Millheiser reflected on the season, he saw elements of it set in relief. He recalled that the team had been focused each week in a way that he had never experienced. They all listened so well, and committed themselves so deeply, embracing every assignment without complaint. Millheiser recalled that he would hear kids on the sideline talking about Tommy at random times, nonchalantly almost, as if they might see him later in the day. He recalled how the players wrote his number on the back of their cleats, and carried out his jersey when they came onto the field. The coach had brought back Tommy's brother Kevin, a 14-year-old who had made varsity that summer as a sophomore. First, when the wound from Tommy's death was so fresh and Kelli and Frank were not ready for Kevin to play again, he worked as a coach, with a coach's shirt and a whistle and drills to run; and then a few weeks later, once the Cutinellas felt it was O.K., Kevin rejoined the team on the field and Millheiser got him out there for the last, emotional, history-making wins.

Millheiser recalled the very end of the season, the Long Island championship game and the big crowd at Stony Brook and the cheerleaders with 54 on their cheeks, and the Shoreham-Wading River players with TC and 54 written on their bare calves and the big 54 flag waving prominently from the stands.

But the most remarkable moment of the year had come earlier, just after Tommy died, and it was a reminder of the importance of the role of high school football and what the game means to the boys playing it, boys in this Long Island community of once and current farm lands. It had been difficult for the coaching staff to continue its routines in the days after Tom's death. "We act like we're adults and we've been through it and we have answers and can be there for the kids, but I'm telling you this was really tough on every single one of us," said Millheiser. "I am going back out there and I'm suddenly aware, in a way that no one is aware before something like this happens, that I am putting kids . . . not in danger really, danger is not what I mean. But I am exposing them to some kind of risk, on any play. At some point again I was going to have the left guard pull right to block for the running back, just a regular play-call, and the players were going to execute it."

After Tommy's death, the coaches had told all the players and their parents that anyone who wanted to stay away from football for a few days, a week, two weeks, however long, and then return to the team, that that would be fine. They would be welcomed back. The coaches understood that anyone might need to be away from the game after what had happened. So they got that message out to everyone, and when the first practice neared Millheiser says that he did not know what to expect. Kevin Cutinella was alongside as a coach but how many of the other kids would show up? What could they get done?

That day after school, Millheiser was out on the field, talking with his assistants. There were still 10 minutes before practice was scheduled to begin. "I kind of stopped talking and started to look around to see what we had. It took me a minute to realize it, but then I did. Guess what? Every last kid on our team was out on the field, and every last kid had his uniform on and had his helmet with him and was ready to play football. Every single kid was there."

NEW ROCHELLE went ahead early and stayed in command of that Thursday night game at Ossining, with Michael Cascio applauding his teammates from the sideline. There was no mention to the assembled crowd of Cutinella's death the day before, and no moment of silence before the kickoff. Earlier in the day, though, there had been discussion about canceling the game altogether. In an impromptu district meeting, a couple of school administrators, so shaken by what had happened in the kindred suburbs on Long Island, had suggested canceling their seasons entirely. "You get schools that have small football teams and that are losing money, and that are getting beat every week," said Steve Young. "Something like this occurs and it's only natural that they think, 'Is it all worth the risk?' It's an over-reaction, yes, but you can understand it."

On the field the Huguenots went ahead of Ossining by 28–0 but then, just before the half, allowed a touchdown that rankled DiRienzo. He warned the team, as they gathered near the far end zone to hear his halftime words, not to be complacent. "We just woke up a sleeping dog and that's a dangerous fucking thing, man," he said. Ossining was due to get the ball at the start of the second half, and DiRienzo, propping up a grease-board to write on, began to address the team, the defense:

"We're a field 50. They come out and we could be field Okie," he said, scribbling arrows and symbols on the board with a blue marker. "But if the tight end wing comes out to the boundary, we're in Cloud over here. And we're in Hug that way. Now if it comes out this way and we check Squat, SAM moves out to number one. We're going to Squat with the SAM and play Cover Four behind him. If it comes out the other way, we're in Hug, Cloud on the backside. There is no adjustment to motion. There is no more Sky. Basically if they are in a Wing-T we're in a cover two."

DiRienzo stopped and spit once on the grease-board and wiped it somewhat clean with his hand. The players were seated or kneeling on the grass. You could smell hamburgers cooking and the old Technotronic song "Pump Up the Jam" played into the night behind them. DiRienzo began again: "We're in a field call and they come out unbalanced to the boundary, then we're in an eight flash. If it comes out to the field, we are in eight slash. You guys got that? Can you guys see these circles?" (Murmurs of "Yeah, coach" from the group.) "Because we really can't let them come down and score.

"Now," DiRienzo said, "if they come out three by one to the field, then, what do you want to do, Coach?" Richie Tassello spoke up, "If 15 is the single receiver on the backside, we're in A-cloud. We are in A-cloud." And DiRienzo continued, "Remember, also it's on the loop with the MAC. If the MAC is out, there's no more thunder. SAM there is no more thunder. You got that?" After all of this DiRienzo added, not kidding in the slightest, "Let's keep it as simple as possible."

Although DiRienzo stresses that he takes each season one game at a time and does not look ahead to such heights as the county championship or playing in the state final at the Syracuse Carrier Dome, he could not stop himself from a last exhortation as the halftime clock wound down: "This next defensive series is very, very important. Make believe we're playing in the Dome right now. We stop them, then we go down and score and we get the fuck out of here."

New Rochelle did all of that, winning by a final score of a 48–14. Forrest ran one in from 30 yards out. Stern caught a 72-yard touchdown pass from Powell. Haitam Coughlin, the Cutinella inscriptions on his headband and lately added on his inner forearm as well, got into the game and broke up a couple of passes.

Afterwards, DiRienzo was reflective. "That news out of Long Island bothers me in a lot of ways," he said. "First of all it is just a tragic accident, so you feel awful for that family. Number 2, there is definitely going to be a backlash against high school football, which I don't like. And Number 3, I still have a son who is playing football."

DiRienzo's Huguenots now had a record of 5–0, four emphatic blowouts among those five wins, and the players were whooping it up on the idling school bus, ready to go home. They didn't have to practice until Saturday—and on that day a few kids, the Cohens and Stern, would be off for Yom Kippur. Early autumn had arrived and the notion that the team might indeed be bound for a state final game at the Carrier Dome was making its way through the team and through the parents around them, and through the community. Given the team's success thus far, it did not seem to be a far-fetched notion at all.

CHAPTER 12

Bullies and Brothers

T NEW ROCHELLE, as at many high schools, there's an added, schoolwide pulse around the annual homecoming game—the pomp-filled pep rally that wipes out the last couple of academic periods on a Friday afternoon; the extended somersaulting cheerleading routines; the band playing its best and longest numbers; kids out selling brownies and raffle tickets to benefit this extracurricular program or that one; and the hopes, of course, for a resounding win by the football team. This year that wish for a win was especially heightened, and extended deep into the New Rochelle community. The Huguenots were hosting the Scarsdale Raiders, a team made up of predominately white and predominately privileged children—Scarsdale's median household income of nearly $210,000 is the highest in Westchester County. This had traditionally been a pushover opponent for bigger, stronger, and better-coached New Rochelle, but in 2013, the Raiders had actually *beaten* the Huguenots, for the first time in 24 years.

"The guys were devastated by that loss," said Gary Powell, Greg's dad, in the days leading up to the 2014 homecoming game. "They were wailing and boo-hooing like kindergartners afterward. They just could not believe they had lost."

Scarsdale, though, was now following up with its best start to a season in years; like New Rochelle, the 2014 Raiders had opened up at 5–0. That proved, as DiRienzo growled to his players early in the week, that "they know what they are doing over there." He added that the upcoming matchup should be "about redemption for how we played last year, not about revenge."

For the players, and for many in and around New Rochelle High, there was an almost personal sense of enmity surrounding the game. The team had felt disrespected at Scarsdale in 2013 in part because, for reasons never articulated, the players and coaches had been relegated to using a cafeteria as a locker room. The Huguenots claimed they had also felt a spray of racially charged comments land upon them as they came on the field and, later, an incident arose in which a former girlfriend of a prominent New Rochelle football player had been vilely taunted by members of the Scarsdale varsity, her image posted alongside crude remarks on social media.

There was also an off-field development that at once pointed up the communities' different mind-sets and concerns, and got into administrative crosshairs: New Rochelle's 2014 Homecoming Game against Scarsdale had originally been scheduled for a Friday night at the school, until complaints arose that the timing wasn't at all ideal for players who were scheduled to take an SAT college admissions test early the next morning. While those in New Rochelle seemed (for the most part) content to have the players bang their heads under the lights, then take a crack at the aptitude exam 11 hours later, the Scarsdale contingent was rather more resistant to that scenario and successfully petitioned the district to change the game time to Saturday night, well after the SAT. (This annoyed the Huguenots for whom a Friday night game is a treat. It's also worth noting that many more Scarsdale players than New Rochelle players were actually signed up to take the test.)

The distaste for Scarsdale—just 5.3 miles (but in another sense, a world) away—was crisp among New Rochelle players, whose hunger for payback had churned for months. Ahead of the game, two Huguenot seniors, Garrett Noake and Tyler Cooney, sent out a taunting video on

Snapchat in which they introduced themselves to the Scarsdale players, ("Hi, I play center for New Rochelle . . .) and vowed, in language best left to the imagination, that the Huguenots would prove themselves much the manlier squad come game day, further suggesting that Scarsdale players were not, in fact, manly at all. The video found its way to Scarsdale coaches who were not pleased in the least.[1]

Noake, the linchpin of the offensive line and Cooney, in the rotation as a guard, were part of a loose clique on the team known as the Powder Boys. These were white kids mainly—among them the receiver Carmine Giordano, the defensive end Frankie Lammers—but certainly not exclusively; the Powder Boys also included a player nicknamed "Night" for the deep darkness of his skin. The clique's nickname came from a practice they had refined, during hell week and then more earnestly in the dorm rooms at Brookwood, in which they would ambush an unsuspecting younger player and wallop him persistently with soiled sweat-socks that they had filled with baby powder. White dust in your eyes, the powder pasted on your cheeks, a minute or two of confusion, even fear, for those players who'd never experienced it. In short, a dose of hazing as initiation.

Beyond the actions of the Powder Boys, other incidents of hazing (or

---

[1] Another, satellite incident illustrated elements of the tension leading up to the game, and of the differences between the towns: Several days before homecoming, a few Scarsdale players stopped off at the McDonald's restaurant on North Avenue, less than a half mile from New Rochelle High. They were wearing school colors, identifiable, and they saw, sitting at a table and eating, a few Huguenots players. As several witnesses recalled, the rival players exchanged words and the Scarsdale boys, undaunted, and bumptious as frat boys, declared that they were looking forward to coming in and knocking down New Rochelle in its homecoming game. The Huguenots in the McDonald's were kids on the smaller side—one was Haitam Coughlin, the lacrosse standout—and as this line of conversation continued, a few decidedly larger and more rumble-ready boys emerged from another table, members of a local gang. "These were kids we grew up with," Haitam recalls. "We all used to play together when we were little kids but then some of us went the football route and those guys went the gang-banging route. It took about three seconds for them to get involved." The New Ro gang guys came up close to the Scarsdale players, inquired whether there was a problem afoot that they might help with, and then, after a portentous pause, suggested that the Scarsdale boys forget their Big Macs and just leave. Without resistance, they did just that.

initiation) went on at various times, and any number of established players were potential perpetrators. You might see a senior intricately knotting together the laces on a younger player's left and right cleat moments before practice; or in the hallway just before the bell, a new member of the varsity being surrounded and apprehended by a few older kids, then wrapped up and carried outside, forcing him to miss class. There was a vulgar prank involving hot sauce and undergarments, and, perhaps most typically, a mischievous sequence that included the hiding away of a players' clothes and the demand that the player then go out and, as one Huguenot phrased it, "show yourself to the world!" That is how it could come to happen that coach DiRienzo might be sitting at a table in the bunkhouse at Brookwood, going over plays with his coaching staff, and suddenly look out the window to see one of his newly established backup tight end/defensive tackle types high-stepping it, barefoot and naked as Adam, through the dry summer grass.

"I guess it depends who you are and what your mind-set is, but it makes us crack up," said DiRienzo. It was mid-October now, a few days before the Scarsdale game. "It's *funny*. I could imagine it might be upsetting to certain kids. Some kids might find it fearful, but I honestly haven't seen that on this team. Kids take this stuff in stride; usually they're laughing along with everyone else. It's like a pie-in-the-face gag. Some coaches might try to shut all that stuff down, really monitor their kids, no hazing at all, but for me those things are a natural part of everything. It's like the more experienced players are saying, 'Come on in, you're one of us now.' And it's a reminder that we all need humility, which we do.

"There's a limit, though, that's for sure," DiRienzo continued. "With that kind of horsing around, there has to be a baseline of respect, a line you won't cross. It has to be about bonding and bringing someone in, not about victimization or alienating someone. That doesn't work. If a player gets upset and tells you to stop, you have to stop. Period. I like to think our guys know that—you don't see them picking on kids who are compromised. I'm fortunate that in my time here, almost 25 years now, none of that stuff has gotten really out of hand at this level. When you look at what happened with that team at Sayreville, that's something else all together. That kind of bullying is off the charts. Terrible. You wonder about the culture there that would allow that. It's horrible for those kids and also horrible for us as a sport. We see all the news about this stuff and we're sick about it."

INTO THE vortex of that autumn of 2014, with its run of NFL domestic violence cases, and the brain damage disclosures and the sudden college retirements and the spate of high school deaths, came this as well: The discovery of an apparent pattern of grotesque bullying within the varsity football program at Sayreville War Memorial High School in Middlesex County, N.J., about 50 miles from New Rochelle. The acts were so repugnant—allegedly repeated incidents of upperclassmen pinning down and digitally sodomizing freshman players—and apparently so preplanned and ritualized that the district's superintendent, Richard Labbe, abruptly canceled the Sayreville football season at all levels. "We are not going to tolerate forms of harassment, intimidation and bullying," Labbe said.[2]

The Sayreville incidents, which allegedly took place over two weeks in September, drew huge local outrage—at the horrific acts, of course, and also from some parents of players not involved in the assaults who were dismayed that their kids' season (which for some players meant the continuing of a college audition) had been "taken away" from them. Some parents of cheerleaders and band members were also upset. Sayreville has what is among the most successful football programs in New Jersey,

---

[2] Such a cancellation was not unheard of in the New Rochelle district. Although the varsity program has indeed been unblemished by a bullying scandal, there was in 2012 an episode at the Isaac E. Young middle school—albeit an episode categorically less deviant and disturbing than what happened in Sayreville. In the Isaac E. Young football locker room, some underclassmen were allegedly taunted, poked at and repeatedly harassed by older teammates as the Guns N' Roses song "Welcome to the Jungle" blared. No sexual or physical assault was suggested, but some of the players were unnerved by the treatment and several parents complained. When the players on the team refused to reveal the names of the offenders, the last three games of Isaac E. Young's middle school season were called off.

having won four state titles since 1997, including three straight from 2010 through '12, and that success has made a sizable imprint. As one student told reporters during coverage of the hazing incident, "Football runs this school. That's all anyone cares about. Football, football, football."

Seven Sayreville players, their ages ranging from 15 to 17, were arrested and charged with crimes including hazing, conspiracy and, in three cases, sexual assault. Head coach George Najjar, who in his 20 seasons had led the team to all of its state titles and had been elected to New Jersey's Football Coaches Association Hall of Fame, was suspended, then later reassigned as a physical education teacher within the district; virtually the entire varsity coaching staff was dissolved.[3]

The response to and coverage of the bullying extended far outside local borders. An article in Britain's *Daily Mail*, which relied on its own reporting as well as that of the Associated Press, appeared under this long, lurid headline: FOUR WOULD HOLD HIM DOWN, TWO WOULD STAND GUARD, THE SEVENTH PENETRATED HIM: VICTIM'S PARENT REVEALS HORRIFIC DETAILS OF FOOTBALL TEAM 'HAZING RITUAL' AT NEW JERSEY HIGH SCHOOL.

Much as the NFL's domestic violence cases and head trauma statistics were casting a dark shadow across all levels of the sport that autumn, the Sayreville hazing was widely identified—by armchair observers as well as by platform pundits—as being emblematic of a football culture that extends from prepuberty to adulthood. One ruminative *New York Times* piece addressed "the recent struggles of the National Football League" and then declared that "the troubles that have shaken the sport at the highest levels arrived [in Sayreville] last week." (Six of the seven players charged pled guilty or were found guilty of lesser assault charges.)

---

[3] Further complicating the situation was the fact that at almost exactly the same time that the bullying news emerged, information came out that one of Sayreville's assistant coaches, Charles Garcia, had been arrested for possession of steroids. The bizarre coincidence appeared to be just that, however—a coincidence. (An investigation into whether Garcia had provided steroids to any Sayreville players would later conclude that he had not.) The bullying case, with all its allegations and revelations, was evaluated and handled purely on its own (de)merit.

Countless media dissections of the Sayreville incident alluded to the NFL, and specifically to the highly public 2013 incident involving the Miami Dolphins' Richie Incognito, a brutishly intense offensive lineman who had allegedly bullied his teammate Jonathan Martin with a series of threatening and racially suggestive texts. Audio emerged of a voicemail in which Incognito, who is white, called Martin a "half-nigger piece of shit" and threatened violence on Martin and Martin's mother and sister. According to a subsequent NFL report, two other Dolphins linemen, Mike Pouncey (who is biracial) and John Jerry (who is black), also engaged in the persistent verbal bullying of Martin. After Martin quit the team and deep waves of negative publicity ensued, the Dolphins released Incognito, who sat out the entire '14 NFL season. (He was later signed, in early '15, by the Buffalo Bills and their newly hired, proudly contrarian, head coach, Rex Ryan.)

Yet for all the visibility of such cases, the suggestion that a high school football team is an especially fertile breeding ground for bullying—whether verbal, physical or to the level of sexual assault that occurred in Sayreville—is far from an established fact. Actually, it's an intellectual leap. "It's true that there is an environment of aggression on a football team, and you can see that that might translate into a type of bullying for some kids," says Emily Bazelon, a senior research scholar at Yale Law School whose extensive writing and thinking on bullying and cyberbullying within the high school culture includes her illuminating 2013 book *Sticks and Stones*. "But you can also see a team like that being supportive and helpful *against* bullying, with the players protecting one another. So much depends upon the culture of leadership, upon the coaches and the student leaders on the team. We can't know this for sure but I wouldn't say there is anything about a sports team that's necessarily conducive to bullying. It depends on so many other factors."

Bazelon's work has not explored bullying in high school sports specifically, and, in fact, very little scholarly work has. One oft-referenced study, done in 2000 through Alfred University, focused on incidents of hazing in various organized groups that high school students are involved in. A survey presented in the study showed that 35% of students who played on a high school sports team experienced "hazing as part of joining the group." (Neither football nor any other sport was separated out for individual study.) That's a significant percentage (and may even reflect under-reporting), but it is far less than the 76% of students who said that they were hazed while joining a high school fraternity or sorority, and far less than the 73% who said they were hazed while joining a "gang."

The sports teams' 35% hazing rate is virtually the same as that reported by cheerleaders (34%) and is not dramatically more than the percentage reported by students in high school vocational groups (27%), church groups (24%), music, art or theater groups (22%) and political or social action groups (21%). Football teams, in other words, are hardly unique when it comes to hazing, although they are often viewed under a kind of public microscope rarely trained upon a neighborhood gang or a school choir or a student Shakespeare troupe.

Other results in the Alfred University survey suggested that not all students deeply minded the hazing. Across the various groups, about 45% said they went along with being hazed because it was "fun and exciting" and because they believed it helped to bring the group closer together. Only 16% said they submitted to being hazed because they were "scared to say no." The percentage of students who reported having "positive" feelings toward their experiences of being hazed (27%) was exactly the same as those who reported having "negative" feelings.

Of course this is all hard to parse, almost inscrutable, because the term hazing—which, as Bazelon reminds us, "is just one of the forms of bullying"—encompasses so many things. A bout of pointed locker-room razzing or a 30-second butt-naked dash across a lawn at Brookwood football camp, as your teammates hoot, howl and goad you along, may to some kids qualify as a lark; being held down by a group of older players while one of them forces his finger into your anus is something else entirely.

At New Rochelle, the Sayreville incident predictably occupied some of the sideline and parental discussion, found its way into the game-day stands, and inspired local reporters to ponder big questions about the present and future of the sport. Yet none of the parents who hovered around the Huguenots that fall—not Kirby or Exzodia Mack; not David or Mary Gaudio; not Michelle Ammons, Tyler Cooney's mom; not Dawn Holder or Donald Baron; not Gerald or Carla Stern; not Gary Powell; not Keith Wheeler Sr.; not Charlotte Anthony; not Mark or Pam Cohen; not Randy or Janice Forrest; not Steve Lilly, Demetrius Rodriguez's dad—not any of these parents expressed worries about hazing or bullying being a detrimental factor in their son's life. "It's not something we've ever seen or worried about at New Rochelle," said Gerald Stern. Jack's older brother, Sam, also played for the Huguenots, then played college football at Hobart. "I don't see coach D standing for anything like that. And I don't feel like it's something our kids have been involved with. The football experience here has built character for my boys, not broken down their character. My feeling is that these kids respect the coach and that he is ultimately in control of the team."

"Yes," said Alex X., "some stuff goes on. Powder Boys and stuff like that. Or kids get heckled when they're new. But it's not bad. If anything I think being on the football team *helps* with bullying. For some kids, quiet kids, walking through the hallways at a big school like New Rochelle can be tough, you know. People pick on each other and there are some pretty tough dudes here. But when you're a football player, everyone knows that if they bother you the whole team has your back. So they don't bother you."

Added Haitam Coughlin, "It's support, and you get it even if you are a kid who doesn't play much, who may be running around getting water for the other guys in practice half the time; you're still part of the team, part of this family. And we would not let a member of the family get bullied."

"If anything Quincy would stop that kind of bullying behavior when it came," said Exzodia Mack. "That's how me and his father raised him, and also that's just how he is. He's going to stand up for the younger kids, or the kids who are trying even if they aren't really making it. But I don't think he even has to do that. Bullying is not a problem on this team. These are solid kids. They may have fun with each other, but they are not going to hurt each other."

Or as Kirby Mack said—in a more simplistic sentiment echoed

almost exactly by Donald Baron in explaining why he had no fear of his son Jared's being bullied—"He's a strong kid. I know that Quincy can take care of himself."

While the Sayreville hazing was seen by the collective ruminati as a window into the soul of the high school game, even into the soul of the entire sport, the incident was, among those at the core of New Rochelle football, regarded as a distant event, practically from another sphere. The same could not be said, however, of another, related development that followed. Not long after Sayreville shut down its football program, the Monroe-Woodbury school district in upstate New York, reacting in part to the tenor of the time, announced it would cancel the last two games of its junior varsity season, also because of bullying-related issues. There had been a pattern of heavy-handed homophobic and racial slurs on that Monroe-Woodbury team, allegedly involving several players and signifying a culture of intimidation. Like New Rochelle, Monroe-Woodbury has a racially diverse student body, and in announcing the cancellation of the games school superintendent Elsie Rodriguez said, "We are very upset about this as a school district. The kids involved have to realize that these statements are not allowed. It's unacceptable."

Along with articulating some of the verbal bullying, a local newspaper, the *Times Herald-Record*, reported that a boy on the team had complained about "one of his sneakers being dumped into a toilet bowl filled with urine." Those events, along with the almost simultaneous cancellation of the season finale at Eldred High, also in upstate New York, after players there had allegedly rubbed their clothed crotches in certain teammates' faces, inspired even more media inquiry and speculation about football's culture. The *Times Herald-Record* published a front page "special report" titled THE HAZARD OF HAZING.

Although Monroe-Woodbury it is not a proximal neighbor to New Rochelle—the schools are 55 miles apart—it is a regional power in its own right and the teams have developed into playoff rivals. They've played each other in state playoff games five times in 10 years, and each team tends to feel that any path to the state title will likely require beating the other.

"To be honest, seeing what happened at Monroe-Woodbury does make you nervous," said DiRienzo. "I don't believe we've had that behavior go on here, just maybe some isolated cases, and we have definitely not had anything like what happened at Sayreville. But when these things occur it reminds you that you have only so much control. I'm not familiar with the program in Sayreville but Monroe-Woodbury is a good, solid program at a good, solid school, and has coaches I respect. When I saw what happened up there I had this nauseous feeling pass through me, like, if it happened there it could happen anywhere."

THE STANDS around the football field were packed for the homecoming pep rally. Students, thrilled to be freed from class, jostled their way gaily into the metal pews shouting what-ups and teasing one another, a couple of thousand or more on hand, overspilling the bleachers. Many kids wore strings of plastic purple beads around their necks and, now and again, sudden ensemble shouts of "New Ro!" burst seemingly spontaneously from the crowd.

Each of the fall athletic teams was introduced and duly saluted but only the football guys got called out individually, the captains first and then the rest of the seniors—who assembled for a midfield pose with their parents and siblings—and then every last player announced. The P.A. broadcaster delivered each name with dramatic intonation, as the player came jogging out with arms raised, clapping, and the crowd cheered and the big, thumping band on the field played loudly into the open air.

It was a bright and beautiful early autumn day, Friday at about 2:15 p.m., and after the last of the football players had been feted and a student hip-hop dance troupe had finished its performance, the homecoming king and queen were announced and brought up onto a small riser to be crowned: Jasper Baskerville, the bearlike senior football lineman, and Cynthia Rodriguez, a cheerleader and Jasper's girlfriend. They had met in the eighth grade and had been dating since the 10th and they were very well-liked, known by their peers and the underclassmen not so much for being cool ("We're not," said Cynthia) as for being kind.

Jasper and Cynthia had made their homecoming aspirations abundantly clear, pinning up bright yellow posters on hallway bulletin boards, and even making T-shirts touting themselves in the election for king and queen. No other football players were in the running and in many of the "campaign posters," as Jasper laughingly called them, he—or else Cynthia—wore his number 56 football jersey. "And it worked!" said Jasper grinning as he stood on the field shortly after the coronation. He was holding a rose he'd been given and he had those beads around his neck and Cynthia, beaded as well, was off to the side tittering and surrounded by several classmates. Jasper had only begun playing football for New Rochelle in seventh grade. "We're so happy right now," he said. "Some kids think it's awesome that we're this interracial couple, but that part doesn't matter to us. We don't even think about it, really. It just makes us feel good that we're popular and all." He shuffled over a few steps and leaned in and nuzzled close to Cynthia. "This season is like a movie!" Jasper added. "We are 5–0, and I am homecoming king!"

The big crowd was dispersing into the afternoon and lines were forming at the ice cream truck parked in back of the school, and up and down the road seniors were sitting in their cars in the parking spaces, windows down and radios on. The football players had begun to head inside for some film work before they would come back out for running and drills. They would be at school all afternoon—right through to a moms' team dinner, and then, afterward, a brief, final postmeal practice session in helmets and pads.

Alongside the football field, athletic director Steve Young was conferring energetically with Jim Benge, a former Marine and former New Rochelle player in his late 40s, who tends to wear fatigues and has tattoos on his calves and back. For nearly two decades, Benge has worked as the team's equipment manager, but he is much more than that; another adult adviser, a core figure in spirit and soul who suffers no bullshit, and also the guy who makes the trains run on time. He had been with the team for nearly two decades; and one suite of tattoos on his leg salutes the state football championships New Rochelle won in 2003 and '12. Now, with Young watching, Benge fussed with some wiring connected to a large whirring generator on the sideline. Two of the 10 temporary flood-light panels that had arrived that afternoon didn't seem to be working. Saturday's kickoff versus Scarsdale was set for 7 p.m., 27 hours away. "We've got to have this buttoned up by tomorrow," Young was saying to Benge. "Actually, we've got to get it done now so that they can get in all their work tonight."

It had been a solid, heady week of practice, one of the more focused of the year. On Monday, in large part a day of conditioning and weightlifting, assistant coach Rich Tassello had led the boys through a tough, pointed workout that included at the outset a set of taxing core-muscle exercises: The players all lay on their backs on the rubber-matted weight-room floor doing prolonged crunches—their legs and shoulder blades raised off the ground, bicycle-kicking furiously, the sort of nasty, demanding chore that forces a degree of concentration on the group. There was no talking among the players, just huffing and grunting.

Tassello kept working them. Do it for 45 seconds, pause for 30, start it again. He kept them at it much longer than he usually did, a tacit reminder that something important, Scarsdale, was waiting at the end of the week. Suddenly, mid-stream, Shameek Miller, his big legs pump-ing through the air, started shouting in his high-pitched voice, "They are not working as hard as we are! They are not working as hard as we are!" By "they" he meant the kids at Scarsdale, and the boys around Shameek, the whole floor full of them, cheered in assent, yelling through their grunts, sloughing off the pain.

Shameek, who had lost all that weight in the year before, had taken off another eight pounds during the season and his asthma was, for the most part, behaving. He didn't always get into the games as much as he wanted to, but he kept practicing very hard and he loved the team, and he said that he felt as good as he ever had. "Only thing is that I have these knots in my hand," he said, standing outside the weight room, still sweaty from the workout. Shameek held out his right hand and you could feel hard deposits inside the flesh in the side of his palm. He said that the hand was tender to the touch. "It's like cartilage or calcium or something in there from banging against helmets. It makes it harder for me to really punch when I'm on the line now, but I'm doing it. Punching through!"

Shameek said that for the moment football was the only thing he could really think about, what with how well the team was doing and the hope in the back of his mind that they could make it to the state final. After the season, though, he said, he was hoping to begin a plumber's apprenticeship through a program at the school. He liked the idea of plumbing, of fixing things, and he said that hanging around at the Hollows, at home or visiting with friends at their apartments, he could see the need for people who were good at that kind of work. He felt sure he could be a very good plumber himself and that was what he wanted to do. "For me," Shameek said, "knowing that I am making it on the football team, it's like then I can make it doing other things too, like in my job and everything."

At the Hollows that week, Shameek had run into Ray Rice, who was making his first visit to the housing project since the uproar over the video. Rice visited over at the high school as well, just before football practice one afternoon, and there, in the parking lot outside the athletic department, he saw some of the guys. "Come on over," Rice called. From the trunk of his car, Rice produced boxes and boxes of new cleats: Nike Superbad Pros, bright purple with a white swoosh. Sweet looking. The shoes were gifts from Rice to the team. Some of the players put them on immediately, and several were also wearing those new Nikes at practice on that Friday afternoon an hour or so after the homecoming pep rally had ended. None of them seemed to have any qualms about accepting the gifts, even knowing what Rice had done to Janay.

"Tyler loves those cleats," said Michelle Ammons, Tyler Cooney's mom. "Plus, he helped carry them inside from Ray's car, which he thought was cool." Ammons knew about the taunting Snapchat that Tyler and Garrett Noake had sent out ahead of the Scarsdale game, and she also knew about the many levels of conflict between the New Rochelle and Scarsdale teams dating back to the year before. "Tyler looks at it like he is standing up not just for himself but also for his teammates," Ammons said. "That Snapchat seems harmless to me, not like real trouble. He only started playing a couple of years ago, that's it, and since then football has changed him. Coach D has changed him. A lot. It's good. He used to get into fights all the time, get into trouble. Now I hardly worry about that at all. He has a self-esteem he didn't use to have. And he is more patient."

The late sun was landing on the bleachers where Ammons sat and she was shading her eyes with one hand as she watched Tyler, number 64, as he worked through his blocking drills. "Football is his life," she went on. "If he won't clean his room, won't do what he needs to do in school, won't do his homework, all I have to do is tell coach D about it. And then, guess what? It gets done. Coach is *tough* on them. He can be *really* tough. But I trust him. I think he keeps them safe and gives them discipline. He's been like a life coach.

"Sure, I do worry about injuries, every mom does. I sometimes wonder if Tyler got a concussion or anything, like everyone's talking about, I wonder if he *would* tell me about it. As close as we are, I don't even think he would tell me, he'd be afraid he wouldn't be allowed to play. That just shows what being on this team has done for him, and the family it has given him: Frankie. Noake, Justice, Alex X. Those kids are always at my house. I mean I don't know what Tyler will do without football. His father lives in Florida and they talk a few times a week but coach D is like that male figure in Tyler's life right now. That works for me."

Tyler's father, Mike Cooney, a mail carrier, had flown up to New York for the Scarsdale game and he too sat in the bleachers, a few rows in back of Michelle Ammons, watching practice. Tyler was a senior and there would only be so many more days like this. "This is first time I've ever seen him play," said Mike. "It's a big one. A big game, a big weekend, a big moment in Tyler's life. He is so excited. Michelle is right—he and I usually talk about three times a week. For this past week, though, he has been calling me every day. Sometimes twice."

Before settling in to watch practice that day, Michelle had dropped off a large pot of macaroni and cheese with Dawn Holder, who was, per usual, at the center of the Friday night meal that several of the players' moms (and a couple of the dads) were staging in the cafeteria near the gym. Lots of high carb food—pasta, corn, garlic bread—as well as grilled chicken, salads, assorted drinks, some fruit, a few stacks of cookies. The cheerleaders were there as well, and so were many of the cheerleaders' and the players' younger siblings. No teachers or coaches were around, nor anyone from the football staff, save for Jim Benge, who had solved the issue with the temporary floodlights and who had been charged, as he sometimes is, with saying some words to jack up the team.

First Benge addressed the group before the meal, saying his own brand of grace. The players, the cheerleaders and the siblings had gathered in a very large circle around him. The food was all prepared. The cheerleaders, by coach D's long-standing policy, would get their dinner first, then the football guys. Everyone standing in the circle lowered his and her heads and joined hands, a human chain. Benge said, "Dear Lord, bless us tonight, that we are together as a family. And dear Lord bless us and let us enjoy this food and have a good time tonight. Because tomorrow we go to war!" Big cheers erupted and the circle broke up and the players, jostling and play-fighting one another, found tables to sit at, while the cheerleaders queued up to get their food on plastic trays, cafeteria style, from the team parents who were serving it.

After everyone had eaten, and just before the players would go out for that last hourlong nighttime practice, Benge spoke again, delivering a rousing, high energy speech. He stood at the front of the room and the players and cheerleaders turned in their seats to face him, and some little brothers and cousins, boys of six or seven, clambered onto some of the football players' laps to watch and listen.

Benge was all fire and vim. He chastised Scarsdale for having had the game time changed from its original Friday night start. ("We should be out on the field whupping their candy asses *right now*, but they had the game moved because of the friggin' SATs! Man, I am so mad.") He reminded the players—as if they needed reminding—of the previous year's loss at Scarsdale, and of the fact that the Raiders were now 5–0, and he warned that if any of the Huguenots intended to go out on the field the next day with "your head up your ass" it would promise to be a long and unfortunate game. Near the end of his soliloquy, Benge, red-faced now, suggested that Scarsdale's players might have to "leave by stretcher or leave by ambulance" because, he noted, "hell is coming." The talk lasted eight minutes or so and the parents, shuffling around off to the side and organizing the leftovers, listened all the while. "My boys love this kind of stuff," said Mike Cohen, laughing. "I kind of love it too."

IF THERE was a test to the solidarity of the team during and around the time of the Sayreville bullying episode and as the Scarsdale game neared, it came not from within but from without. Certain parents had been making it known to their boys and to the coaches and to others around the team who cared to listen that they were dissatisfied with how coach D was apportioning the playing time and running the offense. Yes, the Huguenots were unbeaten, and winning most games handily, but why, father X and mother Y wondered, wasn't my son, or my friend's son, getting more playing time? Why weren't these guys getting more chances to make highlight-worthy plays and amass the personal statistics to prove how good they were?

A faint feeling of irritation crept in among the parental set, the sum of a comment here, an observation there from one onlooker or another. Quarterback Greg Powell, his father Gary reminded people, had the arm to put up big numbers. And while Gary understood, and even respected, DiRienzo's reluctance to pass the ball when the team had a significant lead (as it often did), well, Gary thought, they could pass a *little* more often, couldn't they? Let Greg get his due after all the time he has put in, let him exploit an overmatched defense when it is there to be exploited.

Then there were the running backs. It was obvious to everyone that Forrest deserved to be the Huguenots' leading ballcarrier, but on the downs he didn't get the ball, carries kept going to Jared Baron, an excellent, strong runner who was eating up yards by the half dozen and beating defenses, but who was also, some parents couldn't forget, a freshman. In a sense, Baron was stealing playing time from their senior sons who after so many years had been expecting greater responsibility and limelight. "Do you believe in chronology?" asked Keith Wheeler Sr., watching practice a few days before the Scarsdale game. "Because I believe in chronology. Why is this young guy getting all these chances instead of guys who were there before him? Other guys could be just as good as he is."

Keith Wheeler Jr., fast, and dynamic as a ballcarrier, was not getting utilized to his father's satisfaction. CJ Anthony, tough through the center of the field, wasn't being entrusted enough in short yardage situations. And what about Bryce Davis, who was so quick and aggressive as a cornerback on defense? Shouldn't he get some time on offense as well? There weren't *a lot* of parents griping and there weren't *a lot* of kids in question, but there were a few—enough to subtly, at least temporarily, shift a mood.

"I deal with these kinds of questions a lot, every year," said coach DiRienzo. "You know that it's coming. I tell parents at the start of each season: I am not responsible for creating your son's college highlight film. I'm responsible for winning games with this team at New Rochelle. Lately, for a few reasons, the complaining's been a little more intense than usual. Some parents are reasonable. We can talk. I'll even listen sometimes. Some parents are just out of their minds."

It was inevitable that some of the questions raised by the parents, the dinner-table complaints, might play upon a player's own quiet sense of indignation and find their way to ground level—to the locker room, the sideline, the huddles and the trenches. That explains why, when Bishop Leak assembled the team to deliver the pregame prayer about a half hour before kickoff against Scarsdale, he prefaced it with a few words of caution. "There have been a lot of voices out there, we know that," Bishop Leak said. The members of the Mitey Mites, the seven- to nine-year-old team from New Rochelle's Youth Tackle League, were also in the room. "People saying this thing and the other thing about who should be doing what. You have to get those voices out of your head, you have to shut out all of those voices and all of that noise. There is only one voice that matters and that is the coach's voice. That is the only voice that you need to be hearing. What goes on out there has to stay out there and what goes on in here is ours."

After the prayer, the players charged out onto the field, breaking through a large paper sign that read in three-foot letters REDEMPTION and was held by three cheerleaders on either side. The Mitey Mites, in their own white and purple jerseys, trailed behind, their little legs pumping hard. The game was being streamed through a local web portal, and a few local reporters stood near the field. It was a very clear evening, though quite cold, and the bleachers were maybe three-fourths full.

Three minutes into the first quarter, Jonathan Forrest broke off a 45-yard run. One minute after that, he took the ball 18 yards and into the end zone and the Huguenots had the lead for good. They scored another touchdown in the second quarter and another in the third and a final touchdown with about 11 minutes to play, and all along the defense, Cohen and Holder and Baskerville up front, Demetrius Rodriguez tough off the edge, gave hardly an inch. Final score, 27–0.

Though the game had not been close, it had been intensely physical, the chippiest of the year for New Rochelle and full of extra hits and pushes and tweaks between and after the whistles by players on both teams. Forrest was hit hard but cleanly in the open field just before the half, an onrushing low-helmet to the left leg that led to a swollen and badly sprained knee. He was wrapped up tightly at halftime and limped to the sidelines where he spent the last two quarters, out for the game. In Forrest's absence, Baron did get most of the carries, but Keith Wheeler got some too and scored a touchdown from two yards out. CJ Anthony also got his chances and he too produced a TD. Powell ran one in for the other score.

Wheeler, though, was knocked out of the game in the second half, having dislocated his shoulder on a collision while making a defensive play in the end zone, and Garrett Noake had *his* shoulder badly wrenched as well. Noake's injury happened during the intimate, vicious struggles of the offensive and defensive lines, and from that point on, beginning early in the third quarter, he sat on the Huguenots bench. Noake was shirtless in the cold night—it was 42°—and he was defiant and unsmiling. Becky

Schwartzman, the trainer, had wrapped the shoulder in large ice packs, stretching wide ace bandages across his upper torso. Garrett's brother Griffin Noake, the former Huguenots center who'd gone on to play as an offensive lineman at SUNY-Cortland, emerged from the stands and came onto the New Rochelle sideline to sit beside his brother and try to ease him into a better mood. "Look at the scoreboard," Griffin said. "You guys are killing it."

But Garrett was full of frustration over his injury and he remained unsmiling and said he wished he was still in there giving it to "those assholes," by which he meant the Scarsdale Raiders. For the longest time, Garrett, despite the sharp chill in the air and the ice on his body and the stiffening wind that reddened his pale skin, refused pleas from Becky and from Griffin that he put on a shirt. Finally, in the game's final minutes, Griffin simply stood up and pulled off the oversized Cortland hoodie he was wearing and, without waiting for an O.K., put it over Garrett's head to try to warm him up.

Both teams committed gratuitous penalties throughout the game, penalties that interrupted the rhythm of play and caused some nastiness. Corey Holder kept getting into it with the Scarsdale blockers. He was agitated—for one thing he had not liked the hit on Forrest, a kid he'd been playing alongside since Mitey Mites—and he was getting overaggressive on the line. DiRienzo barked at Holder from the sidelines ("Cut it out, Corey!") and pulled him off the field for a play or two but then put him right him back in.

The smell of reefer drifted out of the bleachers at times during the beginning, middle and end of the game, and the crowd was noisy in its support, cheering their Huguenots. Later the Scarsdale coaches would say that they had felt threatened by fans in the stands, another sign of the animosity between the clubs. When the game ended, DiRienzo walked over and stood maybe 10 yards from the Scarsdale sideline, waiting to shake hands with head coach Andy Verboys. But Verboys didn't come over for some time. He busied himself talking to various people and appeared to be snubbing coach D. Until, after a while—enough time had passed that some onlookers were commenting on the coach's apparent dismissal of DiRienzo—Verboys did make his way over toward DiRienzo, trudging slowly.

When Verboys arrived, the men shook hands and DiRienzo put a hand on Verboys's back. DiRienzo complimented Verboys on the quality of his team, and he apologized for the New Rochelle players who had gotten too rough. Lou said that he knew Scarsdale had been without a few of its important players because of injuries and that if those players had been healthy the outcome of the game might have been a lot different. DiRienzo said all the right things and Verboys mostly nodded. "That's how dad will always do it," said Lou Jr. as he watched the short conversation end. "But shaking Verboys's hand and patting on the back? That's pretty much bullshit. They hate each other. My dad respects almost every coach we go against. But not that one."

Strong feelings from the game lingered on both sides, and a few days later, Scarsdale's athletic director, Joseph DeCrescenzo sent an email to his counterpart at New Rochelle, Steve Young. It read:

Dear Steve, I need to inform you of a few issues that occurred Saturday Night at the football game

1) one of my varsity asst coach's wife and daughter were verbally abused by New Rochelle fans.

2) My head coach and an asst coach were harassed by many fans when leaving the press box. The fans were standing in the aisle leaving no room for my staff to get by. They called for your security to help but with the noise from the lights and the crowd no one could hear them.

3) In addition to the crowd issues my coach will be providing me detailed information and video clips. I will forward you the video showing some of the New Rochelle players taking shots at Scarsdale players after the whistle.

DeCrescenzo had copied the Scarsdale principal on the email, and a phone conversation between Young and DeCrescenzo ensued. In that talk, Young responded to DeCrescenzo's objections by saying that security had in fact gone quickly over to help the Scarsdale coaches get through the stands when they left the press box. Young also fired back, claiming that earlier in the week a Scarsdale assistant coach had tried to get into a second-floor classroom overlooking the New Rochelle field, presumably as a way to watch or film the Huguenots practice. (The would-be spy, Young said, was escorted away by school security.) Young pointed out that while New Rochelle was called for a personal foul in the game, Scarsdale was called for two. Young mentioned by name the Scarsdale coach who during the game had shouted a few times, as a threat, "Wait til they come to our place!" and he added that he had heard how loudly and rudely that same coach's wife had been yelling at the Huguenot players during the game.

"And don't bother to send any video clips," said Young. "I've seen the film." Then he suggested specific plays, by quarter and time of game, that DeCrescenzo might want to look at to see just how improperly *his* boys had behaved.

The back-and-forth accusations left the athletic directors at an impasse, though Young did not at all like the tone of what had been said. In closing the conversation, Young invoked the name of a nearby private high school, one with a level of wealth and an ethnic homogeneity much closer to Scarsdale's than to New Rochelle's. "If you guys don't like coming to the jungle, as you call it," said Young before putting down the phone, "I suggest that you start scheduling games with Rye Country Day instead."

"THAT HAD to be the most intense game of our season," Quincy Mack said afterward. "There was a lot going on. It was good what Bishop Leak said to us about not listening to voices outside the team. But to tell the truth, we knew it already. When all the stuff was going on about who was playing and who was not, and we started hearing it at practice, we got the team together. Me and Demetrius, all the captains. We said how it had to stop, that no one knew who we were but us. We talked about that inner circle again, like coach told us. And the guys all bought in. The complaining pretty much stopped. It was a crazy time around here, the bullying stuff going on and people talking about us, but coach D says that how you handle things in here, in your house, that's the only way to change how people will judge you."

Whatever the judgment of the unbeaten Huguenots was shaping up to be—and now you could hear talk of "States" even beyond the steady onlookers—the Scarsdale win had been momentous. It was, in the hallways as well as on streets throughout the school district, a win for us against them, in which "us" and "them" implied great differences in lifestyle and societal class. On the night of the game, after the players had showered and dressed, some of them had gone over, in small groups, to the local diner, the Mirage, on North Avenue for some late-night food. Each time a new clutch of players arrived, something would happen, a reaction. Like when Greg Powell, Manny Walker and Haitam Coughlin, three juniors and fast friends who had been playing on football teams together for a decade or more, pulled open the front doors and started to walk in. There was the briefest hush in the packed restaurant and then, as everyone recognized them as football players, the people in the diner stood up and started cheering and whooping and clapping. "It felt like out of *Friday Night Lights*!" Coughlin would say. Amid the noise, the boys continued inside and found classmates at different tables to hug and to high-five, and that night all three of them ate for free.

CHAPTER 13

No. 1, and Knowing It

HEY WERE going to beat Carmel—that much the Huguenot players felt sure of. They would win easily, just as they had done so often in this unbeaten season. Years earlier, the Carmel Rams had been a formidable team (a state semifinalist in 1998) and before each season back then the team would go for a late-summer football retreat to a camp in upstate New York, Camp Pontiac. In those years, that's the camp that New Rochelle used as well. "We bunked next to each other and the coaching staffs were close," recalls Todd Cayea, then, as now, Carmel's head coach. "Lou and I were young. We shared ideas. He's a student of this game and he's a passionate teacher. But the most important thing about Lou has always been that he has character and integrity, and he is straight up. Those are the reasons why young people will follow you."

Cayea remains one of the rival coaches that DiRienzo most respects, although Carmel has slipped from regional prominence. In 2014, Carmel, weakened by injuries, cases of academic ineligibility and other internal and external influences, was on its way to a fourth straight nonwinning season. "There are many challenges to coaching football in the public school system nowadays," Cayea said before the Rams hosted the Huguenots. "Kids on a football team now are not the same as they were when we were ramming heads back in Camp Pontiac in the late 1990s. They just aren't. More distractions. But Lou finds a way to relate to the kids, to keep evolving and to stay even-keeled, which explains why he has sustained this for so long.

"This season," Cayea added, laughing, "he just happens to have a team that's driving him crazy." The two coaches talk from time to time throughout the year. "He feels like he has to jump through hoops to motivate them."

"IT'S GOOD to be confident but there is a problem with being over-confident," coach Keith Fagan was saying on the New Rochelle practice field a few days ahead of the Friday night game at Carmel. There was a break between drills and a small group of kids, helmets off, stood around him—Greg Powell, Tyler Cooney, Demetrius Rodriguez, a couple of others. Fagan was urging the kids to stay focused in practice, to remember that they always needed to prepare. "You have to keep your head in this thing every day," he was saying. "If you're just doing things out here because the coach tells you to, you're not going to get anything out of it. You have to believe in this. You need to practice like the game is here already, see yourself in the real moment, make all of what you do today count tomorrow."

"But we're doing that!" said Powell. "Aren't we doing that?

"No," said coach Fagan. "No, you're not."

There was an afterglow around the team from the win the Saturday before. Beating Scarsdale had lifted New Rochelle's ranking to No. 1,138 in the United States, to No. 14 in New York, and, most pertinently to their mood and immediate surroundings, to No. 1 in their division and the favorite to emerge from Section 1 and advance to the state playoffs. That, along with the less-than-daunting prospect of playing downtrodden Carmel, seemed to have produced a level of satisfaction, even complacency on the part of the players. All week practice lacked intensity; there was an emotional incompleteness, compounded by a physical one. An unusual number of injured, high-profile Huguenots were hanging around the perimeter of the field. "Our walking wounded," said Fagan. "Our depleted troops. A season of football can do this to you."

Jonathan Forrest, whom teammates had taken to calling "Jonny Franchise," was limping around gingerly with a Grade 1 MCL sprain after taking the open-field hit against Scarsdale. Garrett Noake and Keith Wheeler each had their wrenched shoulders heavily wrapped. Jasper Baskerville's tender right knee—he'd been playing through it for a couple of weeks—was now too swollen to run on. "That's four key guys out right there, eight starting positions because they play both ways," said coach Fagan.

That wasn't all: Nigel Bailey, the dreadlocked junior, stood on the sideline with his left arm in a sling, nursing a fractured growth plate. Bryce Davis was playing although he still wore a hard cast supporting his left wrist, and Corey Holder's fracture and torn labrum had not yet healed, leading the coaches to limit his repetitions. Kicker Robbie DeRocco, whose right hip kept clicking when he moved it and who was experiencing numbness all through his right thigh, stood on the sideline too. "At least you guys don't have to be out there getting your brains scrambled," said Phil Spivack, a curmudgeonly assistant-coach/scorekeeper type, trying to keep the injured guys loose.

Another player, a lineman who hadn't played much all year and who had been a behavior problem at times, mouthing off to coaches and even earning an internal, one-game suspension in the middle of the year, was not in uniform because of what he described as "a lot of anxiety issues and feeling depressed." He had been battling these feelings, he said, for some time. The year before, his mother, who worked a local job, had been arrested for DWI in an incident that had drawn gawking media coverage. That was one ongoing source of his feeling uncomfortable, the boy said—that the kids in school joked about this, not the football players so much, but students in the lunchroom and in the hallway. There were other issues too, he said, relating to his situation at home, and he had gone to see a school psychologist a few times.

None of this, though, translated into much sympathy from teammates. A player suffering from anxiety—not unlike a player suffering from a not-obvious concussion—can engender charges of malingering among the young and skeptical. These, after all, are not wounds you can immediately see nor easily measure. To some of the Huguenots, the kid seemed healthy enough on that afternoon, and this was a day when, given the other injuries on the team, he could have been of real use on the practice field. "Anxiety?" one teammate said that day. "Yeah, right. Call me when you have Ebola."

Summer was long gone, yet the trees outside the practice field were still thick with celadon leaves, flecked only gently with reds and browns. The pond lay behind the trees and the sun's reflection sat flat on the water. There were still a couple more weeks before daylight savings time would end. In some sense it had been a long season of football, dating, for this particular group, back to the spring and encompassing those hard weeks of August. ("Championships are won in months that don't end in R" was among DiRienzo's adopted maxims.) Yet at the same time, the relentless, game-week-into-game-week hamster-wheel pace of the season proper made it difficult to believe the schedule of games was nearly over. After playing Carmel, win or lose, the playoffs would begin.

DiRienzo stepped away from the center of practice and stood on the field in his gray sweatshirt and black ball cap, surveying. He was dissatisfied with the tempo, and with areas of sloppiness that he saw. In all of his successful seasons of coaching at New Rochelle, the two state title years included, DiRienzo had never had an undefeated team. Not once. Now his Huguenots were aiming to go to 7–0. "I don't know," DiRienzo said. "Sometimes I wish we'd lost a game early on, just so that these guys could get a little scare into them, a little more awareness. A tough loss can do more to wake up a team than anything you try to teach them."

DiRienzo turned and paced off a bit, in thought. His left leg still ached at times from the ulcer surgery (in September he'd had it drained) but he hadn't used a cart on the field since shortly after the team got back from Brookwood. "Just can't do it," he said. "I'll let it really heal up after the season." Overhead a flock of Canadian geese suddenly appeared, wings beating, and flying together in a textbook V. They were headed south perhaps, or somewhere. DiRienzo looked up. "Perfect formation, every time," he said, laughing a little. "I wish all my football players were like that."

"WHERE'S FORREST? Coach, do you know where Jonathan Forrest is?" It was less than an hour before kickoff on that Friday night at Carmel, and as New Rochelle finished its pregame warmups, and the players started heading back to the locker room, three local Carmel-area kids—middle-schoolers by appearance—came up to Huguenots assistant Greg Foster at the side of the field. They were hoping to get Forrest's autograph, one of them said. "See, look," he added, holding up an iPhone, "I've got a picture of him as my screen saver!"

"He's inside," Foster told the boys. "He'll be out a little later. He's not in the game though. He's hurt."

Forrest and the other injured players who had been forced to miss practice that week—along with two other Huguenots who'd now been felled and quickly quarantined with the flu—were officially out of the game, all save for Jasper Baskerville, whose knee swelling had somewhat subsided and who was acutely aware that he was deep into the evensong of the high school football journey he so embraced and revered. "I'm not missing a single down if I don't have to," he had said during the week. Jasper was thinking he might go on to play in Division III; the football program at nearby Western Connecticut State had some interest. But he was not counting on it.

It was Jasper, barreling out in his big 56 jersey, who led the Huguenots out of the Carmel High locker room and onto the field, an assignment usually entrusted to Forrest and Corey Holder. A short time later, at the coin toss, only two of the three active captains—Demetrius Rodriguez and Quincy Mack, but not Holder—went out to meet the head referee and the opposing captains at the center of the field. DiRienzo had held back Holder as a punishment. "Coach says it's because I was playing dirty last week against Scarsdale," Holder said from the sideline, shrugging discontentedly. "He saw me doing some things on film he didn't like. So he said I couldn't lead the team out this week. I couldn't go out for the toss. I guess I did play dirty. But I was just fighting back after what they were doing to us! Coach says he doesn't care if we are right or wrong, we can't play dirty. We have to play the game the right way. I understand what he is saying. But I still think those guys had it coming."

Many of the parents had made the hourlong drive north to Carmel: Keith Wheeler's parents (even though Keith wouldn't play with his bruised shoulder). The Cohens. The Macks, including Quincy's sister. Donald Baron of course. Dawn Holder. Michael Cascio's mom, Gail. The Sterns. The parents greeted one another as they settled into the stands, and they talked among themselves about the undefeated season and about the traffic they'd endured on the drive up, and about some ongoing situations at the high school. Like their sons, these parents were unlikely social partners, from varied circumstances, thrust together by common high school demands, by football. They would never have known one another otherwise. Their social circles would never have overlapped.

Steve Lilly, Demetrius Rodriguez's dad, came to the game too. He had driven straight up after his shift at the Albert Einstein-Weiler Hospital in the Bronx, though by the time he arrived, midway through the first quarter, Lilly had just missed Demetrius's touchdown, an elegant, 27-yard, over-the-middle snare of a pass from Powell. The play opened the scoring in the game.

Lilly had come right down onto the sideline to let Demetrius know he was there and Demetrius lit up when he saw him. He walked straight over and wrapped his father in a solid embrace and told him about the touchdown. "I am so proud of this kid," said Lilly shortly afterward. "He's got his older brother Tyler and his younger brother Aidan, and the rule I give them is the three Fs: Focus. Follow through. Finish. They all do that—and that's because of sports. Wrestling. Football."

Tyler was a sophomore wrestler at SUNY-Cortland. Aidan played jayvee football for New Rochelle. "We talk about being the best at whatever you're doing," said Lilly. "On the field and in life. I'm working at Einstein. I'm a janitor there. And I want to be the best fucking janitor they have. It's like that. It's important." Lilly didn't get to many of the games—work often kept him away—so Demetrius had been thrilled he'd made it.

"Thanks for coming, Pops!" he'd said as he'd let go of that embrace.

The Rodriguez touchdown was the first of four in rapid succession for the Huguenots. Jared Baron broke off a 54-yard scoring run, CJ Anthony rushed in from 13 yards out, Powell scored on a quarterback keeper. Carmel went the entire first quarter without getting a first down. At the start of the second quarter, New Rochelle had a 27–0 lead and DiRienzo began filling the lineup with second- and third-stringers. He began running short-yardage plays into the center of the line. "That's Lou. That's the integrity," Carmel coach Cayea would say after the game. "He wasn't going to burn us."

In the second half, DiRienzo turned the play-calling over to coach Foster. "If you're in third-and-long you can run a pass play," he said. "You don't have to, but you can." Then DiRienzo walked far down the sideline, away from the area of play. The lights were bright around the field and in the stands everyone's breath steamed into the air. DiRienzo's sister Carmen had come to the game and the two of them stood together for a while talking as the game moved into the fourth quarter and wound inexorably down. The final score was 33–0, and the matchup had not, for even the briefest moment, been any kind of fight.

And while DiRienzo forbade the team from cheering or celebrating on the field—it would have been unseemly after an outcome like that—he did gather them together in the end zone, each player on one knee, surrounding him. "We are 7–0 and we are Number 1 in Section 1, and we know that," DiRienzo said. "But our season really starts now. We lose next week and we're done. Try to remember that. You're off tomorrow, no practice. Have fun tonight, but represent yourself well, walk proud and stay focused. People look at you when you're on top. We get right back to work on Sunday. Have your fun, but remember that there is a fine line between fun and trouble."

The team rode the bus back to New Rochelle together, still in their uniforms. DiRienzo wasn't along. He'd gone to the hospital with one of his players, a seasonlong backup who had gotten into the game at tailback, made his first carries of the year and then, in a routine pile-up near the end of the final quarter, broken his foot. On the bus, the boys were loose and happy, debating with exaggerated earnestness about what music should be played. Coach Fagan took over and settled on an old-school country-western mix, which drew an eruption of groans and sardonic cheers. There was laughter and constant chatter all the way home. "That bus ride was awesome," the senior receiver and cornerback Jack Stern would say later. "I think it was one of the best times of my whole career. We were so happy. And we were so together."

IN THE days that followed, Jonathan Forrest was not giddy like the others. Never the loud or rambunctious type, he seemed wholly without levity as he continued to nurse and rehabilitate his injured knee. After years of being a central life force on the team, a leader deeply entrenched in guiding and sustaining the day-to-day and week-to-week, Forrest was suddenly removed, sidelined. He could not lead in the way that he had always led, by example. Except for the foot injury he had worked through at the start of the season, the sprain that had curtailed him at Brookwood, this MCL situation was the first significant injury of Forrest's four-year varsity career.

In the week leading up to New Rochelle's first playoff game—the Huguenots would be at home on Saturday afternoon against a team from farther upstate, Mahopac High—Forrest attended practice but could not participate. He wore his jersey and sweatpants, listened in when the coaches went over particular plays and strategies, and each day briefly rode a stationary bike that Jim Benge had brought out and placed next to the field. Forrest rode the bike on very low resistance, per Dr. DeLaMora's orders, and he did not stay around for the entire three hours of practice. When one Huguenot father—John Hinchey, Chris's dad—came out a bit late to watch the team on Monday, he asked Kirby Mack and the other dads, "Has there been a Forrest sighting?"

Forrest spoke softly when he spoke at all. He said he was hoping to get back out there for the second playoff game (as Dr. DeLaMora had suggested he might be able to), but around the field he seemed sapped, discouraged. On Tuesday of that week Forrest tweeted that he had received his eighth collegiate offer, from the University of Rhode Island. On Wednesday he tweeted, "Just wanna be in college already."

While the other injured players had returned to practice, Forrest was joined on the sideline by a talented, swift junior who all year had been a valuable secondary contributor to the offense: Rashon McNeil. He had come to the team as a transfer student for 2014, but now, suddenly, he had been ruled ineligible for football, as well as for classes. The school district had determined that McNeil did not in fact live in New Rochelle; he lived in the Bronx and was traveling to the high school each day. McNeil had not worked particularly hard to hide this reality. His Twitter handle, for example, didn't stem from his surname—as in "jforrest_21" or "Holder_Era"—but was simply "bronxrebels7". And while his profile photo showed him muscling up in a New Rochelle T-shirt, the description below said that he was "Class of 2016, DB/WR/Ath Bronx NY." McNeil's plan all along was to move into New Rochelle that December, but for the time being he was still a Bronx resident, ineligible and off the team.

Steve Young and DiRienzo were questioned about whether they had been aware of McNeil's living situation, and thus his ineligibility, and both said they had not. The matter hadn't been much pursued by school officials or by external administrators. In the New Rochelle system, the discovery of illegally enrolled students, kids who commuted from somewhere else, was not at all uncommon. "I'd say the district does 400 house checks a year," Young suggested, a number confirmed by principal Reginald Richardson. "Kids bring in a bill or something that says they live at a certain address, but when you go to that address they don't really live there—it's an aunt's house or some other relative's or friend's or something."

Most of these illegal, nonresident students are not football players. Many are not athletes of any kind. New Rochelle High sits less than five miles from the New York City border, from the Bronx, a borough where at some high schools students pass through metal detectors on their way into the building, and where some dropout rates are alarmingly high. New Rochelle suggests a better, safer alternative to those city public schools. (Parents living within some other Westchester school systems, Mount

Vernon and Yonkers specifically, sometimes illicitly send their children to New Rochelle as well.) That's why a mom might put her teenager on a public transit bus, from the Bronx to New Rochelle each morning, hoping for a better education, a taste of suburbia, a path to a fuller life. Competitive sports issues surrounding nonresident or illegally recruited athletes are small—and in the larger scheme even insignificant—parts of the whole. Though he was now ineligible, McNeil still came to practice each day, wearing everyday clothes, hanging around with whoever was free, or squeezing a football and watching the drills. This was his family, he said, and there was nowhere else that he wanted to be.

McNeil was on the sideline for that home playoff game against Mahopac, too. He wore black jeans and a blue hoodie and he sat beside Forrest on the bench, a lighter presence beside Jonathan's still gloomy mien. Sometimes McNeil would toss a football with one of the guys, warm him up. Coach D was happy to have McNeil there; he didn't want to take the game away from him—"It's big for this kid"—and he also imagined that McNeil, lithe and long, with good hands, would be a factor the following season when he became eligible. Coach liked the idea that McNeil's apprenticeship, even if now somewhat sidetracked, was continuing.[1]

The Huguenot players had arrived at the school at 9 a.m. that day, way early for the 2 p.m. start. Their collective wake-up alarm had gone off the night before, when coach D had abruptly and prematurely curtailed a late, indoor practice—a startling decision less than 18 hours before the playoff season would begin. This had come at the end of another on-and-off week of practice for the Huguenots, another struggle for the coaching staff to get the group to concentrate consistently. "We push them, we pull them, we kick them, we yell at them, we talk with them, we hug them," said coach Fagan. "But they're kids. It's up to them."

On Friday evening the team was practicing inside the gym. "We were a little sloppy, and a couple of guys had made some really dumb mistakes

---

[1] McNeil did move to New Rochelle a few months later, as had been intended, and as a senior the next year, he indeed proved to be an important—and completely legal—part of the Huguenots offense.

on a play," Haitam Coughlin would later recall. "One of the guys on the line made a joke about it, and a bunch of kids cracked up."

Coach DiRienzo was not in the least amused. "Everyone go sit your asses on the bleachers!" he bellowed. And then, before the players could even get there, DiRienzo exploded again, "Oh, forget it, everyone just go home, get outta here," and he walked straight out of the gym.

"We stood around looking at each for like 10, 15 minutes," said Coughlin. "Then we kind of realized there was nothing we could do, so we left."

The team by now had developed a leadership council, a group that formed organically over the course of the season, and was made up of the captains plus several others—Jasper, Powell, Stern, Cowan. The group left the aborted practice that night and found DiRienzo in the football space, already watching game film and spitting tobacco into a Styrofoam cup. The players vowed to DiRienzo that they would come back the next day early, to try to right this wrong, and get prepared for the game against Mahopac. They said they knew they needed it. That was why the whole team showed up by 9 o'clock—still a couple of hours later than DiRienzo, but in good time nonetheless—for a session and a run-through that the coaches later said was as disciplined an effort as they had seen all year.

"Throwing them out of practice like that is serious," Louis Jr. said on the sideline just before the Mahopac game began. "He was really frustrated. My dad threw us out of practice once or twice during the years I was on the team, but never on the night before a game. And before a playoff game? No way."

It was a beautiful sunny football Saturday and the bleachers were nearly full when the Mahopac players ran onto the New Rochelle field two-by-two, holding hands. Each of them wore high pink socks, a reference to breast cancer awareness month, following the lead of the NFL. The Mahopac Indians ran a wing T option offense and the coach's son played on special teams; they had won three straight games, each by 20 points or more. That run lifted Mahopac to 5–2 on the season, a typical record for a typically solid team, although the thought among all of those who thought about such things was that New Rochelle would win this game, and comfortably.

The New Rochelle cheerleader, Dymond, sang the national anthem and Mantey Boahene gave a few words of encouragement to the team, the last little pep-blast on the field. Mantey said that he hadn't been able to be with the team the week before because he was "laying my stepfather to rest" and he urged the Huguenots to "Win the game! Do me a favor and win the game!"

Demetrius caught an early touchdown, but then Mahopac responded with a 15-yard scoring pass, taking a 7–6 lead and putting New Rochelle in the unfamiliar position of trailing. A few possessions later the Huguenots got the football on their own five-yard line. Noake was back in at center, his shoulder good enough to go, and Dylan Cohen and Corey Holder were bursting strong off the offensive line, and New Rochelle started pushing Mahopac around. Baron kept running for solid gains—nine yards here, five there, a break outside for 30. Wheeler ripped off a couple of nine- and 10-yard runs himself, and then Baron went into the end zone from two yards out and the 95-yard touchdown drive—the game-turner—was complete. Powell bulled his way in for the two-point conversion.

"You're leading 14–7, but you have to act like you're losing 14–7," said assistant coach Rich Tassello, addressing the defense at halftime inside the football space. "Do not let up. Keep doing just what you are doing, because they are unable to move the ball right now. But they will if you let up." Coach D added, "You do not have time to be fatigued. You have 24 minutes to either move on or go home crying. You have to dig deep."

Through the cinderblock walls you could hear the Mahopac coaches screaming at their players. Delivering their own halftime message, like bloody murder, really, screaming at the kids to play better, to play harder, to get certain things done. "Damn, listen to all that hollerin'," said Wheeler, setting off a roomful of snickers.

New Rochelle got the ball to start the third quarter and on the opening drive, with Baron leading the way moved deep into Mahopac territory. Some older New Ro regulars standing outside the fence at the far end of the field had taken to taunting Mahopac with, "He's in ninth grade, he's in ninth grade" each time Baron touched the ball. Powell then finished the drive by throwing a short touchdown pass to Demetrius. The score was 21–7 New Rochelle, and that's how the game would end.

Mahopac had not played badly, had led for a chunk of the first half, had quieted New Rochelle's Forrest-less offense for long stretches ("If we're going to continue to advance, we need to get a lot better offensively," DiRienzo told a local reporter after the game) and had, on the surface, made a game of it. But all the while New Rochelle had been playing defense, an intent, methodical, gang-tackling level of high school defense that left Mahopac little room to move, or breathe, the kind of defense that DiRienzo's teams are known for. All told in the game, Mahopac's rushing offense had produced zero yards. Zero.

"We did dig deep," DiRienzo said to the team when the game was over and the fans had begun to spill down from the bleachers. "You dug deep." The players knew that they would be in for practice the next day, extra running to seal the punishment for Friday night's foolery at practice. "Go see your families," coach D said. "And be back here tomorrow like we talked about. I'm proud of you."

CHAPTER 14

Arlington

**HATEVER THE** outcome of the 2014 Section 1 Class AA semifinal game—to be hosted by New Rochelle on the afternoon of Saturday, Nov. 1—it would be the final game on home turf for the Huguenot seniors. The semifinal also would be a rematch of sorts with the team from Arlington High, a 3,300-student school 65 miles due north from New Rochelle, deep into hilly Dutchess County, the uppermost region of Section 1. Arlington and New Rochelle had met two months earlier in an informal preseason scrimmage but the more significant link between the teams ran deeper: Arlington's coach was Dominick DeMatteo, the eldest son of the venerable Tony DeMatteo, Section 1's all-time winningest football coach, a towering figure throughout the region, and a 72-year-old man of great influence on Lou DiRienzo's professional life.

During DiRienzo's high school years in Tuckahoe, when he was working long summer days for his father at the quarry and weighing what he might do with himself in future years and how he might acknowledge his own limitations ("the advanced education life was for my sisters,

195

not for me") while at the same time leveraging the strength of his own balance—that "maturity and openness and stability even as a kid" as his sister Carmen describes it—he attended a football camp run by the DeMatteo brothers, Tony and Donald. "And that pretty much changed my life," DiRienzo says. "That's basically where all this started for me. Already back then Tony DeMatteo was a man of stature. When he spoke he commanded attention. That has not changed. You're drawn to him. You learn so much from listening to him, from watching him. The DeMatteo brothers showed me how to coach kids the right way, the way I felt I wanted to do it."[1]

In 1988, when he was a few years out of college and on his path as a high school coach, DiRienzo took a job as Tony DeMatteo's assistant at Roosevelt High in Yonkers. Less than three years after that, at the age of 28, DiRienzo got the head coaching position at New Rochelle. "My time under Tony DeMatteo at Roosevelt equipped me to be a head coach," he says. "It was an apprenticeship, and it gave me skills and tools that I still use."

Tony is now the coach at Somers High in Section 1; on his list of his disciples—he has been a head coach in the section for close to 50 years and has inspired dozens of former players and assistants to coaching lives—no one is more prominent than Lou. The two men still meet and talk often. They go to football conferences together, and they still have what DiRienzo calls "that mentor-pupil relationship."

Dominick DeMatteo, who is about a decade younger than DiRienzo, was a player on those late 1980s Roosevelt High teams ("So I've known him since he was a kid," DiRienzo says) and in 2014, just five days after the Huguenots returned from the retreat in Brookwood, Arlington and New Rochelle scrimmaged at a neutral site. For that meeting, played without quarters or official score, Lou had prepared New Rochelle to

---

[1] Donald, also a respected and beloved high school football coach in the area, died in 1999 of lung cancer. A few years later, a four-and-a-half-mile portion of the New York state highway system, a stretch running through lower Westchester, was designated the "Don and Tony DeMatteo Parkway."

defend Arlington's 21 personnel offensive package—two running backs, one tight end, two receivers. Over the course of the season, however, Arlington had begun turning at times to a 12 personnel package (one running back, two tight ends), to better spring one of their players who had emerged as a big-play runner.

"Quincy and the fellas are at our house watching film of that offense every night," Kirby Mack said three days before the semifinal showdown. "They talk like they're a little worried, but I think Arlington doesn't have shit. Yeah, they can run the ball a bit, but no one runs on New Ro. Nobody."

Kirby sat at a small stone table, 40 yards back from the practice field, with a few of the regulars—Donald Baron, Keith Wheeler Sr., John Hinchey—recalling old days and Section 1 playoffs past, and assessing the current New Rochelle team. They speculated about whom the Huguenots would play next, in the final, after beating Arlington: It would be a rematch with John Jay perhaps, or else a game against neighboring Mamaroneck, which was having its best season in memory behind a dangerous running back, Marquez Jackson-Allen, who had played youth football in New Rochelle's Youth Tackle League.

A bag of unshelled pistachios sat on the table and the three fathers worked and ate the nuts, little fillers for gaps in the conversation. Teachers or students who walked by often raised their hands in greeting to one or another or all of the men. Wheeler Sr. stood rather than sat, and he was consistently the most animated of the four, full of his usual second guesses and particular complaints. He was concerned, for example, that New Rochelle's offense was too predictable, not exotic enough. "We need a gadget play," Wheeler declared. "Every good team has to have gadget plays to break things up." The men chewed that one over for a while—just what kind of trick play might it be? A flea-flicker, probably, or a halfback pass, and who would be best to execute it? "Keith can throw the ball if he has to," Wheeler said of his son.

At one point the klatch got interrupted. The mother of a junior varsity player had come over from watching jayvee practice and she was in a state of mild concern. She had heard, she said, that the Arlington High football program was in trouble, that it had been beset by injuries. She said that a rumor had sprung up that Arlington might have to forfeit this upcoming game.

The suggestion engendered immediate dismissal from the men, some quick jokes and laughter. But the jayvee Mom stuck to her story, and to the details, creating a few minutes of confusion until some searching on smartphones revealed the facts: There was indeed a high school named Arlington with a football team in just the dire condition that the mother had described. Only this high school was in Riverside, Calif. The year before, one of that school's players had died from a head injury suffered on the field. This had caused a dramatic drop in football participation at the school, and then, during the 2014 season, a run of injuries to other players, including several concussions, had indeed forced the cancellation of the season, after eight winless games. All of this had been chronicled in a *New York Times* article on troubled high school football programs that had appeared that very morning, Oct. 29, 2014. The Arlington Lions of Riverside, Calif., were perhaps a symbol of parlous times in the sport, but the Arlington Admirals of Dutchess County, New York, were alive and thriving and coming in as scheduled to play the Huguenots for a berth in the Section 1 Class AA final.

THE PRACTICE schedule for New Rochelle was now six days a week, beginning with several hours of conditioning on Sunday. Quincy Mack, CJ Anthony, Demetrius Rodriguez, Justice Cowan and numerous others, seniors especially, were getting to school each day before 7 a.m. to lift a little, to go over more film, get some football work in before first bell. DiRienzo would be at school by that time too, hustling from weight room to film room to administrative offices, talking with players, taking early phone calls from parents, and trying to remind himself to prop up his bad leg whenever he could.

The kids, as their parents attested, were not having to be rousted out of bed in the morning these days, nor pushed out the front door. They woke, they ate, and they were ready to meet the day. As a team the Huguenots seemed high on the collective effort, energized by the mission before them. Practices were marked by proactiveness: players hushing themselves before a coach began to speak, or lining up for tackling drills before being asked, or scenes such as Chris Hinchey, still doing his Rudyesque best, running out unbidden behind the goalposts to field and retrieve balls as Robbie DeRocco kicked them one after the other after the other, pushing to regain his field goal form, to work his way back from the thigh and hip trouble that nagged at him.

"They're all so focused on this," said Charlotte Anthony, CJ's mom. "Football is CJ's life, and it's 24/7. I find him in his room when he should be doing homework and he's drawing out football plays in his notebook. Or he's watching tape." Charlotte, who is British, is herself a dedicated athlete and competes in Tough Mudder endurance races. She might have preferred that CJ played soccer, as her younger son did ("It's the more beautiful game," she says, laughing), but that had not happened; the prominence of CJ's father Jeffrey as a local youth football coach ensured it. Still, Charlotte likes the way that football "helps manage CJ's temper." She says she carries no real fear of his being seriously injured. "He is so physically fit," Charlotte reasons. "And he knows the game so well. When he did have an injury, to his left leg, he worked so hard through physical therapy to get himself back."

Charlotte had helped put together the Friday night team meal, which this week fell on Halloween, so that a few plastic pumpkins and some sprays of fake cobwebs adorned the gym. After the spaghetti and meatballs and salad, trays of cupcakes with orange-and-black icing came out and Quincy and Demetrius took it upon themselves to carry the trays from table to table, offering them up. In his fire-up speech, Jim Benge talked about how "Dominick DeMatteo will have his team ready to play tomorrow" and also conjured up some allegedly dirty tactics Arlington players had engaged in back at the August scrimmage. "This is payback," Benge said, "and you have not played your best football yet."

A late practice again followed the dinner, outside under temporary lights, and at the end of it DiRienzo brought the team together and warned the boys to steer clear of Halloween antics. It was a chilly night and black, without stars. "No shaving cream, no running around, spooking around, none of that," coach D said. "Go right home and get yourself some rest. I'll tell you what," he added, deadpanning. "You can each have one piece of candy. That's it."

RIGHT UP until that Friday before the game, Jonathan Forrest remained less than 100% sure that he would play against Arlington, and that uncertainty continued to dominate the conversation and chatter among those around the team. By Saturday morning, though, Forrest was declared fit and able, and after the pregame run-through he got some late treatment on his knee and upper leg from Becky Schwartzman. When Forrest walked into the football space a half hour before game time, the rest of the team was already there, in uniform, holding their helmets, sitting in the chairs. It was unusually quiet and most of the players were looking down, idle or fiddling absently with their hands.

"Hey, Forrest, how you feeling?" Demetrius called out as Jonny came in, echoing a question that had been asked many times by many people over the preceding days.

"Pretty good," Forrest said quietly.

"Well," Demetrius replied, and then he paused just so . . . "I don't caaaaaaaaare!" The quip sent loud laughter bouncing through the room, its perfect timing just the icebreaker the boys needed. A short time later, with some last spirited words from Reverend Leak ringing in their ears, they ran out to the field, along the way reaching up to tap a square sign that had been pinned above the doorway leading from the school. The sign read 48 MINUTES TO PLAY. A LIFETIME TO REMEMBER.

This was the coldest game day of the football season, no question, and rainier even than the afternoon that Ray Rice had come back to the sidelines. The unkind elements had taken their toll: The crowd in the New Rochelle bleachers was sparse, maybe 175, maybe 200. There seemed to be an equal number of people across the field on the Arlington side, grouped together under school-maroon-colored umbrellas, having driven the long way down to see their underdogs play. Arlington's mission in this game, as one of their top defensive players said, was to "shock the state."

The biting wet-gray weather and the small crowd lent a strange and slightly surreal aspect to the game—"There was something weird about it from the start," Haitam Coughlin would say—and the conditions may partly explain why Arlington fumbled the routine opening kickoff, immediately turning the ball over to New Rochelle. Soon after, CJ Anthony caught a short pass from Powell in the slot just inside the Arlington 10-yard line, swirled and shook off a couple of tacklers until he dived, airborne and ball extended with both arms, past the pylon. Touchdown. CJ landed hard, left shoulder down, and he got up grimacing even as he pumped his right fist in celebration. He headed straight through the sideline and through his teammates' head-tapping, butt-slapping congratulations until he found Becky. "My shoulder," he said to her, working off his helmet with his good arm, "Get it right, so I can go back in. Please." DeRocco meantime, his leg still balky, missed the extra-point attempt. Four minutes into the game and New Rochelle led 6–0.

Anthony, it turned out, wouldn't return. The pain from a sprained AC joint in that left shoulder soon led him inside the school where, as tears filled his eyes and he tried to fight off anger and disbelief, he was fitted with a temporary sling and allowed to return to the sideline. That injury disquieted the team, and so did something else: Forrest, though he had appeared sharp in the final practices, couldn't get himself right. He struggled to accelerate—a yard gained here, stopped at the line of scrimmage there—and he did not play at all on defense, using that time to stretch on the sideline, massage the knee, or ride the stationary bike that had been set up for him. When he ran the ball, Forrest couldn't get outside, and a few times he seemed inclined to go down early rather than fight through traffic for more yards. He was being very un-Forrest-like, trying to minimize contact. Pain from an injury can do that to a football player. "Haven't never seen him like this in my life," Corey Holder said to Bryce Davis during a timeout.

Not long after Anthony's score Greg Powell threw an interception that led to Arlington's tying the game at 6–6. After that, though, Powell guided New Rochelle on a solid touchdown drive, passing to Wheeler, passing to

Stern, and ultimately scoring on a keeper from four yards out to put New Rochelle ahead 13–6 with less than a minute to go in the opening quarter.

Now Jasper Baskerville was injured too, having taken a blow to the side of the head that he said he had brought upon himself. "I was hitting them hard, and on one play maybe I hit too hard," he said to Becky, "and then my whole right side went blurry." A concussion was feared (though later it was ruled out) and Schwartzman sat Jasper on the bench and asked him to try to follow her moving index finger with his eyes. He was not allowed back in the game until after the half.[2]

Three starting players were out and Mack was visibly limping on the field. Anthony, wearing a gray hoodie, still had on his eye black. His jersey, his helmet and his shoulder pack sat rumpled in a heap on the wet ground near the bench where he had pulled them off, creating the appearance that CJ had evaporated, his purple outfit lying there empty where he once was, like the black hat and cape of the wicked witch after she is melted by water in Oz.

---

[2] For the trainer Schwartzman, it had been a demanding and gratifying season. She had been more than proficient, excelling to the point that there was no question she would be asked to return as New Rochelle's head trainer. Yet the load of fall sports had been taxing. There had been a concussion on the soccer team to assess, and one on the cheerleading squad as well, and then there was football, with all of its concussion-related concerns—Michael Cascio's in particular–and the ongoing flow of injuries small and large, and the nonstop coach and player calls of "Becky! Becky! Get over here!" The potential for catastrophic injury on the football field haunted her a bit, Schwartzman allowed, especially since 2011 when, while she was studying at SUNY Cortland, a 16-year-old high school football player named Ridge Barden died after sustaining a head injury during a game a few miles from Cortland's campus. "I didn't have anything to do with treating him," Schwartzman said. "But I knew the trainers and some of the paramedics who did. They were shaken up. One minute the kid is making a tackle and the next minute he is dead. And even though they did everything right, there was nothing they could do to stop it." Schwartzman followed not only the technical and industry news in training and athletic medicine but the popular stories, too—she had read the piece about the Arlington High in California, for example—and it was not unusual for her to bring up such news on the sidelines, out of earshot of the coaches and kids. A few days before this semifinal game, for example, she talked about a high school football player from Tampa who the weekend before had had his leg amputated after a freak on-field knee injury led to blood clots. "Crazy," said Schwartzman. "Sometimes it's just crazy."

Even undermanned, the Huguenots were stingy on defense, allowing only one Arlington drive of any significance the rest of the first half. And New Rochelle appeared to have even that drive stopped, forcing Arlington into fourth-and-long. The Admirals, though, converted that play by connecting on an 18-yard touchdown pass—a sudden, improbable jab that made it 13–13 at halftime. Dominick DeMatteo's kids had indeed come downstate to play.

The Huguenots were quiet and uncomfortable as they assembled in the classroom at the half. "We are in a football game, boys, a 48-minute football game like I told you we were gonna be," DiRienzo said. He called out gruffly to Jim Benge to "get some fucking water for these guys," and Benge, grumbling that working for DiRienzo was like having another wife, went and got some bottles and brought them in to be passed around. Coach D worked on the grease board for a while, setting up a play for the first offensive series, adjusting the pass defense.

"I don't know," he said finally, capping the marker and turning to face the group straight-on, "this game could be 26–26 after 48 minutes. I don't know. I can tell you that I don't like the looks on your faces though. This is the game we are in, right now. I can't make you want to play it—that has to come from inside each one of you." A pause as coach D looked around the room. "This is not the time for talking anymore. This is no time for talking . . . ."

Back out on the sideline, rain still falling intermittently and the team about to take the field to receive the kickoff, Demetrius Rodriguez exhorted everyone to give extra effort on every play. Suddenly Justice Cowan started yelling, "This is not going to be the last football game we ever play. I am not fucking losing! I am not fucking losing!" Moments later that kickoff was up. Wheeler caught the ball and, weaving, ran it back, past midfield and then some—all the way to the Arlington 16-yard line, thrilling the undersized crowd in the bleachers and sending a bolt of jubilation through the New Rochelle sideline. "Here we go, boys! Here we go!" Demetrius crowed.

But the stirring runback yielded little return. On third-and-6, Forrest took a three-yard loss back to the 15-yard line, and on fourth-and-9,

DiRienzo, unhappy with the kicking conditions on the field, left the offense out to try for a first down—Powell carried for seven yards. Two yards shy. Arlington took over on downs with the score still tied. Late in that third quarter Powell threw his second interception of the day—to the same player who caught the first one, a 5' 10" All-Section Arlington cornerback named Ryan Denardo. He stepped in front of Jack Stern at the 24-yard line, leaped for the catch and ran the football all the way back into the end zone, a pick-six that put New Rochelle in a position it had not been in all year: Trailing by a touchdown, 20–13, with just 15 minutes to play.

A few of the dads in the crowd, Kirby Mack and Keith Wheeler Sr. and Mike Cohen, had made their way down from the bleachers and were now standing at field level, on the far end of the sideline. Some of New Rochelle's second- and third-stringers stood huddled together to keep warm. Benge, in his purple slicker, wore a soft, brimmed hat with a camouflage pattern. The former Huguenot Chris Cowgill was among the onlookers, along with a pack of other alums, and as the fourth quarter advanced they kept shouting out encouragement to the team. "They live to beat New Ro, but that is not happening!" Cowgill sang out.

It was Baron now who carried the ball—no longer the hobbled Forrest—and it was Baron who, with 7½ minutes on the clock, swung to the right side behind his blockers, got to the edge and shucked past the defense to disappear down the far sideline and on into the end zone, 54 yards and a spray of wet earth behind him. Touchdown!

The New Ro cheerleaders broke into a frenzied routine involving high leaps and the singsong spelling of words in unison. CJ Anthony, his eyes bloodshot from tears, stepped forward to join his teammates in celebration, and the rain had even stopped for a while. The team had not been tested much all season, not since the overtime game against John Jay, Week 3, but they were being tested now. They still needed the extra point to tie the score, no sure thing given DeRocco's bad leg. But the kick went up and it was good. 20–20.

"Let's get this done, boys, let's get this done," said Haitam Coughlin, pacing and clapping. Coaches Fagan and Violante were moving up and down the sideline too, for different angles of view. Fagan was on the headset talking urgently about what plays to call for the offense. The injured Jasper, after a phone call with Dr. DeLaMora, had gotten back in there, helping to fortify both sides of the ball. A little group of Mighty Mites players, Mantey Boahene's boy and others, had stopped their usual horsing around and turned to watch the end of the game.

New Rochelle did just what it needed to do, forcing and recovering an Arlington fumble near midfield with 1:20 remaining in the game. The Huguenots had the end of regulation by the throat. They might score here and come away winners or at the least they would send the game to overtime and, as the better team and playing on their home field, they would like their chances.

The first two plays of New Rochelle's postfumble possession, a run and an incomplete pass, got nothing. Now it was third-down-and-10 with 30 seconds to play. Powell, taking the shotgun snap from Noake, passed once more, throwing the ball over the middle of the field, maybe 15 yards beyond the line of scrimmage. Demetrius Rodriguez appeared to be the intended target, but the pass was badly underthrown. The only player with a chance to catch it was a standout senior linebacker for Arlington named Bailey Faldetta. He made the interception easily, alone in the center of the field, and then he took off downfield. Faldetta returned the ball not 10 yards or 15, or 20, but 56 yards, all the way to New Rochelle's 11-yard line where Dylan Cohen finally wrapped him up.

Groans and shouted expletives went up, and then a bizarre, disbelieving near silence enveloped the New Rochelle sideline as the offense came off the field and the defense went on. Across the field the Arlington side was giddy, the players high-fiving one another and butting helmets in their own, joyous, pinch-me disbelief. Two snaps later Arlington lined up for a short field goal. Up. Good. Final score: Admirals 23. Huguenots 20. New Rochelle's season was over.

After he had thrown that interception, his third and most fateful of the day, Powell had come to the sideline and sunk jelly-legged onto the bench, distraught and sobbing. His teammates, Shameek Miller and Manny Walker, came over to him. Shameek, who 10 weeks earlier during that hot afternoon scrimmage on the lower field at Camp Brookwood, had himself been in tears on the sideline, brought his face right up to Powell's. "You're good, man. You are good," Shameek said "It's all right. You're good. This is going to be O.K." Powell, though, was lost in his emotions. He put his head down and into his hands, inconsolable.

The teams lined up for the postgame handshakes, and at the end of the lines coach D and Dominick DeMatteo embraced and exchanged a few words, their shared values and histories implicitly acknowledged before they headed off separately to address their teams. The Huguenots were assembled in the far end zone. "They made one more good play than we made," said DiRienzo to the stricken group. The boys had taken a knee and were looking toward him, one last time. Some of the players were red-eyed and sniffling. Others had a hollowed look. Powell kept on sobbing, so that coach D, as he tried to get the team settled, admonished, "Greg, stop all that." Tyler Cohen and Alex X., Jasper and Holder. All there with empty faces. Anthony stood in his gray hoodie with his arm in a sling and Dylan Cohen knelt beside him.

"There is nothing I can say now that will be sufficient," DiRienzo said. "They made one more good play than we made. As you walk off this field, you keep your head up. You walk with dignity. You walk with class. There is no finger-pointing. We all made mistakes. I made mistakes, you made mistakes. We made them together. When I talk to you about commitment," he continued, his voice cracking the way it does, "when I talk to you about the inner circle, this is when you will need that more than ever. Remember that, whatever people say, nobody's opinion counts but mine and yours. Nobody's opinion counts but mine and yours. Let's go home."

———

THE BOYS went off past the cheerleaders who wore white rain ponchos over their uniforms and stood in two lines, putting on brave faces and applauding. A few moms, Dawn Holder not surprisingly among them, had also come onto the field and they too clapped, reaching out to give this boy or that one a hug. "You've had a great year," Dawn kept saying. "We love you."

The weeping continued in the locker room for many of them. Powell went off by himself into the shower area shouting and cursing and pounding the walls. Alex Gaudio, the big guy who had played only a handful of downs all year, sobbed in great, body-racking heaves. It didn't matter whether you were a star of the team or the last man on the bench, the loss was felt by everyone together. Demetrius wept stoically and Cowan wept with a vengeance, and Chris Hinchey wept too. Others mourned less conspicuously, bereft in expression, shocked, moving slowly and without purpose around the crowded room. Gradually players started peeling off their uniforms, their cleats, their shoulder packs and their thigh pads and getting dressed in every-day clothes. It was not simply the loss of this game, but the end of the whole experience, the abrupt disbanding of the team as they knew it. Benge came into the locker room and set down a large container filled with individual bags of Halloween candy that the cheerleaders had packaged up for the team.

The players each took a bag (sometimes two) as they left, individually or in groups of two or three. Some went over to see coach D to shake his hand. DiRienzo was in the football space, his face reddened by the cold and his ragged emotions, spitting tobacco into a cup. He kept going over the various X's and O's of the game with Keith Fagan, recounting the particular play-calls and the details of what they had done right and what they had failed to do. "I've been on both sides of this kind of game," DiRienzo said. "I get as emotional as the kids do."

Forrest stopped over to shake hands with coach D as well, a last brief stop before slipping out. Maybe it was the way his season ended, or maybe it was the uncertainty ahead, the knowledge that his injury and limitations over the final games had cooled some of his college suitors, but for whatever reason Forrest was not as present in the collective postgame grieving as most of the others were. He dressed quietly and said a few goodbyes and see-you-Mondays, and then he was gone. Later that afternoon, though, Forrest tweeted out a few thoughts about his time playing football at New Rochelle. One tweet showed Forrest and coach D embracing on the field. Another tweet began, "Best 4 years of my life, hands down."

Shameek had come into the hallway outside the locker room. Some parents were there, some siblings and various others. Shameek was saying to everyone and to no one in particular that he did not want there to be no more practice. In fact he wanted to have practice again the very next day, he said, so the team could "fix this." Jasper was in the hallway now too, waiting for CJ who was giving him a ride home. Jared Baron emerged and shook hands firmly with some of the adults there and then walked, his back straight, out the door. As the minutes wore on, the numbers thinned, and the sounds of distress stopped echoing through the locker room.

Among the last to leave was Quincy Mack. After his handshake with DiRienzo, he walked alone down the empty school hallway and out the door to meet his father, who stood waiting just outside. Quincy was alone—that is, save for two boys of about 10 years old who trailed 15 feet behind him. "I don't know who they are," Quincy said to his dad.

"That's the fan club," Kirby explained. "That's two young boys thinking, Yeah, I want to be a linebacker like that too."

Quincy wore a black rain jacket, and a pair of Beats headphones rested on his shoulders, somewhat askew. He came over and hugged Kirby and then hugged another man who was there talking with Kirby, James Valentin. He had coached Quincy back in Mighty Mites and then had gone on to serve a tour as a soldier in Iraq. Now Valentin was back and coaching youth football players 90 minutes north, near Poughkeepsie. The connection to Q was still strong from their football days together. "There is going to be life after this loss," Valentin said to Quincy. "There will be, there always is, even though you don't think so now."

Quincy plays baseball too. He's a powerful batter and he loves that sport, the feel and rhythm of it. He said that now he would take one week off so his body could heal, but that then he couldn't wait to join the baseball team for fall workouts. Quincy was standing under the eave of the school building, as the rain had begun to fall again, straight down through the breezeless air. Valentin held a striped umbrella.

And yet as much as he did love baseball, Quincy said, nothing could compare to the camaraderie, the commitment, the energy and the love—yes, this was a word he used—of that football team. "My team-mates are like brothers to me, and seeing them hurt is what makes this loss hurt me even more."

Quincy said how the every-dayness of the football team, being on the field or in the film room, getting hit, hitting and helping people back up, was what made it all worthwhile. He talked about how he had come over from Mount Vernon and that he had been genuinely moved when the players named him a captain. Quincy said he took his position as a team leader very seriously, that he thought about it every single day and that he would miss that role now that it was gone. He talked about how much coach D and the coaching staff meant to him and to all the players—what an inspiration to see the work that these coaches put in, how DiRienzo "was always there early in the morning for us" and how he "cared about all of our lives. He helped us stay on our grades, he talked to us about what schools to go to. He paid attention to us."

Quincy knew he might have a chance to play either baseball or football at a college somewhere, Division III or junior college most likely, and he said that despite the physical toll of football—he still had that pin in his hip, and the limping on the field came from severe back pain he had been nursing for weeks—he would definitely play football not baseball if forced to choose. He liked to hit, he said. He liked that contact.

Quincy paused. Justice Cowan came out of the building and stopped there under the eave and the two boys embraced, holding it without ex-changing a word. Then Justice walked off into the cold, rainy afternoon. And as Quincy watched him go, he declared suddenly that he wished he could relive all of what had happened over the past few months on the football team, the ups, the downs, the great highs and the hard parts even. "Yeah, I wish it were summer again right now and the season hadn't started," Quincy said. "I wish I could do it all again."

CHAPTER 15

To Play or Not to Play

**HEY WERE** back in school that Monday, glum and reeling and battered, but back in school. Quincy still moved gingerly, and CJ had his arm in a sling, and Forrest limped like a man with a wooden leg. Although the team was saluted for its fine season during the morning announcements, there was no celebrating. All day the hallways were quieter than they usually were when the football guys were around, "almost like a mute button was pressed," one senior at the school said. "It was pretty weird actually." A few teachers stopped by to see DiRienzo and sympathize about the loss—paying a condolence call as it were—but there was nothing like the usual football-season bustle near the coaches' rooms or outside the gym.

The players all came down there after the final bell, though, going into the boys' locker room, the security guard greeting them quietly as they passed. There was gear in the lockers that needed to be retrieved, and each player pulled out his pack and his white jersey and his purple jersey, and his helmet and whatever other pads or protective pieces he had been using at the end of the year. They gathered these things, each of them, and then trudged out of the locker room and into the hallway—a sporadic, strange and silent march—and over to Jim Benge in the equipment room to turn it all in. "All right," Benge would say as each kid's gear came to him, marking it off on a sheet on a clipboard. "O.K."

A few of the players had "forgotten" their white jerseys, and Benge, aware that this happens every year, nodded and said, "By the end of the week, all right, or else I have to come after it." Corey Holder allowed to a couple of teammates that his jersey had not exactly been forgotten, that he just wasn't quite ready to give it back. For Corey and for many of the boys that jersey, meaning the number stitched upon it, had become an identity—in the games, during practices, when they wore it to school on Fridays, everywhere. Garrett Noake had a purple decal of his 53 adorning his backpack; Jack Stern, number 11, sometimes got referred to as "Ones."

They should have been going out there to the field to run the linebacker drills or the TNTs. They should have been setting up chairs around the screen in the football space to break down game film ahead of a rematch with John Jay–East Fishkill. They should have been needling one another and lacing up their cleats on the locker room benches, while coach Foster or coach Violante yelled for them to get a move on. But they weren't doing any of that. None of those things had purpose anymore. The kids all wore their school-day clothes and carried their backpacks, and after the gear had all been returned they made their way toward the classroom where coach D was going to address the team, the seniors first and separately from the rest.

DiRienzo barely mentioned what had happened in the game against Arlington 48 hours before. There was no advantage in reliving that, he said. There were about two dozen seniors in all, a little more than half the team. He talked to them about always remembering the importance of having that inner circle of people they could trust. He reminded them how young they were, starting out in adult life, and that they should listen only to those people who had their "best interest in heart, who care about you and are invested in what's best for you." This wasn't advice about just football, coach D said, "it applies to your further education and it applies to your job, whether you become a sanitation worker or the CEO of IBM. Listen to the people on the inside who know you. Not to the people on the outside who don't."

He told the seniors that he needed them to get their transcripts together and their SAT scores and to make an appointment to come and see him so they could put things in their folder and update their college plan. "I need about 20 minutes of your time. It doesn't matter if you are wanting to play football next year or not, I will look at what you have and listen to what you are thinking about, and I will help you get into school," he said. He suggested that if they *did* want to try to play football somewhere they should make sure that they got their best highlight film put together and posted on the Hudl site where recruiters could find them. "See coach Fagan for that. I do not know how to make those tapes." DiRienzo said he was available every day before school, and between 12:30 and two in the afternoon, and then again at the end of the school day. He wrote those times in clear print on the whiteboard and then stood looking at them for a moment so that the kids did too.

"Make an appointment and come see me, and we'll get everything straight, make sure you have an idea and a strategy for what you want to do," DiRienzo reiterated. The plain gray ball cap he wore might as well have said "guidance counselor" on it. "Make that appointment. I may remind you once, but I am not going to hunt after you. It's your job to do this if you want my help."

He talked more about the process and procedure around preparing and applying for college, and said how the kids should make sure to tell their parents to apply for FAFSA, the federal student financial aid package. A couple of players asked questions about the deadlines and DiRienzo's entire address, those questions included, lasted 10 minutes, maybe 12. Then the kids got up from the chairs and left the football classroom, essentially for good.

For the underclassmen, though, the younger boys who came in soon after the seniors were done, essentially 19 juniors and freshman Jared Baron, coach D had a longer, saltier message. He brought up college and school matters with them too, about the importance of getting their grades in order right away. "If you got a 65 in your English class, you have to make that up in night school this year, not as a senior." And he told them about his office hours and that they too should set up appointments to talk with him about their hopes and ideas for college.

But to this group DiRienzo did have a lot to say about the football season just past, and about the season now in front of them. They could learn more from the game against Arlington than they could from the big wins against North Rockland or Ossining or Mahopac or any of them, DiRienzo said. "I don't know that Arlington won that game on Saturday. I think we lost it. That will leave a bitter taste in your mouth. It should. I know it leaves a bitter taste in my mouth. The discipline that it will take to get rid of that bitter taste begins from the time we step into that weight room until the end of the next season." He paused and looked around the room. Everyone seemed to be paying attention. Coach Fagan was in there too, standing quietly in the back.

"We'll start weight room work on Monday. It's voluntary," DiRienzo said. "I'm going to be in there with you. I'm not going to be there for just two guys, but I know there were 10 of you here in the weight room yesterday so that's a start. Now you'll take the rest of the week off to get your heads right, and we will start this up fresh."

DiRienzo continued by recalling some of the things that had happened during the season that he didn't want to see happen again. Like the hoo-hawing that had led him to throw the team out of the gym during that Friday night practice a few weeks earlier. That had simply been a waste of time he said, growing increasingly annoyed as he thought back on it. That kind of messing around made practice "as useless as tits on a bull. Have you ever felt tits on a bull? I didn't think so.

"I apologize if I'm a little edgy," DiRienzo added, "but this is the way I feel today. If you don't like this demeanor than maybe you should figure out something else you're going to do in the fall. Because I'm going to hold you accountable for everything. I'm going to make sure my coaches hold you accountable in every single individual drill. There's not going to be any more of, 'I'm going to talk to this guy to get him motivated.' You have to motivate yourself. Get in the fucking drill! Either be ready to go or go do something else.

"I am no longer going to be a social worker. I had to be that this year, but I have X'd that out of my job description. I'm not a social worker and I'm not here to help you make your daddies happy. Been there, did it, don't like it. I know I'm being a little edgy, but I want you to know from now on, this is the direction we're going. My responsibility as the head football coach at New Rochelle is to win football games."

The kids looked taken aback. They were still raw from the loss. As a group they had almost broken into laughter at coach D's tits-on-a-bull allusion before realizing that he was not in fact joking in the least. Coach Fagan had had to check a grin himself at times at what DiRienzo said. "Not be a social worker?" Fagan said later that afternoon with a chuckle. "*Of course* he's going to be a social worker. He's said stuff like that before because he gets frustrated when the kids don't lay it all out. But he's a sucker for them and how they are feeling and processing things. Yes, he wants to win. He cares about that a lot. He gets feisty and he cares about discipline as a value and as a means to an end. We all do. But not be a social worker? Hah! You watch. In two days he'll be sitting in here talking with a kid about what's going on at home. He can't help it."

After leaving the meeting, many of the underclassmen made their way outside, leaving from the back of the school. A few joined a group of girls who'd been waiting for them, and some of the others headed out to the parking area, to meet some kids who were hanging around in their cars with the windows down. It was a gray day for the most part, but not cold. The football field was empty, save for one corner of it where a group of six guys in a circle kicked around a soccer ball among themselves. Out in front of Chicken Joe's on North Avenue a crowd of teenagers had congregated, just hanging around. Holder was there with Demetrius Rodriguez and Bryce Davis and Justice Cowan, and they were showing each other things on their phones. CJ might have been around too, but he had gone to the doctor to get an MRI on his shoulder.

DiRienzo often reminded his players that anyone could come see him privately for any reason. "I'm here every day," he would say. This gave a sense of solidity and reliability, something the players could count on. And at the end of his talk to the juniors that afternoon he had looked over at Powell and said "Greg, come on back." That's where the two of them were now, sitting side-by-side in the football space, watching film of the Arlington game, watching Powell specifically. "You see right here?" coach D said, freezing the image. "Right here you have to plant your foot before you throw. When you don't plant your foot, that's when the ball is going to tail off. That's when you get into trouble. This is something that we're going to fix."

THE HUGUENOTS would have a very successful year in 2015, once again going undefeated through the regular season. In late September they won at Arlington, 33–6. On Halloween they won at Scarsdale 33–7. New Rochelle was 11–0 by the time it reached the Class AA state semifinals—the ninth time in 15 years that DiRienzo's team had made it that far—and there, playing up at a neutral site in Kingston, N.Y., the team lost to Saratoga Springs in the most heartbreaking way. Several missed chances late in the game (including a drive that ended at the one-yard line) left the Huguenots trailing 32–29 in the final minute. And though it appeared that their kicker, a kid named Omar Pulido, had hit the game-tying field goal with 37 seconds to play, Saratoga's coach had called timeout just before the snap. New Rochelle had to try the kick again and this time Pulido missed, sending the ball wide to the right. "We didn't lose because of a lack of preparation. We didn't lose because of a lack of effort. We played hard," DiRienzo said after the game, adding of his players: "They are crushed. Sometimes life hurts. . . . It's how they rebound from it."

New Rochelle's deep run in 2015 was led partly by the dynamic play of Rashon McNeil and Keelan Thomas, both seniors who had been shut down in '14 due to eligibility issues, and also by Jared Baron, who was now, as a sophomore, a prominent ballcarrier and a high-impact line-backer. The most crucial leader, though, was Powell, who had matured into a smart, poised and driven quarterback, ultimately becoming a third-team All-State selection. Powell had made himself into a strong candidate for a Division II scholarship, and he believed, as ever, in even bigger possibilities. His Twitter profile included the declaration "DI Bound" as well as an adaptation of Forrest's 2014 mantra, "On a Mission to a Free Tuition."

"Greg took that loss to Arlington at the end of 2014 personally," says DiRienzo. "He came back determined to do things differently and to create more positive outcomes. He's the epitome of the lessons learned from that game."[1]

Many of the graduated seniors from the 2014 team came around in 2015, joining alumni like the Cargills and Mantey Boahene on the sideline during games, or using the weight room and visiting with coach D. Quincy Mack was playing at Lackawanna junior college in Pennsylvania before a hip injury ended his season early. Jasper Baskerville played at Division III Western Connecticut, and Garrett Noake at Division III Utica in New York. Corey Holder had gotten into ASA College in Brooklyn, a two-year school that produces Division I players. He had made the travel team.

Others among the pivotal 2014 New Rochelle seniors enrolled in college but were not playing football: Jack Stern at Towson in Maryland; Demetrius Rodriguez at Westchester Community College; Keith Wheeler at Monroe College in New Rochelle; CJ Anthony at a state college a few hours north; Bryce Davis at Blinn, a junior college in Texas.

Jonathan Forrest, it turned out, did not go to school or play football at all that following year. The forgettable, injury-hobbled coda to his senior season had changed his perspectives and opportunities and led him to enroll in a prep school where he planned to spend a semester, taking classes and reestablishing himself on the field so as to go on to college from there. But in late summer Forrest tore his left hamstring while running. It was a bad tear, and while he avoided surgery—"just a lot of rest and a lot of rehab," he said—the injury scotched his prep

---

[1] The Cohen twins were stalwarts on the 2015 team as well, both Tyler and Dylan distinguishing themselves. Early in the year Dylan missed a game with a suspected concussion—an event that per his mother's stipulations might have ended football for him. But he was soon deemed fit to play, a concussion not firmly established and returned to the field the following week.

school plans. Finally he accepted an offer from Temple University as a preferred walk-on for the 2016 season.

A little more than a month after that 2015 state semifinal game, on Christmas Day, the movie *Concussion*, starring Will Smith, came out in theaters across the country. DiRienzo did not go to see it. He knows the basic story line—just about everyone in football does—and he doesn't like that it portrays the game as a cauldron for brain injuries. Coach D will point out that the NFL has made important, safety-minded rules changes since the early 2000s when the movie takes place, that is, when Dr. Bennet Omalu, working with the University of Pittsburgh, was discovering and categorizing repeated cases of extensive brain damage in former NFL players. Omalu's pioneering work, as *Concussion* distills, suggested that because of the nature of the sport, such damage would inevitably afflict hundreds, even thousands of players. Time has borne this out. Whether the NFL's crackdown on helmet-to-helmet hits and its abolition of wedge blocking on kickoff returns, and its codified, more sensitive concussion treatment protocol will significantly reduce the number and severity of brain injuries remains to be seen, or may never be known.

DiRienzo, understandably, did not feel eager to see a movie with a message and an aura that is, in the end, a threat to his livelihood, to the family trade. As he tells his seniors at the end of each season, "You are moving on to the next phase of your life. For me there is no next phase. I coach football at New Rochelle. That's what I do. I do it in June, in September, in February, in March, in all the months of the year." Both of DiRienzo's sons, Louis Jr. and Andrew, were closing in on teaching degrees and deciding whether to try to begin their football-coaching lives in the college game or in high school.

"What we are doing at this level is not what is happening in the NFL," says DiRienzo. "So I don't like the implication that it is. High school football gives kids something unique. Something they aren't going to get any other way and something very valuable. We who are in this profession and associated with high school football have to believe that something special and vital is going on here. Or else why are we doing this? That's what it is all about."

"WOULD YOU?" people often ask me. "Would you let your son play football?"

I do not in fact have a son. I have two girls, and a nephew who played three years of football at a public high school near Boston. When I'm asked this question it is in the larger, societal spirit in which the question tends to be understood, and in which this narrative is framed.

I came to writing this book without an agenda, but with high curiosity. And now, on the other side of inquiry and immersion, of sifting through the "to play or not to play" question far beyond the point of distraction, I am without an agenda still.

I've talked with people who see football as a blight, boxing-like, and an ill that society could and should do without; they'll exaggerate football's risks, overstate the brutality of the culture. I've talked to others who swear by football to the point of rationalizing away or even dismissing its dangers, to shrugging off the violence at the heart of the game. In truth, though, it's not as simple as either view. It's complicated. The question of whether young men will continue to play football in the droves that they play it now, and whether, from an ethical standpoint, they *should* play it, may be the existential debate at the center of American sports.

One year after Tom Cutinella died following his on-field collision, former classmates gathered in vigil at Shoreham-Wading River High. A scholarship has been set up in Tom's name, to be awarded each year to a student who, among other things, exhibits "characteristics of kindness, modesty [and] selflessness." Tom was also publicly remembered, right about that time, at the annual Tunnel to Towers 5K race in New York City, an event born of the 9/11 tragedy that raises money for veterans and first responders, and a race that Tom had run in.

About two months later, on Dec. 17, 2015, in Knoxville, Tenn., a 15-year-old kid named Zaevion Dobson threw himself in front of three girls he was not related to, shielding them from a spray of random bullets. The girls were not hurt. Zaevion was killed.

Is the fact that Tom Cutinella twice volunteered to run in that Tunnel to Towers charity race and the fact that at age 16 he told his parents he wanted to become an organ donor consistent with the kind of person who commits to the task of being a lineman on a high school football team? Did the fact that Zaevion Dobson was a devoted football player, a sophomore fullback and linebacker on the varsity team at Fulton High, have anything to do with his instinct to protect?

It is not a surprise to learn also of a coach in Israel who uses football drills and games as a means to prepare high school boys for potential military battle. "The mentality of football is very similar to what you try to instill in elite combat units," the coach, Itay Ashkenazi, told the Associated Press. "Most of them coming in, they don't know football . . . . They fall in love with the values we try to build up, you know, the team concept, the getting tough mentality and physicality." High school football is a construct that puts young men through hard physical, psychological and social pressures that they learn to handle and sometimes thrive on. Other sports do that, but football is its own arena with its own demands, its own risks and its own rewards.

Nor is it a surprise that during the 2015 season 11 more high school boys died playing football—of heat stroke, from a broken neck, from brain swelling, from blunt force trauma to the head. That is, as ever, more deaths than in all other high school sports combined. And the injury rate in football continues to be higher than in any other high school sport by an order of magnitude.

So might it be that that autumn of 2014 was indeed a tipping point for the game and its future? Was it around that time that football, as an institution, finally plateaued? It's too early to tell of course. Stories continue to come in of youth and high school football programs shutting down, but so do stories of such programs developing and expanding. Participation numbers show clear signs of instability but they are not yet indicative of a long-term trend. Rome was neither built nor did it decline in a day.

It was in the autumn of 2014, on Oct. 27 as many high school football seasons were nearing their playoffs, that filming of the movie *Concussion* began. And it was all the uneasy news surrounding football that fall—not least the reveal that the NFL had acknowledged that so many of its players were bound for brain damage—that intensified the study of concussions: more grants, more research, and the brains of more and more players being donated for assessment.

In 2016, *The New York Times* told the story of Tyler Sash, a retired New York Giants safety who, after behaving erratically for several years, had died from an accidental overdose of pain medication at his Iowa home. Sash was 27 years old. He had appeared in only 27 NFL games, credited with 19 tackles. When he was cut from the Giants in '13 at age 25, his effectiveness lessened by multiple shoulder surgeries, he had played football for 16 years. The vast majority of that football came at the amateur level—youth league, Oskaloosa High, three years at Iowa. Sash had talked about his uneven mental state, his trouble concentrating and keeping calm, and when his autopsy came back from the brain center at Boston University, the results were just as the family feared: heavy markings of chronic traumatic encephalopathy, C.T.E.

One projection of football's future is that its constituency will continue to divide. The kids who play the game, and their parents, will be those who see the sport as a way to advance, to gain access to higher education they otherwise would not have; to get, in the rare cases, a shot at a Division I program or, rarest of the rare, the NFL. But kids who don't have the physical ability to aspire to a high level, or who have other pathways to college and the means to pay for it, simply won't play football. Why risk it? There's not enough to be gained. You might view this as a practical application of prospect theory. You might call it common sense.

Yet it's an unhappy divide. The notion of football as a sport overwhelmingly played by the have-nots and consumed by the haves is not an easy notion to bear. Something will be deeply lost.

If I let my son play football, I would embrace all that the game could give him—the strength, the knowledge, the sheer fun—but I wouldn't kid myself. I would accept that my son would at some point suffer a concussion, quite possibly several. However much I trusted him, I'd know there would be a chance he wouldn't tell me or anyone else if he did suffer one. And he would sustain other injuries playing football too, caused by violent impact. I'd have to feel comfortable with the risk.

If I let my son play high school football I would of course want him to have the best and most safety-oriented helmet available, but I wouldn't kid myself. I'd understand that that helmet, however firmly constructed, could not protect his brain. I would trust that helmet the way the atheist prays in the foxhole, figuring it couldn't hurt.

If my son did play football I'd want him to play for a responsible, intelligent coach who abided by the values of discipline and honesty, who had a kindness to him and who thought of his players' safety before he thought of winning a game. But I wouldn't kid myself. I'd know that no coach, however scrupulous and well-intentioned, could eliminate the risks of the game.

"Would you let your son play football?" rings differently to every person in every circumstance, defying an objective answer. I now believe, and for this I'm grateful, that I understand the question.

ON SEPT. 27, 2015, Kelli Cutinella, Tom's mother, ran in that annual Tunnel to Towers 5K race. It had been a year since Tom's death. Kelli missed her son deeply, of course, and she felt this was a way to get closer to him. Tom's father Frank was at the race too, and so was tangible evidence of the legacy that their child, as an organ donor, had left behind. Kelli ran in the race alongside a 23-year-old woman, Karen Hill, who had received Tommy's heart.

Kevin Cutinella, Tom's younger brother, was still playing football, a captain at Shoreham-Wading River. He was a starter on both sides of the ball as a junior in 2015, a quarterback and a linebacker, and he helped Shoreham-Wading River once again go undefeated and win the Long Island Championship. Tom remains heavily present in the team's consciousness and spirit, and for the Cutinella family football remains part of daily life. Kevin was on the sideline when Tom absorbed his fatal hit in '14, and though he expressed some early apprehension about continuing to play football he has embraced the game as vital for the joy he has in playing it and for continuing his brother's legacy. Both Kelli and Frank are in full support. They describe Kevin as "the most courageous person we know."

Frank and Kelli also support their youngest son, William, and their daughter, Carlie (who ran with Kelli in that Tunnel to Towers race) with the same pride and strength. William was a seventh-grade football player at Shoreham-Wading River when Tom died, and he has decided not to return to the sport, choosing to play soccer instead. "When our children want to do something or not do something we talk about it as a family," says Kelli. "And we usually stand by the decision they make. If Kevin said tomorrow that he did not want to play football anymore we would be behind him. And if William said he wanted go back to football we would be behind him too."

The Cutinellas still believe that football is a wonderful and important game, full of values that they hope their sons embody and will embody for life. They also believe that high school football is more dangerous than it needs to be. Frank has met with athletic directors from across New York, advocating for rules changes to encourage the shared responsibility that a community has when it sends its children onto a football field. The gist of the rules changes, which in 2016 will be implemented in Suffolk County, where the Cutinellas live, is to require coaches and designated parents to report targeted or helmet-to-helmet hits when they go unnoticed by the referee—and also that such hits should result in ejection. The Cutinellas have not allowed video of Tom's last play to go public, but on the film, they say, you see that he was the victim of such a helmet-to-helmet hit, the kind that happens so often during a football game. Immediately after the blow, before its repercussions could be known or even suspected, the hit was celebrated, as per football norm, by opposing players.

Even if their rules changes can begin to shift football culture in their local schools, Frank and Kelli know that nothing they do will make high school football truly safe. Their hope is that in Tom's name they can make it at least incrementally safer. That is a big hope to hold on to.

On Feb. 5, 2016, two days before Super Bowl 50, NFL Commissioner Roger Goodell spoke with the media. During the session he was asked whether it was safe for young people to play football. "If I had a son, I'd love to have him play the game of football," the commissioner said. And then he added: "There's risk in life. There's risk in sitting on the couch."

The statement, in its arrogance, resounded through the world of high school and youth football. ("He is not making things any easier for us," coach D said in New Rochelle. "You have to think there was a better way to answer that question.") And Goodell's words were echoing especially loudly for the Cutinellas the next day. It was 11 a.m. and there was snow all over the backyard of their Wading River home and a newspaper, Long Island's *Newsday*, was open on the table to the article about what the commissioner had said. Frank kept looking at it and shaking his head. He himself played football in high school, and the game has been an integral part of Kelli's maternal life three times over, since Tom was 7. Neither of the Cutinellas, sitting on chairs in the kitchen of a house that once had four children bounding about but now has only three, could understand what might drive a man of Goodell's stature—however protective of profit he might be, however empty of character—to say something as dismissive as that. *There's risk in sitting on the couch.*

"I love football and this family loves football and we won't speak against the game," said Frank. "But we aren't naive. We understand why participation numbers have been declining around here. And when you hear a commissioner talk the way that he talks it does make you wonder where this is all going."

In the next-to-last game of Shoreham-Wading River's 2015 season, Kevin, carrying the ball down the sideline on wet turf, had injured his left ankle. He missed the team's final game and needed surgery. Kevin was expected, however, to be fully recovered by the time the football season rolled around again, to take the ball and to step out onto what it is now known as Thomas Cutinella Memorial Field at Shoreham-Wading River. There is a plaque to Tom at the field, and on it are words taken from a speech he gave to his teammates early in that 2014 season. "Teams are more important than individuals," reads the speech, in part. "To win, there must be commitment, compassion, faith, accountability, respect and love."

Most anyone in the high school football community who passes by that plaque recognizes those words to be true and affirming. And that is why, for now anyway, this year and next year and surely for years to come, on Cutinella Field at Shoreham-Wading River and on McKenna Field in New Rochelle, and on fields in your town and my town and the town next door, another high-school football season will begin.

The Team

NEW ROCHELLE HUGUENOTS, 2014

PHOTOGRAPH BY DANIEL MOXEY

FRONT ROW *(left to right)*: Bryce Davis, Carmine Giordano, Jasper Baskerville, Demetrius Rodriguez, Jonathan Forrest, Corey Holder, Quincy Mack, Garrett Noake, CJ Anthony

SECOND ROW: Amir Sharif, Tyler Cooney, Frankie Lammers, Michael Cascio, Alexeij Xhokaxhiu, Keith Wheeler, Spencer Pressley, Kevin Ramirez, Alex Gaudio

THIRD ROW: Nigel Bailey, Akkad Ivey, Tyler Cohen, Justice Cowan, Marlon Riley, Robby DeRocco, Jared Baron, Dylan Cohen, Manny Walker, Mykal Rasheed

BACK ROW: Rashon McNeil, Chris Hinchey, Justin Cossifos, Jayson Prince, Mikaiel Ebanks, Greg Powell, Keelan Thomas, Danny Williams, Haitam Coughlin, Miles Harvey, Kevin Singletary, Eric Stenroos

Acknowledgments

CKNOWLEDGMENTS START at New Rochelle High School, and with head football coach Lou DiRienzo, who afforded me crucial and illuminating access and who tolerated me (and my many questions, and my poking around) with great patience. Similarly, to DiRienzo's staff, big gratitude for each coach's own patience and accessibility: Keith Fagan, Greg Foster, Rich Tassello, Brian Violante, Vic Chiappa, Ray Rhett and the one and only Jim Benge. Also, nods to Bishop Fetson Leak, Becky Schwartzman, Dr. Sergai DeLaMora, Phil Spivack, Carol DiRienzo and Carmen DiRienzo. I'm grateful to the administration at New Rochelle, without whose help this story would not have been possible: In particular thank you to athletic director Steve Young, for his generosity of time, and to principal Reginald Richardson.

The players on that New Rochelle team, whose names are found throughout the narrative of this book, let me in and did not blink. A salute to all of them. Many of those players' parents provided insights and candor and while many of their names are also found throughout the book, special appreciation goes out to these: Kirby and Exodia Mack, Donald Baron, Dawn

Holder, Greg Powell, Keith Wheeler Sr., Michelle Ammons, David and Mary Gaudio, Mike and Pam Cohen, Charlotte Anthony, John Hinchey, Gail Cascio, Randy and Janice Forrest, Steve Lilly, Chiara and Leonard Xhokaxhiu.

To Tanza Kirkland and Jamar Thomas, my deep thanks for their openness and our conversations during such an excruciating period of life.

And great thanks as well to Kelli and Frank Cutinella, for their own openness and their willingness to talk about real, hard things in a terribly difficult and trying time.

For his observations and perceptiveness, thank you to Sam Silverman. Also, from the gridiron: Steve Butler, Todd Cayea, Andy Verboys, Dominick DeMatteo, Samuel Kornhauser. And for sundry insights, small and large, thank you to Shari Maurer, Lynda Radosevich, Laura Bittelman-Procops, Steve Silverman, Patrick James Studdert-Kennedy, Anant Nambiar, James Valentin, Adam Deutsch, Benjamin Brody, Selena Roberts, Ralph Russo, Maura Sternklar, Michael Sternklar, Norman Goldberger, Jacques Steinberg and Bruce Goldberger with his fine eye.

Innumerable people were helpful in making important connections that aided my reporting. Among them: Matthew Hiltzik, Alison Gilbert, Richard Sgaglio at the Burke Rehabilitation Center, Maria Ober at Boston University's School of Medicine.

Thanks to Jay and Scott Fielder from Brookwood and to some important alums: Mantey Boahene, Fred Campbell, Chris Cargill, Courtland Cargill, Andrew DiRienzo, Lou DiRienzo Jr.

For making things clearer and often distilling them, thanks to Barry Jordan, Robert Cantu, Emily Bazelon, Wayne Jordan and Kevin Knifflin.

Thank you also to those of you who spoke with me but asked not to be acknowledged by name.

We all have an inner circle. To mine:

Many thanks to my literary agent, Andrew Blauner, for his intelligence, his commitment and his sound sense—qualities, among many others, that surround whatever work we do together.

David Bauer, whose editorial view and acumen succeeds from the 10,000-foot perspective, right down to ground, helped me, and this book, on every level.

At *Sports Illustrated* and Time Inc. Books: Thank you to Steve Koepp for his astute direction and to Margot Schupf for supporting and believing in the book. The peerless Stefanie Kaufman makes every project better, stronger and more professional, and this one is no exception. Ben Baskin's diligence and attention went above expectations and was invaluable. So too was the attention to words and shapes and images of Kevin Kerr, Stephen Skalocky, Erick Rasco and Cristina Scalet. Thanks also to Paul Fichtenbaum, Chris Stone, Stephen Cannella and Peter King at SI. And for their creativity and savvy, many thanks to Anja Schmidt, Courtney Greenhalgh, Bryan Christian, Courtney Mifsud, Tanya Farrell, Gary Stewart and Anne-Michelle Gallero.

And then the inner, inner circle: This book, like so many things, came about only through the love and great understanding of Amy Levine-Kennedy, Maya Kennedy and Sonya Levine. And through the permanent wisdom of Kathrin Perutz and Michael Studdert-Kennedy, the progenitors, with their lasting impact.

Kostya Kennedy
New York, 2016

Selected Bibliography

Selected Books, Articles and Papers

Araton, Harvey. "Town Ponders Season's End." *The New York Times,* Oct. 12, 2014.

Baugh, Christine M. et al. "Frequency of Head-Impact–Related Outcomes by Position in NCAA Division I Collegiate Football Players." Journal of Neurotrauma, Volume 32, Issue 5, August 2014.

Belson, Ken. "New Tests for Brain Trauma Create Hope, and Skepticism." *The New York Times,* Dec. 26, 2013.

Belson, Ken. "Concussions Show Decline of 13 Percent, N.F.L. Says." *The New York Times,* Jan. 31, 2014.

Brown, Roger. "Casey Cochran Reaches New Heights in Connecticut." maxpreps.com, Nov. 15, 2011.

Cantu, Robert and Hyman, Mark. *Concussions and Our Kids.* Mariner Books, New York, 2012/2013.

Conner, Desmond. "UConn QB Casey Cochran Done with Football, a Few Thoughts from His Dad." *The Hartford Courant,* Sept. 8, 2014.

Cournoyer, Janie and Tripp, Brady L. "Concussion Knowledge in High School Football Players." *Journal of Athletic Training,* Volume 49, No. 5, Sept./Oct. 2014.

Dawsey, Josh and Terlep, Sharon. "What the Sayreville Teaches Us

About High-School Locker Rooms." *The Wall Street Journal,* Nov. 12, 2014.

DeLillo, Don. *End Zone.* Penguin Books, New York, 1986.

Dugan, Sarah et al. "This is Your Brain on Sports: Measuring Concussions in High School Athletes in the Twin Cities Metropolitan Area." *Minnesota Medicine,* Volume 97, Issue 9, September 2014.

Eichelberger, Curtis. "College Athletics Safer Than Ever Through Concussion Research, Awareness." National Football Foundation, Oct. 28, 2014.

Fainaru-Wada, Mark and Fainaru, Steve. *League of Denial.* Crown Archetype, New York, 2013.

Gessel, Luke M. et al. "Concussions Among United States High School and Collegiate Athletes." *Journal of Athletic Training,* Volume 42, Issue 4. October 2007.

Gregory, Sean. "Is Football Worth It?" *Time,* Sept. 29, 2014.

Harbaugh, John. "Why Football Matters." baltimoreravens.com. April 22, 2015.

Helling, Steve. "6-year-old Football Players: Too Young to Tackle?" *People,* July 7, 2014.

Interdonato, Sal. "Army Coach: Football 'safer game these days.' " *Times Herald-Record,* Jan. 24, 2015.

Jones, Carolyn. "New Law Tackles High School Football Collisions Head-On." *San Francisco Chronicle,* July 22, 2014.

Kaplan, Emily. "Steve Gleason Goes Deep." theMMQB.com, Nov. 20, 2014.

Klemko, Robert. "When the Game Goes Dark." theMMQB.com, April 22, 2014.

Klemko, Robert. "If You Give a Mouse a Concussion . . ." *Sports Illustrated,* April 17, 2014.

Kniffin, Kevin M., Wansink, Brian and Shimizu, Mitsuru. "Sports at Work: Anticipated and Persistent Correlates of Participation in High School Athletics." *Journal of Leadership and Organizational Studies,* Volume 22, Issue 2, May 2015.

Layden, Tim. "The Danger Zone." *Sports Illustrated,* Sept. 1, 2014.

Longman, Jeré. "Your School Lost Every Game? Hey, Better Luck in the Postseason." *The New York Times,* Nov. 20, 2014.

Macur, Juliet. "Burying Young Players Isn't Part of the Game." *The New York Times,* Oct. 8, 2014.

McAllister, Thomas W. "Even Without a Concussion Blows to Head May Affect Brain, Learning and Memory." *Neurology,* Dec. 11, 2013.

Moore, Jack. "Welcome to the Concussion Industrial Complex." Vice Sports, Nov. 17, 2014.

Pennington, Bill. "Concussions, by the New Book." *The New York Times,* Nov. 30, 2014.

Rodriguez, Justin. "Football Takes a Hit." *Times Herald-Record,* Jan. 26, 2015.

Solomon, Jon. "Congressman Urges NCAA to Have Concussion Penalties." cbssports.com, Nov. 12, 2014.

Witz, Billy. "Program Crumbles, One Season after Player's Death." *nytimes.com,* Oct. 30, 2014.

Selected Publications and Websites

abcnews.com; *Associated Press; Atlanta Journal-Constitution*; baltimoreravens.com; *The Buffalo News;* buzzfeed.com; The Center on Brain Injury Research & Training; Centers for Disease Control and Prevention (Morbidity and Mortality Weekly Reports and Heads Up: Concussions in High School Sports materials); *The Charlotte Observer*; *The City Review* (New Rochelle); *The Clarion-Ledger* (Jackson, Miss.); clearedtoplay.org; CNN.com; Concussion Legacy Foundation (various releases); connect2concussion.com; dailymail.com (*The Daily Mail,* U.K.); harrisfhc.com (Buffalo Junction, Va.); *The Hartford Courant*; *Houma Today* (Louisiana); *The Journal News* (Westchester, New York; "Small Team Battles For Its Future" and others); lenapelifeways.org; lohudblogs.com; *Los Angeles Times*; maxpreps.com; High School Sports; momsteam.com; nbcnewyork.com; mprnews.org (Minnesota); nj.com; msgvarsity.com; *The New Rochelle Sound Report*; newrochelle.dailyvoice.com; (New York) *Daily News*; *The New York Post*; *The New York Times*; news4jax.com (Jacksonville); *Newsday*; nfl.com; pbs.org (League of Denial: The

NFL's Concussion Crisis); *People*; *Pittsburgh Post-Gazette*; *Riverhead News-Review* (Long Island, N.Y.); sfgate.com; silive.com (Staten Island, N.Y.); *Sports Illustrated* (Sept. 29, 2014, NFL Poll; and others); *Staten Island Advance*; stophazing.org; *The Suffolk Times* (Long Island, N.Y.); swata.org; *Tampa Bay Times*; *Time* (Sept. 29, 2014, and others); *The Times-Herald Record* (Orange County, N.Y.); triblive.com (Valley News Dispatch); upworthy.com; *USA Today*; *The Wall Street Journal*; *The Washington Post*; wbur.org; weather.com; *Westchester Magazine* (New York); wivb.com (Buffalo, N.Y.); woodtv.com (Grand Rapids, Mich.); wptv.com (West Palm Beach, Fla.); wset.com (Lynchburg, Va.); wtvr.com (Richmond)

Other Resources
HBO: *Real Sports with Bryant Gumbel*

National Center for Catastrophic Sport Injury Research: Annual Surveys

National Federation of State High School Associations: Participation Statistics

National Operating Committee on Standards for Athletic Equipment

NYU Library (Bobst)

UConn Athletic Communications

Southwest Athletic Trainers' Association

Youth Sports Safety Alliance

About the Author

KOSTYA KENNEDY is the author of *The New York Times* best-sellers *Pete Rose: An American Dilemma* and *56: Joe DiMaggio and the Last Magic Number in Sports*, both of which won the CASEY Award as best baseball book of the year. A former senior writer at *Sports Illustrated*, and now an editorial director at Time Inc., he edited the 2015 best-seller *Super Bowl Gold: 50 Years of the Big Game*. He teaches at NYU's Tisch Institute of Sports Management, Media and Business, and he lives with his wife and children in Westchester County, N.Y.

www.kostyakennedy.com
@KostyaKennedy